HOW *to* DRIVE

A Text for Beginning Drivers
Fourteenth Edition

Includes tips on:

- Managing visibility, time and space.
- Developing an effective visual search pattern.
- Driving in adverse conditions.
- Identifying traffic signs, signals and markings.
- Economical driving and modern drivetrains.
- Preventing distracted driving.
- Avoiding aggressive driving and road rage.
- Selecting insurance coverage.
- Traveling with a trailer.
- Maintaining vehicle systems.

HOW *to* DRIVE

1

CONTENTS

HOW *to* **DRIVE**

PREFACE

In the United States, almost 90 percent of people over the age of 16 are licensed drivers. As the primary mode of transportation, driving gives us a sense of freedom and flexibility to travel when and where we want. It is an activity that most people enjoy, and one that must be correctly learned and properly practiced if injury is to be prevented.

Your safety and the well-being of those who travel with you are the primary concerns of AAA as we wrote the fourteenth edition of How to Drive, the definitive text on how to develop and master risk-management skills based on managing visibility, time and space in all driving situations. Since the 1930s, AAA has been committed to preparing new drivers for the challenges of the road.

Written in clear, concise language for beginning drivers, How to Drive emphasizes the information and processes needed to drive safely in today's traffic environment. How to Drive contains information about:

- Managing risk
- Traffic signs and signals
- Traffic rules and regulations
- Identifying desired and alternate paths of travel
- Safety restraint systems
- Interacting with other roadway users
- Alternative drivetrains, including diesels and hybrids
- Driving economically
- Distracted driving
- The effects of alcohol and other drugs on driver performance
- Drowsy driving
- Road rage and aggressive driving
- Responding to driving emergencies
- Driving in adverse conditions
- Trip planning and special skills needed for towing a trailer
- Purchasing and insuring a vehicle
- What to do in the event of a collision

This edition of How to Drive reflects more than 70 years of experience, which AAA has gained in developing driver education materials such as Responsible Driving, Licensed to Learn, Teaching Your Teens to Drive, and Dare to Prepare.

The 14th edition of How to Drive is designed to be used as part of an instructional package that includes the How to Drive Instructor Guide (Stock #350509) and How to Drive Test Book (Stock #350309).

For more information about the availability and price of How to Drive, contact your local AAA club and ask for Stock #350209.

HOW *to* **DRIVE**

INTRODUCTION

Driving is a complex and often demanding task, even for skilled and experienced motorists. To drive safely you must control the vehicle, comply with traffic laws and regulations, monitor traffic conditions, watch the behavior of other drivers, keep an eye out for children, pedestrians, animals and cyclists, and maneuver in all kinds of weather and road conditions.

You must also obtain information from continually changing environments, decide what action to take, initiate that action, assess the consequences, take remedial action if necessary, and constantly repeat the process. Good drivers perform these steps in a timely manner.

Heavy traffic, speeding drivers, emergencies, bad weather, distractions and fatigue, as well as emergencies created by others, place additional demands on you as a driver. Traffic crashes are the number-one killer of young people ages 15 to 20. Novice drivers account for four times more crashes than drivers with just five more years experience. These statistics mandate that every driver be prepared. How to Drive will help the beginning driver, peers, parents and mentors be safe and effective in the driving process.

ACKNOWLEDGEMENTS

AAA Driver Training Programs and other AAA National Office staff wish to thank the following individuals for their contributions and dedication to the 14th edition of How to Drive:

Robin A. Bordner
Traffic Safety Center of Southwest Michigan
Sturgis, MI

Edwin W. "Ned" Ferris III
Driver Education and Traffic Safety Instructor
Instructor Training and Mentoring
Intellectual Property and Courseware Design and Development
Frederick Community College
Frederick, MD

Debbie Prudhomme
Training Wheels Driver Education
Maple Grove, MN

Allen Robinson, Ph.D.
CEO, ADTSEA
Highway Safety Center
Indiana University of Pennsylvania
Indiana, PA

Additionally, AAA Driver Training Programs and other AAA National Office staff wish to recognize the following individuals for their contributions toward enhancing the 14th edition of How to Drive:

◆ Michael Borkowski
◆ Tom Crosby
◆ Kathy Downing
◆ Chuck Mai
◆ Sandra Maxwell
◆ Joseph Perfetto
◆ Helen Sramek
◆ Ken Glaser

HOW *to* **DRIVE**

CHAPTER 1

Managing Risk When Driving

Chapter Objectives

- ◆ Explain the freedoms and responsibilities that accompany a driver's license.
- ◆ Describe the crash and fatality risks of new drivers.
- ◆ Describe common errors committed by new drivers.
- ◆ Explain how your perception of your driving ability can influence crash involvement.
- ◆ Explain how knowledge and awareness of risk can influence a driver's behavior.
- ◆ Describe how better management of visibility, time and space can lower risk when driving.
- ◆ Identify and discuss the characteristics of risk.
- ◆ Identify the three stages of Graduated Driver Licensing (GDL).
- ◆ Identify the role of parents and mentors in achieving the objectives of GDL.
- ◆ Explain the purpose and content of a Parent-Teen Driving Agreement.

HOW *to* **DRIVE**

A Driver's License — What Does it Mean?

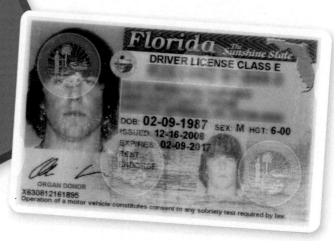

The license. What does it mean to have a license to drive? To most drivers, regardless of age, it means freedom to come and go when and where they please. It means choices and opportunities. But along with these opportunities comes responsibility.

What does driving mean to you?

Driving safely. Driving safely is a complex and often demanding task, even for experienced, skillful drivers. To drive safely, drivers must monitor traffic and traffic-control devices while observing and anticipating the actions of other drivers, pedestrians, cyclists and animals. They must know and comply with traffic regulations and control their vehicles under all types of weather and road conditions. In addition, drivers must search for and obtain information from frequently changing environments, decide how to effectively respond to various situations, assess the consequences of alternative responses, initiate action, make adjustments as necessary — and constantly repeat the process to minimize risk.

Good habits. A skillful, experienced driver performs these steps as a matter of habit, minimizing the need for corrective action. Fortunately, not all driving is done under conditions that require advanced driving skills or a constant, intense level of attention.

Additional demands. Increased speed, dense traffic, poor weather, distractions, stress and fatigue can all place additional demands on a driver. Any of these factors can lead to mistakes and situations for which the driver is not prepared or is incapable of handling, thus increasing the chance of a crash.

It does not happen overnight. Considering the demands placed on today's drivers, completing a driver education course and obtaining a driver's license does not mean a driver will drive safely. A license indicates only that the individual has demonstrated basic knowledge and ability needed to control a motor vehicle. Research shows that, on average, it takes a new driver about five years to develop the driving ability demonstrated by the average driver. In fact, nearly half of all new drivers will either be charged with a traffic offense or be involved in a collision during their first 12 months of driving. Many of these collisions will result in injuries or fatalities.

The Facts About Teen Driving

The facts. Each year, approximately 40,000 people lose their lives in motor vehicle collisions, which is equivalent to two jumbo jets crashing each week. Additionally, traffic crashes are the number-one killer of young people ages 15 to 20. Nationally, more than 3,500 teenagers die in motor vehicle crashes each year. Of those, more than 60 percent are not wearing safety belts. Per miles driven, novice drivers have a crash rate four times higher than experienced drivers.

Research shows that, on average, it takes a new driver about five years to develop the driving ability demonstrated by the average driver.

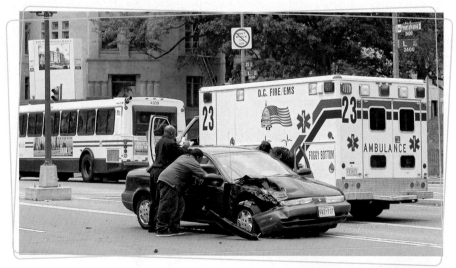

HOW *to* **DRIVE**

Primary Crash Factors

The data. An in-depth review of 2,000 crashes involving 16- and 18-year-old drivers in California and Maryland revealed the top errors committed by these drivers and showed that 16-year-olds had a crash rate 2.6 times higher than 18-year olds. The table below highlights the 10 errors most commonly committed in crashes involving 16-year olds.

Percent Involvement	Errors Committed
20.8%	Did not pay adequate attention to the path of travel
13.7%	Drove five or more miles per hour too fast for conditions
6.6%	Tried to drive through a curve at too high a speed
6.3%	Performed inadequate searches at intersections and pulled in front of cross traffic
6.1%	Did not pay adequate attention at intersections and were struck by other vehicles
5.6%	Used improper evasive action — too much or too little steering for vehicle speed and capabilities
3.9%	Failed to maintain a sufficient visual lead
3.9%	Failed to see action developing at the side of the roadway
3.9%	Were following too closely
3.3%	Failed to yield the right-of-way

Note that distracted driving could have played a role in any of the above errors. It is estimated that approximately 25 percent of collisions involve some form of driver distraction, and young drivers are even more susceptible to becoming distracted while driving.

Fatal-collision picture. To further illustrate the youthful-driver crash problem per 10,000 licensed drivers, an analysis of the "Maryland Teen Driver Fatal Accident Picture" project revealed that 16-year-old drivers have the highest fatality rate:

Age	# Drivers	Fatality Rate (per million miles driven)
16	21,314	10.0
17	35,595	8.6
18	41,172	7.3
19	45,697	7.6
All ages	3,388,055	3.9

Judging risk. One of the major differences between new and experienced drivers is the ability to judge the level of risk — the chance of injury, damage or loss — associated with a driving situation. A lack of awareness or ability to assess traffic or roadway conditions too frequently results in a late, inappropriate or total lack of response. A similar problem appears more frequently among drivers over 65 years of age.

"Risk" is defined as the chance of injury, damage or loss.

The odds. Unfortunately, people who are unaware of the risk involved in an activity or who refuse to accept the evidence of risk are not likely to take action to manage the level of risk. Few drivers are aware that up to one out of every 10 vehicles is involved in a crash each year. In fact, more than 30 percent of drivers believe the odds of being involved in a crash are less than one in a thousand.

Overestimating ability. Another factor influencing crash involvement is gross over-estimation of one's driving ability. About 85 percent of all drivers rate themselves as better than average, with a lot of control — or almost total control — over their vehicles. Even drivers who have just received their first license rate themselves as good drivers, capable of handling any situation. This overconfidence may negatively impact a driver's ability to assess the true risk in any given situation. Because of this perceived superior ability, more than 90 percent insist that if they were to be involved in a crash, the crash would be due to someone *else's* driving error, something wrong with the vehicle or roadway, or just plain bad luck. **In reality, driver error causes more than 90 percent of traffic crashes.**

Risk Assessment

One of the major differences between new and experienced drivers is the ability to judge the level of risk.

Guidelines. Although it is nearly impossible to determine with complete accuracy the level of risk in specific driving situations, there are guidelines that can help you assess risk more accurately and determine a more appropriate response. A driver who effectively manages risk will always follow these guidelines while driving:

◆ Consider the chance or possibility of a dangerous situation developing.

◆ Identify possible alternative actions and consider the consequences of each.

◆ Prepare to change speed or change direction to manage or control the situation.

Risk prevalence. Every minute you are behind the wheel, you are at risk. There is always a possibility that something can go wrong. Collisions can occur along any type of roadway. To manage risk when driving, it is essential that the driver be alert to conditions and objects that could affect the level of risk. To manage risk, you must be aware of the four characteristics of risk:

◆ Risk is always present   ◆ Risk is affected by all road users

◆ Perceived risk differs from actual risk   ◆ Risk can be managed

Risk is always present

More than 50 percent of all vehicle-occupant fatalities occur in single-vehicle crashes, most of which occur on relatively straight, rural stretches of roadway.

Assessing risk. How would you compare the level of risk in situations A and B above? Surprisingly, the chance of a crash is about the same in A and B. Because of the intersection, most people consider situation B to be the more dangerous. Situation A *appears* to be safer: the road is straight, there is no intersection, and there are no apparent threatening objects or conditions. *However, more than 50 percent of all vehicle occupant fatalities occur in single-vehicle crashes, mostly on relatively straight, rural stretches of roadway.*

Some major factors. Even situations that appear to be risk-free do in fact involve risk. Drivers usually recognize that there is some additional risk associated with an intersection, but few perceive the actual risk when driving on a straight, narrow country road. Assumptions of low risk, lack of perceived threat and reduced attention appear to be major factors that contribute to risk and consequences in situations of this type. In this case, drivers can become complacent and underestimate the actual risk involved.

Running off a straight roadway. This type of crash most frequently involves young drivers and drivers over 65 years of age. In these cases, the driver runs off the road and fails to respond or responds incorrectly. Improper use of the brakes or inaccurate steering input can cause the vehicle to lose traction and strike a fixed object or overturn. While such events involving young drivers usually occur after dark, those involving older drivers are more likely to occur between 1 and 5 pm.

What could happen in these situations that would increase your risk?

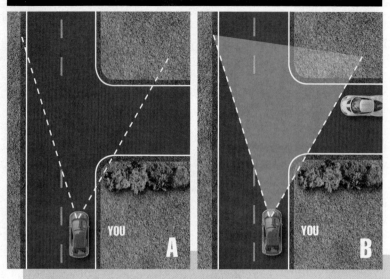

Perceived Risk Differs from Actual Risk

Whenever visibility is limited, be alert and respond to the risk by adjusting your speed, position and visibility rather than driving blindly into a crisis situation.

Blocked vision. How would you compare the level of risk in situations A and B above? When viewed from the driver's perspective, the chance of a crash could mistakenly be perceived as about the same in A and B. However, with knowledge of the second vehicle's presence, you can better assess the higher degree of risk involved in illustration B.

In both illustrations, blocked vision is the factor that should signal increased risk. Whenever a driver's ability to see is restricted, the driver must adjust speed, position and visibility as appropriate rather than driving blindly into a dangerous situation. When your vision is blocked, it should be a cue for you to *assume* that there is an approaching risk hidden from you, and adjust accordingly. For an added measure of safety, as you approach the intersection, move as close as safely possible to the center of the roadway to give yourself a better line of sight, and ease up on the accelerator.

Enhancing your visibility. One way to reduce risk in situations of this type is to drive with low-beam headlights turned on at all times if your vehicle is not equipped with daytime running lights (DRLs). A vehicle with low-beam headlights or DRLs on during daylight hours is visible to oncoming vehicles at almost twice the distance as the same vehicle without headlights turned on. In addition, at intersections, your presence can be detected by other drivers about one second sooner. At driving speeds, that extra second can allow more time for evasive maneuvers, if needed.

Risk is Affected by all Road Users

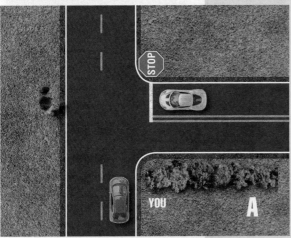

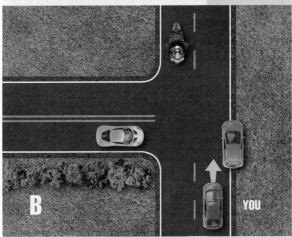

It is important to remember that actions of roadway users — pedestrians, animals, bicyclists and drivers — affect all other users.

All road users affect risk.

Depending on their actions, roadway users can increase or decrease risk for themselves and other road users. The actions of all roadway users — pedestrians, bicyclists or drivers — affect all other users.

Other roadway users. How would you assess the level of risk in situation A? How about in situation B? Depending on their actions, the other roadway users can increase or decrease the level of risk for the others.

◆ In situation A, the pedestrian could dart across the roadway into your path of travel. Also, the other driver might not see you and try to turn left across or turn right into your path of travel.

◆ In situation B, the vehicle approaching from the left may attempt to turn left in front of you. Also, the vehicle parked on the right could enter traffic in front of you.

◆ In both instances, driving with headlights on, easing off the accelerator, sounding the horn in a friendly manner and flashing your headlights could help minimize risk to you and the other roadway users. The safest approach to driving is to automatically assume that other roadway users will always take the action that puts you at the most risk.

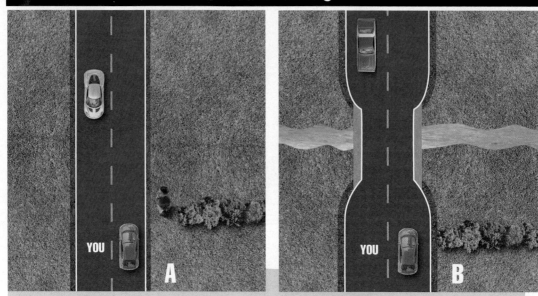

Risk Can be Managed

By separating multiple risks by time and space, you can effectively manage your risk and decrease the chance of a collision.

Separating potential hazards. Situation A is best managed by slowing to avoid meeting the pedestrian at the same time you meet the oncoming car. If the pedestrian steps into the roadway as the oncoming car approaches, you will want enough space between you and the pedestrian to be able to stop or turn the vehicle if you need to. By slowing and letting the oncoming car pass *before* you meet the pedestrian, you separate threatening objects. In addition to slowing you could also sound your horn and flash your headlights to alert the pedestrian and the other driver of your presence.

The best action you could take in situation B would be to decrease your speed such that the oncoming vehicle clears the bridge before you arrive at the bridge. The narrow bridge represents an increase in risk, as does the oncoming vehicle. By slowing down, you separate these two by time and distance, allowing you to address each separately, thus reducing your risk.

The key to reducing risk is managing time, visibility and space. Ensuring that you give yourself enough time to make adjustments, maximize your visibility of the traffic scene and allow adequate space between you and other elements on the roadway can significantly reduce the risk to you and to others. Drivers can effectively accomplish this by:

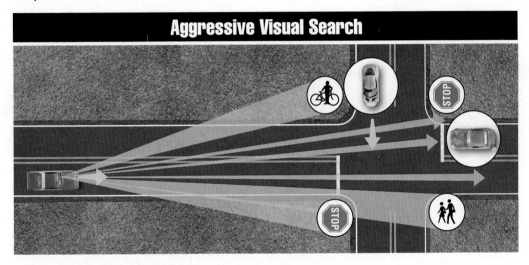

Aggressive Visual Search

1. **Making an aggressive visual search.** Managing risk starts with an aggressive visual search of the roadway and off-road areas. A systematic search includes:
   - Searching 20–30 seconds ahead along your intended path of travel for objects or conditions that could increase the level of risk.
   - Being aware of the level of traction and identifying an alternate path of travel 12–15 seconds ahead into which you can steer if a threatening situation should develop.

2. **Making good decisions with this information.** Using the information gained through your visual search to manage risk is also critical, including:
   - Predicting the actions of other highway users that could increase the level of risk.
   - Assessing the consequences of alternative responses.
   - Determining the best course of action.

HOW to DRIVE

3. **Acting on your decisions.** The final step is to execute your maneuvers, adjusting speed and/or position, and communicate your intentions well in advance. This involves:

◆ Making accurate and appropriate adjustments to speed and direction.

◆ Communicating with other roadway users.

To give yourself enough time to accomplish these, always leave enough distance between your vehicle and the road user ahead. Keep in mind that the closer you get to an object, the more steering input you will need to maneuver around it. Sudden braking and/or following too closely result in nearly 30 percent of all reported crashes annually.

The Licensing Process

Graduated Driver Licensing and Risk

What is Graduated Driver Licensing (GDL)? Graduated Driver Licensing is an approach to ease new drivers into driving by providing practice and skill development under low-risk conditions. As drivers become more experienced, they are gradually allowed to drive under increasingly complex conditions. This process of incrementally increasing a new driver's privileges has been shown to reduce teen crashes, injuries and deaths. Done properly, parents play a key role in these licensing efforts.

How GDL works. GDL programs are designed to help beginning drivers by promoting the development of basic knowledge and skills. By providing structured learning over an extended period of time, GDL programs allow novice drivers to gain the skills, experience and judgment abilities needed to become safer drivers.

The licensing stages. Nearly all GDL programs go through three licensing stages: a learner's permit; an intermediate, probationary or provisional license; and an unrestricted "full" license. License applicants typically spend 12 to 24 months in the first two stages before becoming eligible for an unrestricted license.

The learner's permit. States generally require new teen drivers to hold a learner's permit for a period of six months to a year, although the permit itself may be valid for much longer. During the learner's permit period, the new driver typically must enroll in an approved driver education program and practice basic driving skills under the supervision of a licensed instructor or adult licensed driver. Applicants may drive only when accompanied by an adult licensed driver, and no other passenger can be in the front seat. Some states restrict learner's permit drivers from having any additional passengers or from driving late at night.

Many states and provinces require novice drivers to practice driving for 50 or more hours with a parent, guardian or adult mentor before they can be tested for an intermediate license. Also, learner's permit holders must often remain free of moving violations and at-fault crashes for several months or more before moving to the next stage. In many jurisdictions the permit holder must restart the required learner's permit period for any conviction for a moving violation or at-fault crash.

Intermediate stage. During the intermediate, probationary or provisional license stage, the new driver is generally allowed to drive unsupervised, but with restrictions designed to help reduce the level of risk and distractions. Nearly every state prohibits intermediate license holders from driving during certain nighttime hours, when the chance of a crash is greater. Most states restrict whether new drivers may transport young passengers. Some states require the driver to take a second driver-training class during this stage. Many require the driver to be free of moving violations and at-fault crashes for a number of months before being eligible for a full license.

Full license. After meeting the requirements of the intermediate, probationary or provisional license stage, drivers may obtain a full license. This usually happens around age 17 or 18. For more information on state GDL systems and licensing requirements, visit *www.AAA.com/PublicAffairs*.

How Can Parents Be Involved?

A matter of communication. For driver training to be effective, parents and teens must communicate with each other. Be sure to adopt a parent-teen driving agreement, emphasizing that driving is a privilege, and review the agreement together periodically.

Be a good role model. Also important is to be a good role model as a parent. Behavior is learned, not innate. Parents and teens who both commit to safe driving behaviors can help reduce risk for all drivers in a family.

Conduct supervised practice driving. Developing safe driving abilities is critical — but these skills are only the basics. Novice drivers need much more assistance and experience to become accomplished drivers. To improve, they have to have numerous opportunities to practice and master each new skill in multiple settings and under different conditions. Consistent, supervised practice driving conducted over an extended period of time can help new drivers build on the skills they have learned.

Driving coaches. Parents, guardians or other adults who are at least 21 years of age, with a good driving record for the past five years or more, are in the best position to provide extended, guided practice. Working as teams with their new drivers and driver education instructors, mentors can help instill driving behaviors that will reduce motor vehicle crashes. The most effective way to coach a teen driver is to synchronize the practice driving with the topics being taught in the teen's driver education program.

Tools for driving coaches. There are several programs available to help the mentor make supervised driving sessions more productive and less stressful. AAA's *Teaching Your Teens To Drive* parent-support program contains everything needed to help mentors serve as effective coaches. The program presents 13 individual lessons and provides up-to-date information on safe driving. It is important to be aware that more than one session in a vehicle may be required before the new driver demonstrates an acceptable level of performance for that lesson. More tools and useful information for parents can be found on *TeenDriving.AAA.com.*

To make the most of each practice session, here are some helpful hints for the adult coach:

◆ Choose and pre-drive appropriate routes for each lesson.

◆ Before starting each lesson, make sure the new driver understands the objectives of the lesson.

◆ Remain calm, patient and alert.

◆ Properly demonstrate maneuvers, when needed.

◆ Provide directions well in advance. Tell where the action is to take place, and then describe the action; e.g., "at the next intersection, turn right."

◆ Use language that prevents confusion. For example, use the word "right" to mean direction and "correct" when answering a question.

◆ Monitor traffic in all directions while also monitoring the actions of the new driver.

◆ Pull off the road and park in a safe location when reviewing performance.

◆ Use a checklist to evaluate the new driver.

◆ Use *commentary driving*, a technique in which the new driver verbally describes what he or she sees ahead along or adjacent to the path of travel that could require an adjustment of (1) speed and/or (2) position. This technique helps the mentor gauge the driver's ability to perceive the full traffic scene and to anticipate actions.

HOW *to* **DRIVE**

Parent-Teen Driving Agreements

A parent-teen driving agreement is a written agreement between parents and their new driver to outline responsibilities and rules related to the teen's safe driving. These agreements can provide an excellent way to set goals and expectations that encourage safe driving and help both parents and the new driver avoid misunderstandings about vehicle use. There are many factors to consider when implementing a parent-teen agreement. Guidelines for a parent-teen driving agreement include:

- Adopting restrictions appropriate for the family, such as:
  - Avoid high-risk driving situations during the initial months of solo driving; e.g., adverse weather, congested traffic, unsupervised long trips.
  - Limit all nighttime driving and gradually allow limited amounts as the new driver progresses.
  - Prohibit use of alcohol or other drugs by the driver or other persons in the vehicle.
  - Require all vehicle occupants to wear safety belts at all times.
  - Restrict the number of teenage passengers in the vehicle.
- Never driving when fatigued, angry or upset.
- Acting promptly if there is an infraction of the agreement. Be firm but gentle.
- Being consistent when applying consequences for infractions and not negotiating consequences that have already been established in the agreement.
- Being positive. Focus on the new driver's safety and welfare as a main concern, and reward responsible behavior. Parents and the new driver share the same goal — helping the teen become a safe, responsible driver.

To obtain AAA's Parent-Teen Driving Agreement, visit *www.AAA.com/PublicAffairs.*

The value of supervised practice driving. Becoming a safe driver requires extended, supervised practice during and after completion of driver education. The effort of conducting supervised practice driving is a minimal consideration when weighed against the risks posed by and to new drivers. Parents who support GDL and conduct supervised driving can help new drivers survive the first few years as they gain the valuable behind-the-wheel experience needed to become safe drivers.

It is up to you. The material in this chapter has been designed to help you assess and manage risk when driving. How well you apply the information is up to you. While it is impossible to completely eliminate risk in driving situations, there are ways to reduce it. Always remain vigilant for potentially risky situations and adjust your speed and position as needed.

HOW *to* **DRIVE**

Managing Risk When Driving

Study and respond to each of the following questions. Then review the chapter to see if your responses are correct.

Multiple Choice:

1. Approximately how long does it take a new driver to reach the driving ability of the average experienced driver?
   a. The length of a driver education course
   b. Six months
   c. One year
   d. Five years

2. Each year, approximately _____ people are killed in motor vehicle-related collisions in the U.S.
   a. 75,000
   b. 40,000
   c. 25,000
   d. 10,000

3. More than __ percent of all vehicle-occupant fatalities occur in single-vehicle crashes.
   a. 25
   b. 50
   c. 75
   d. 90

4. Approximately what percent of crashes are caused by driver error?
   a. 39
   b. 55
   c. 63
   d. 90

5. Nearly half of all new drivers will either be cited for a traffic offense or be involved in a collision during their first 12 months of driving.
   a. True
   b. False

Short Answer:

1. List three guidelines for assessing risk.

2. List and explain the four characteristics of risk.

3. Explain how to perform an aggressive visual search.

4. Define "Graduated Driver Licensing" and explain each of the three stages of licensure.

5. Explain how adopting a Parent-Teen Driving Agreement can benefit (a) a teen driver, (b) the family and (c) the driving population as a whole.

CHAPTER 2

Getting Acquainted with the Vehicle You Will Drive

Chapter Objectives

♦ Perform pre-driving checks and sequence.

♦ Safely enter a vehicle when parked.

♦ Describe the functions of the various information devices.

♦ Identify and describe communication, visibility and convenience devices.

♦ Identify and describe passenger-protection systems.

♦ Operate vehicle-control devices.

♦ Adjust the vehicle to fit you.

Forming good habits. Certain checks and procedures must become habits if a driver is to safely and efficiently operate a motor vehicle. The first habit you need to develop is preparing yourself, your vehicle and your passengers for travel.

Pre-driving checks. The pre-driving checks identified below should be performed every time you drive. Checks under the hood, under normal driving conditions, should be performed at least once a month or as recommended in the owner's manual.

Approaching the Vehicle

◆ Have your keys in hand before approaching your car or entering the parking area. If you have a keyless-entry remote with a panic alarm button, keep it in your hand, with your finger poised above the activation button.

◆ Be alert to other pedestrians and drivers.

◆ Search for signs of movement between, beneath and around objects to both sides of your vehicle.

◆ Make sure other drivers see you. Walk well away from parked vehicles.

◆ If parked at the curb, face traffic as you approach the driver's door.

If parked at the curb, face traffic as you approach the driver's door.

Outside the Vehicle

◆ Before entering, check around the vehicle for obstacles that might interfere with safe movement of the vehicle.

◆ Check the driveway, parking area or street for children or other pedestrians. Several hundred children are killed annually by backing vehicles.

◆ Inspect the headlights, brake lights, turn signals and taillights, windshield, and side and rear windows. Clean if necessary and replace any bulbs or lenses that are not working or are broken.

◆ Visually inspect your tires for obvious signs of a problem, and notice which way the front wheels are pointed. Be sure to check your tire pressures at least once each month, as visual inspection alone may not reveal an improperly inflated tire.

◆ Check under the vehicle for fluid leaks.

◆ Look inside the vehicle before entering, especially the back seat, to enhance your safety and protect yourself against carjacking and other dangers.

1. Engine-coolant reservoir (radiator fluid)
2. Windshield-washer fluid reservoir
3. Power-steering fluid reservoir
4. Drive belts (tension and wear)
5. Engine-oil filler cap
6. Engine-oil dipstick
7. Transmission-fluid dipstick (automatic transmission only)
8. Brake-fluid reservoir
9. Battery (clean and level charge)
10. Air-filter assembly

Consult your vehicle's owner's manual to verify what components under the hood should be inspected. Perform these checks at least once a month or as recommended in the owner's manual. Failure to conduct these checks can lead to unsafe operating conditions and costly repairs.

It is important to develop a routine for preparing to drive. Key steps include:

1. Place your key in the ignition.

2. Make sure all doors are closed tightly and locked. In addition to preventing unwanted persons from entering your vehicle, locked doors can help reduce the chance of occupants being ejected from the vehicle in the event of a crash.

3. Check windows; clean and/or defrost as needed.

4. Check for packages or other objects that could block your view or strike an occupant in the event of a quick stop or crash. Secure loose objects in the trunk or use a cargo net (commonly found in SUVs).

5. Adjust the seat, steering-wheel/column, accelerator/brake pedals (if applicable) and head restraints.

6. Adjust the inside and outside mirrors.

7. Fasten and adjust safety belts and make sure all passengers fasten theirs.

8. Adjust air vents, windows and/or temperature control.

9. New drivers should avoid the distractions of the radio or auxiliary music system — leave it off for now.

Your instructor may suggest procedures slightly different from these. However, the important thing is to select a safe routine and then repeat the process until it becomes a habit.

Ignition and Security

Ignition switch. This switch is on the right side of the steering column or, in some vehicles, on the dashboard. The switch locks the steering wheel and shifting lever and enables the driver to start and stop the engine. It can also be used to provide power to other convenience and safety systems. In some new vehicles, electronic chips in the ignition switch and key serve as anti-theft devices. Some newer vehicles also offer keyless, or push-to-start, ignition systems.

Door locks. In vehicles equipped with manually operated locks, each door has its own locking device. In vehicles with electric door locks, each lock usually can be operated independently, and there also is a master control switch, often located on the driver's side armrest. Child-proof rear door locks are generally an option on four-door vehicles.

Adjusting the Vehicle to Your Preferences

Seat-adjustment controls. If manually controlled, the adjustment lever that allows the driver to move the seat forward or back is typically at the lower front side of the driver's seat. A second lever or knob, which adjusts the seat-back angle, is generally at the left rear side of the driver's seat. In vehicles with electric power seats, the controls are usually on the lower left side of the driver's seat, or in a control cluster on the driver's armrest or door panel.

Body position. The position of the driver's body relative to vehicle controls is critical. You should be seated in a comfortable, upright position, squarely behind the steering wheel. The seat should be positioned forward or back, up or down, so that you can easily operate the accelerator, brake and clutch pedals without having to lift your heel from the floor. Sitting too close to the steering wheel interferes with steering, increases fatigue and causes stress.

In vehicles equipped with a driver's side air bag, sitting closer than 10 inches from the steering wheel increases the chance of arm, neck or facial injury in the event of an airbag deployment. You can determine proper distance from the steering wheel by extending your arm in front of you and adjusting the seat forward or back until the top of the steering wheel is in line with the palm of your hand. In many vehicles not equipped with adjustable pedals, drivers less than 5 feet 5 inches tall may need to use pedal extensions.

You should be seated in a comfortable, upright position, squarely behind the steering wheel.

The area around your car.

From the driver's seat, there is a relatively large area immediately surrounding every vehicle that the driver cannot see. This space consists of the area between the vehicle and the nearest point where you can see the ground when seated behind the steering wheel. When properly seated, you should be able to see the ground within 12–15 feet to the front, one and one-half to two car widths to the right side, and one-half to one car width to the left side. The rear window and trunk design of some cars may restrict vision area to the rear. In some vehicles, the nearest visible ground point may be nearly 40 feet. To compensate for this space, it is important to learn where the vehicle's unseen boundaries exist to help prevent collisions. Proper adjustment of the vehicle's features should help to maximize your view from inside the vehicle in all directions.

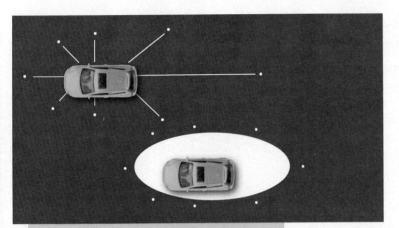

Immediately around every vehicle is space the driver cannot see when in the driver's seat. It is important to learn where the vehicle's unseen boundaries exist.

Steering wheel/column adjustment.

In many vehicles, the angle of the steering wheel or the entire steering column can be changed by using a lever on the left or right side of the steering column. An adjustment lever on the underside of the steering column permits the driver to raise or lower the steering column for better steering wheel angle and height. In a number of newer-model vehicles, the steering column is also telescopic, allowing the driver to adjust the distance between the steering wheel and the driver's chest.

Drivers should strive to maintain both hands on the steering wheel at all times.

Steering Wheel Hand Position and Grip

You should be able to adjust the seat so your left hand rests around 9 o'clock, and your right hand rests at about 3 o'clock, as on the face of a clock.

Hand position. The position of your hands on the steering wheel will vary, depending on the design of the steering wheel, the seat height and the length of your arms and legs. However, you should be able to adjust the seat so your left hand rests around 9 o'clock, and your right hand rests at about 3 o'clock, as on the face of a clock. This positioning allows for optimum control when turning the steering wheel. Alternatively, some drivers may prefer a slightly lower hand position, closer to 8 and 4 o'clock, depending on the position of the steering wheel spokes and personal preference. This mid- to low-hand position will help drivers maintain symmetrical leverage on the steering wheel while minimizing the chance of injury in the event the airbag deploys. Drivers should strive to maintain both hands on the steering wheel at all times.

Grip. You should grip the steering wheel with your arms bent at the elbows. Your grip should be gentle but firm. Grip the steering wheel by the outside of the rim, using both hands. For better control and road feel, use your fingers instead of the palms of your hands and keep your thumbs up along the face of the steering wheel.

Mirror Settings and Use

Adjusting the mirrors. Developing proper visual search habits requires proper positioning and use of mirrors both inside and outside the vehicle. Keep in mind that mirrors are intended for detection and not for gathering detailed information.

The inside mirror. Adjust the inside mirror so that it covers the entire rear window. To use the inside rearview mirror you should have to move only your eyes, not turn your head. Drivers six feet tall or taller may find it helpful to rotate the mirror 180 degrees (upside down) if possible, so that the day/night switch is on the top of the mirror. This action usually raises the bottom edge of the mirror about 1–2 inches and can substantially reduce a major blind area to the front for tall drivers.

Mirrors are intended for detection and not for gathering detailed information.

Side-view mirrors. Adjust side-view mirrors to reduce side and rear quarter-panel blind spots as much as possible.

◆ **Adjusting the driver's side mirror.** Place your head against the left side window (see illustration), and set the mirror so you can just barely see the side of the car in the right side of the mirror.

◆ **Adjusting the passenger's side mirror.** Position your head so that it is centered under the inside rearview mirror, or just above the center console.

Set the mirror so you can just barely see the side of the car in the left side of the mirror. If the vehicle is not equipped with remote mirror-adjustment controls, you may need assistance when adjusting the passenger-side mirror.

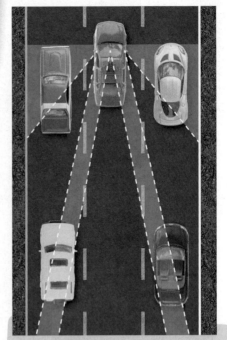

Developing appropriate visual positioning and use of mirrors.

Using the mirrors. Using these settings, the driver can observe what is directly behind the vehicle by using the inside mirror. By using the side mirrors, the driver can see directly into the spaces adjacent to each of the vehicle's rear corners as well. This enhanced visual contact should increase the driver's field of awareness, which can help detect the presence of other nearby roadway users.

With these mirror settings, you will have almost seamless visual contact around your vehicle. For example, when being passed by a vehicle in the next lane to your left, you will see it progress (a) from the rearview mirror, (b) to the left side mirror, (c) to your side vision:

1. Vehicle first observed in rearview mirror
2. Vehicle moving from rearview mirror to left side mirror
3. Vehicle in left side mirror
4. Vehicle moving from left side mirror into peripheral vision
5. Vehicle fully visible in peripheral vision

Remember, even properly adjusted mirrors will not eliminate all blind spots. You must make a final check to the sides before you make any lateral move. Turning your head to use the side mirrors should be limited to quick glances to detect the presence of objects and not to search for detailed information. This does not mean that you should not look over your shoulder to make critical time-space judgments when you move from a stopped position at the curb or merge onto an expressway.

HOW to DRIVE

Occupant Protection

Safety restraints. Lap and shoulder belts, when properly adjusted, are among the most important safety features in a motor vehicle. Safety belts are designed to help slow occupants' rate of deceleration in a frontal collision. Safety belts also help keep vehicle occupants securely in place, with the driver firmly behind the steering wheel and in control in case of a collision or during an emergency maneuver. When worn properly, safety belts also provide added comfort, reduce fatigue and help keep the driver more alert.

Proper use. The safety belt provides maximum protection and comfort when you are sitting up straight with your back firmly against the back of the seat. The lap belt should fit snugly across your hips and not be allowed to ride up on your abdomen. After fastening the belt, be sure to take up any slack. Never use one belt for two people. Do not place the shoulder belt behind your back or under your arm. As a passenger, do not ride in the front seat with the back of the seat in a reclining position. In the event of a crash, your body could slide forward, increasing the chance of both neck and abdominal injury.

When you fasten your safety belt, insist that your passengers do the same.

Properly adjusting your safety belt is one of the most important habits you can develop.

1. Position across hips, not abdomen.
2. Pull up shoulder belt to take up slack.

A properly installed infant seat is strapped into the backseat, facing the rear of the vehicle. This position offers the most protection for the infant in the event of a crash.

Head restraints. Head restraints reduce the risk of neck injury due to whiplash from the impact of a rear-end or frontal collision. If your vehicle is equipped with adjustable head restraints, make sure they are properly positioned. Normally, the top of the head restraint should be adjusted to a point slightly above your ears and — if possible — within 3 inches of the back of your head when you are seated in a normal upright position. To reduce the chance of injury, avoid leaning forward while you drive.

Air bags. Air bags are designed to work in conjunction with safety belts and help absorb crash forces to minimize impacts to the body. Normally, air bags are located in the steering wheel and in the dashboard on the passenger side. Air bags also may be located over the side doors, under the dashboard, in the sides of the seat and in the door panels. Drivers should be positioned 10–12 inches from the steering wheel, and passengers should be positioned 15–18 inches from the front passenger side air bag. Check the owner's manual for air bag safety information.

1 **INCORRECT**

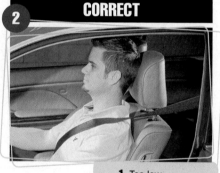

2 **CORRECT**

1. Too low
2. Just Right

When used with safety belts, air bags provide much greater protection against impact with the vehicle's interior structure. This is particularly important in a frontal crash — the most violent type of collision. Crash data show that driver contact with the steering-wheel column is a major cause of serious injury and death.

Air bags provide a great deal of protection against impact with the vehicle's interior.

Because their bones and muscles are not fully developed, children under 13 years of age are safest in the back seat. Never place a rear-facing infant seat in a front passenger seat protected by an air bag unless the air bag has a shut-off switch. Frail, elderly passengers should ride with the passenger's seat moved as far back as possible.

Gear selector lever. In a vehicle with an automatic transmission, the gear selector lever is located either on the right side of the steering column or on a console between the front seats. In a vehicle with a manual transmission, the gearshift lever is generally on the center console or on the floor to the right of the driver.

Using overdrive gear. The highest gear on most transmissions is an overdrive gear, designed to maximize fuel economy. Unless you are towing a trailer or carrying a heavy load, it is best to leave the transmission in overdrive gear (on vehicles equipped with an automatic transmission). The transmission will automatically downshift as needed to maintain power as demanded by the driver.

Accelerator pedal. This foot-operated pedal is mounted in the front right corner of the driver's footwell. Speed is controlled by the amount of pressure applied by the right foot.

Brake pedal. Located to the left of the accelerator pedal, the foot-operated brake pedal slows the vehicle when the driver applies pressure. How much and how rapidly the vehicle slows is determined by how much pressure the driver applies and the amount of friction between the tires and the road surface.

Clutch pedal. In cars with manual transmissions, the foot-operated clutch pedal is located to the left of the brake pedal. When depressed, the clutch pedal disengages the transmission's drive gears so the driver can shift gears manually.

1. Accelerator pedal
2. Brake pedal
3. Clutch pedal

Parking brake. The purpose of the parking brake is to hold a parked vehicle in place. The parking brake may be a foot-operated pedal on the floor to the far left of the brake and clutch pedal, a hand-operated lever to the far left side of the driver's seat, or a hand-operated lever on the right of the steering column or on the floor or center console. To set a foot-operated parking brake, push down firmly on the pedal.

Depending on the vehicle, one of two methods is used to release the parking brake pedal. In some vehicles, you push down on the pedal until a click is heard, at which time the pedal automatically returns to its uppermost or released position. In other vehicles, the hand-actuated brake release lever may be above the foot pedal on the underside of the dashboard. To set a hand operated floor or console-mounted parking brake, simply pull up or back firmly on the lever. To release the brake, grasp the lever firmly with your fingers, and depress the button on the top of the lever with your thumb, then lower the lever.

Cruise/speed control. This device allows you to select and maintain a constant speed without having to keep your foot on the accelerator. The controls are either on the steering wheel or on a lever on the side of the steering column. The control options are on/off, set/accelerate and coast/resume. Speed control can be cancelled at any time by touching the off switch or by pressing the brake pedal. Although cruise control can be useful in maintaining a constant speed, drivers must learn to use the device properly and be alert to changes in the speed of other vehicles. Cruise control should not be used in heavy traffic, or in rain, snow, icy or other slick-surface or reduced-traction conditions. This will allow drivers to maintain maximum control over speed adjustments during these conditions. Check your owner's manual for instructions on using the cruise control.

Cruise control should not be used in heavy traffic, or in rain, snow, icy or other slick-surface or reduced-traction conditions.

The horn. Pressing on the steering wheel in the middle or in the areas to the side of the air bag usually operates the horn.

Turn-signal lever. Located on the left side of the steering column, the turn-signal lever is moved up to signal a movement to the right. It is moved down to indicate a movement to the left. While the signal usually will turn itself off after a right or left turn, the driver may have to manually cancel the signal after a slight turn such as a changing lanes.

Hazard flashers. The purpose of the hazard flashers is to warn other drivers of a problem or to increase awareness of the presence of a vehicle. The switch for the hazard lights is usually on the top or right side of the steering column, or on the dash near the center. When operated, both front and rear turn-signal lights flash.

Windshield wipers and washers. The control switch for the windshield wipers and washers may be on the dashboard, on the turn signal lever or on a separate lever arm on the right side of the steering column. Actually, two switches are involved: one controls wiper-blade speed, and the other controls the washer fluid. Some vehicles also feature a wiper for the rear window.

Headlights. The headlight switch also controls power to the parking lights, taillights, side marker lights and the license-plate lights. The switch may be on the left side of the instrument panel, on the same lever as the turn indicator or on a separate lever. In many vehicles, a separate switch controls the dome light and dashboard light intensity.

One example of a headlight switch

High/low headlight switch. This switch is typically mounted on the left side of the steering column and often the same as the turn-signal lever. It is operated by moving a lever forward or backward to switch from high- to low-beam headlights. On some pickup trucks and older cars, the switch is mounted on the floor, beneath the parking brake, and is operated by pressing on the switch with the left foot.

Additional Features

Heater, defroster and air conditioner. The controls for these devices are in a cluster on the instrument panel. Some vehicles have separate controls on the instrument panel that operate these features in the rear of the vehicle.

Hood release. The lever to release the hood is usually on the left side of the driver's compartment under the instrument panel. In some vehicles it is under, or just to the right of, the steering column. A second latch, located in the grill or under the front edge of the hood, is designed to prevent the hood from opening when the vehicle is in motion and must also be operated to open the hood.

Trunk or hatch release. On many vehicles, the release may be a lever on the floor just to the left or right side of the driver's seat. It could also be located on the driver's door panel or in the center console. In other vehicles, the release mechanism is a button in the glove box.

One example of a trunk release button

Fuel-door release. To prevent theft of fuel and protect against anyone putting damaging substances into the fuel tank, many vehicles are equipped with a fuel-door security system. The release button or lever may be on the floor to the left of the driver's seat, in the center console or in the glove box. It could also be located on the driver's door panel.

Gauges and lights. The gauges and lights on your vehicle's instrument panel provide important information about the vehicle's safety and operational condition. Although gauges and indicator lights are not in the same location on all vehicles, their functions are the same. Become familiar with your vehicle's instrument panel before you drive your vehicle. Read your owner's manual if you are unsure of the location or proper use of any of your vehicle's controls or instrumentation. Make it a habit to glance at the dashboard occasionally as you drive to ensure all systems are functioning properly. Develop the habit of quickly glancing at the gauges instead of staring at them.

Make it a habit to glance at the dashboard occasionally as you drive to ensure all systems are functioning properly.

The dashboard. Look at the picture of the dashboard on the next page. Items on the dashboard are identified by a number designation. Using the owner's manual for your family's or friend's vehicle, compare the presence and location with that shown. Test yourself by describing the purpose of each item.

Other devices. As with the instrument cluster, become familiar with the location and operation of devices such as the radio, window controls, air conditioner, headlight-dimmer switch and turn-indicator switch. Practice using the instruments and controls while the vehicle is parked so you can locate, reach and use them without having to search and take your eyes off the road ahead for more than a few seconds at a time.

1. Fuel gauge

2. Location of the fuel door

3. Low fuel indicator

4. Tachometer

5. Anti-lock brake system

6. Check engine light

7. Battery-voltage warning light

8. Gear-selection indicator

9. Automatic transmission indicator light

10. Left-turn indicator

11. Right-turn indicator

12. Hazard lights/flashers

13. Oil-pressure gauge

14. Theft/security system ON light

15. Headlight high-beam indicator

16. Air bag function light

17. Safety belt indicator

18. Door-ajar warning light

19. Odometer

20. Trip odometer

21. Speedometer mph/kmh

22. Parking brake indicator

23. Trip odometer reset button

24. Engine-temperature gauge

25. Instrument panel light dimmer

HOW *to* DRIVE

TEST 2

Getting Acquainted with the
Vehicle You Will Drive

Study and respond to each of the following questions. Then review the chapter to see if your responses are correct.

Multiple Choice:

1. How often should the pre-driving checks identified for approaching the vehicle, outside the vehicle and inside the vehicle be performed?
   a. When you first buy the vehicle
   b. Every so often (at least once a week)
   c. Every time you drive
   d. Only if something goes wrong

2. When approaching your vehicle parked at a curb, you should:
   a. Approach the driver's door from the rear of your vehicle, with your back to oncoming traffic.
   b. Approach the driver's door from the front of your vehicle, facing oncoming traffic.
   c. Never enter using the driver's door.
   d. Keep your keys concealed.

3. Under normal driving conditions, checks under the hood should be performed how often?
   a. When you first buy the vehicle
   b. Every time you drive
   c. At least once a month or as recommended in the owner's manual
   d. Only if something goes wrong

4. In vehicles equipped with a driver's-side air bag, sitting closer than ____ inches from the steering wheel increases the chance of arm, neck or facial injury in the event of a crash.
   a. 10
   b. 12
   c. 14
   d. 16

5. The top of the head restraint should be adjusted to a point:
   a. Slightly above your ears
   b. Slightly below your ears
   c. At the base of the neck
   d. As high as the adjustment will allow

Short Answer:

1. List the steps involved in safely approaching your vehicle.

2. Explain how safety belts can help protect vehicle occupants in the event of a collision.

3. Explain the optimal seating position behind the steering wheel.

4. Explain how to set the vehicle side mirrors, and how they help drivers monitor the space around their vehicles.

5. Describe eight items that can appear on the instrument panel.

CHAPTER**3**

Understanding Vehicle Space Needs, Natural Laws and Balance

Chapter Objectives

◆ Identify vehicle operating space.

◆ Explain the benefits of selecting and monitoring a planned path of travel.

◆ Describe the impact of surface conditions on traction.

◆ Describe natural laws and their effects on traction and vehicle movement.

◆ Explain the impact of steering, acceleration and braking inputs on vehicle suspension balance, weight distribution and traction.

The Controls:
Accelerating, Braking and Steering

The controls. As a driver, you control the speed and placement of a vehicle through three main input channels: accelerator, brakes and the steering wheel. Each of these controls is easy to operate, but smooth, coordinated use is developed with practice. Practice will help you become familiar with the differences in the "feel" of the vehicle you drive. It will also help you notice how your body and the vehicle react to abrupt braking, steering and acceleration, compared to smooth operation of the same controls. Remember that smooth operation of brakes, accelerator and steering depend on proper adjustment of the seat and steering wheel, as well as an upright position behind the steering wheel, as described in Chapter 2.

Direct your attention 20 to 30 seconds ahead and to both sides along your intended path of travel.

Visual input. Few people appreciate the degree to which attention to driving and a directed visual search influence their chance of being involved in a crash. It is important to remember that the eyes see what the brain directs them to look for. When driving, you should be searching for objects or conditions within, along or closing on your planned path of travel. To operate a vehicle smoothly and safely you must develop the habit of directing your attention 20 to 30 seconds ahead and to both sides along your intended path of travel. This will allow you to identify objects or conditions that could increase the level of risk.

Relating to other objects. Just as important as developing smooth control of steering, braking and accelerating is knowing your vehicle's placement in reference to other objects on and off road. You should be able to determine whether you can safely move into a planned space ahead, to the side or to the rear of your vehicle.

Operating space. At all times, you will need adequate operating space in front of, to the sides of, and to the rear of your vehicle. It is important to maintain open space in these areas so that you can move the vehicle there, if necessary. Operating space can be thought of as a space cushion, extending in each direction from the vehicle.

The need for space. As speed increases, the operating space required also increases, especially space to the front of the vehicle. As you travel faster, having additional space will allow you more time to respond to a situation.

Miscalculating space. If you incorrectly judge the amount of space needed to operate a vehicle in a given situation, the possible outcomes range from a minor fender bender to a destroyed vehicle with potential for serious injury. Adjustments in speed and position must be made in direct proportion to your operating space requirements.

Adjustments in speed and position must be made in direct proportion to your operating space requirements.

HOW to DRIVE

Targeting Line of Sight, Planned Path of Travel

Planned path of travel. To allow enough distance to stop in response to threatening objects or conditions, you must identify a planned path of travel, or *visual control zone*, 12 to 15 seconds ahead. An alternate path into which the vehicle can be steered if the planned path of travel is blocked also must be identified. Under most conditions a following interval of three or four seconds will enable you to adjust speed or position appropriately. However, three to four seconds may prove insufficient if the alternate path involves leaving a paved roadway and braking to a stop on the shoulder. Under such conditions it is critical that you be aware of any vehicle to the rear, including its size, lane position and distance behind.

Referencing Vehicle to Path of Travel

Visual referencing. A visual reference point relates some part of the roadway to some part of the vehicle. Good space judgment depends on your ability to visualize space, accurate visual referencing, knowledge of space needs and driving experience. Experience and visual referencing are the most important factors in developing good space judgment. Each driver may see the relationship of roadway surface to the vehicle somewhat differently, depending upon the position of the driver's body, the driver's size and the vehicle type. Variables that can influence perception of reference points are eye dominance, seat adjustment, seat height, head movement and vehicle type. The visual reference points, however, will be similar for any vehicle.

Road Surface and Traction

Traction. Traction is the adhesion, friction or grip between the tires and the road surface. Without traction, a driver cannot steer, brake or accelerate. A loss of traction may cause a loss of control that can result in skidding.

Traction varies. Traction varies with the vehicle's speed, tire condition and roadway surface. As a driver, you control your vehicle's speed and the condition of your tires. However, you have no control over the road surface or its condition, so you must learn to recognize conditions that may indicate a change in traction, which in turn will require a change in speed or direction.

Surface material. Road surfaces produce different amounts of traction. The following are ranked in order, from the greatest traction to the least:

1. Concrete
2. Asphalt
3. Brick or polished concrete
4. Dirt
5. Gravel
6. Sand over hard surface

Traction is the adhesion, friction or grip between the tires and the road surface.

Conditions that can affect traction:

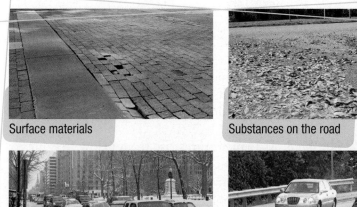
Surface materials

Substances on the road

Surface conditions

Roadway design

Substances on the road. Any substance on a road surface can reduce traction. Be alert for sewer covers, paint, vinyl strips, tar, wet leaves, sand, loose gravel or mud. These substances will almost always reduce the level of adhesion or traction available. (Sand spread over an icy road is an obvious exception.) Oil, tar, radiator overflow and rubber left by frequent vehicle starts and stops at intersections all have an adverse effect on adhesion.

Any substance on a road surface can reduce traction.

Surface conditions. Poor road conditions such as rippled surfaces or potholes can contribute to a loss of traction. Be especially alert when the road is wet. At the beginning of a rainstorm, dirt and oil can rise and mix on the roadway surface, making the road extremely slippery. At speeds as low as 35 mph and a water depth of only 1/12 inch, "hydroplaning" can occur. This action, similar to the phenomenon that makes water skiing possible, occurs when the tires rise up on a wedge of water. Your speed, tire inflation, width, tread and the depth of water on the road all influence the speed at which a vehicle will hydroplane. In all situations, it is the driver's responsibility to prevent his or her vehicle from hydroplaning.

Temperature changes. As temperatures rise from below freezing to about 32 degrees, icy and snow-packed areas become more slippery. Wet ice is much more slippery than dry ice. Intersections are likely to be slicker because starting and stopping vehicles polish the ice.

Other factors. In addition, bridge surfaces, overpasses and shaded areas may freeze before other road surfaces. Wind gusts and strong crosswinds can make steering on a slick surface difficult. Large buildings or embankments may block the wind, cause a sudden change in wind direction or shade an icy area from the sun. Patches of ice or wet leaves can cause unequal traction. Under such conditions, even moderate braking or acceleration may result in loss of traction that can lead to a sudden skid.

Bridge surfaces, overpasses and shaded areas may freeze before other road surfaces.

Road design. Roadway design features, such as banked or crowned roads, can have an effect on traction and control. A crowned roadway is a road that is higher in the middle than at the sides. A banked roadway, usually found at a curve, is higher on one edge than the other.

Roadway Design Can Affect Traction

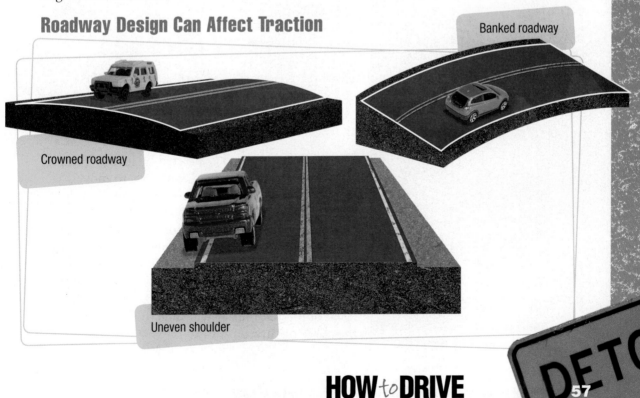

Banked roadway

Crowned roadway

Uneven shoulder

DETO

Shoulders. Roadway shoulders frequently provide the only escape path in an emergency. However, the shoulders of most highways provide less traction than the road surface. As a result, you need to be aware of shoulder conditions whenever you drive. Shoulders may be rough or soft; covered with loose materials such as dirt, cinders or sand; or littered with broken glass or other waste. When steering off the road onto the shoulder, expect a reduction in traction. Braking with two wheels on the road and two wheels on the shoulder will result in unequal traction and may cause skidding.

> The shoulders of most highways provide less traction than the road surface. When steering off the road onto the shoulder, expect a reduction in traction.

Shoulders may not be even with road surface.
A common problem is that roadway shoulders are not even with the road surface. In such cases, particularly where the difference in the surface level is three inches or more, extreme caution is advised. A driver trying to steer a vehicle back onto the road may catch (scrub) the inside wall of the front tire on the edge of the road, resulting in steering problems or loss of control.

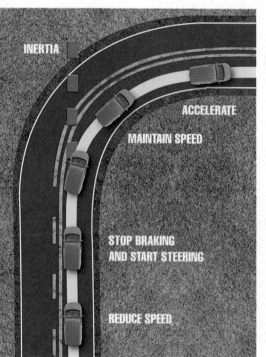

INERTIA

ACCELERATE

MAINTAIN SPEED

STOP BRAKING
AND START STEERING

REDUCE SPEED

Natural Laws and Traction

Inertia. Traction also is affected by inertia. Simply stated, an object in motion continues to move straight ahead until acted upon by some outside force. This force creates problems when a driver changes a vehicle's direction too suddenly. As the car travels around the corner, inertia tends to keep the car moving forward in a straight line, rather than allowing the car to follow the curve or turn. Unless traction is great enough to overcome the force of inertia, the car will slide to the outside of the curve or turn.

Five factors influence the effect of inertia:

1. Sharpness of the turn or curve
2. Speed
3. Size, height, weight and load of the vehicle
4. Roadway slope
5. Roadway surface condition

Gravity. Gravity, the invisible force that keeps our feet on the ground, also affects vehicle traction and performance. Gravity's downhill pull affects a vehicle's ability to accelerate and maintain speed on hills. When going up a hill, you must accelerate to keep a constant speed and overcome the force of gravity. On a slippery hill, acceleration may result in a loss of traction.

Driving downhill. Conversely, when you drive down a hill, the force of gravity tends to boost speed, which increases the stopping distance. A crowned road that curves sharply right or left can be especially dangerous if located on a downgrade. On such a road, traction must overcome both the force of gravity and inertia.

Kinetic energy. Movement requires energy, and the faster an object moves, the more energy is needed. Kinetic energy, the amount of energy needed to propel a vehicle, is affected by the vehicle's weight and speed. Kinetic energy also directly relates to decelerating a vehicle. First, braking distances needed to stop a vehicle increase by the square of the amount the speed is increased. For example, if a vehicle's speed doubles from 20 mph to 40 mph, the distance needed to stop the vehicle increases by four times. Second, the force of impact in a collision also increases by the same ratio: the square of the increase in speed. That means that if a vehicle's speed is doubled, the forces involved in a collision will be quadrupled.

Braking distances needed to stop a vehicle increase by the square of the amount the speed is increased. For example, if a vehicle's speed doubles from 20 mph to 40 mph, the distance needed to stop the vehicle increases by four times.

Vehicle-Suspension Balance and Traction

Single-vehicle crashes. More than 50 percent of occupant fatalities occur as a result of single-vehicle crashes. Basically, the vehicle leaves the roadway and strikes a fixed object or overturns. Almost without exception, these crashes involve improper steering or braking or a combination of the two. Improper steering or braking or both can upset a vehicle's balance, which can lead to a loss in traction and an unintended path of travel.

A matter of balance. Vehicle suspension balance refers to the distribution of the weight of the vehicle on the chassis. A transfer of weight from one point of the vehicle to another occurs whenever the driver accelerates, brakes, turns or performs some combination of these actions. The amount of weight change and the driver's ability to control the vehicle are influenced by the rate of acceleration, brake application, steering input, surface traction or combinations of these factors.

Weight distribution. The vehicle's weight can be shifted from the center of the chassis, with the weight distributed approximately equally over the front and rear tires, to a position where weight is concentrated over the front, rear, left or right tires. When the vehicle is stopped, or traveling straight at a constant speed, its suspension and traction are stabilized.

Vehicle at rest or moving at a constant speed.

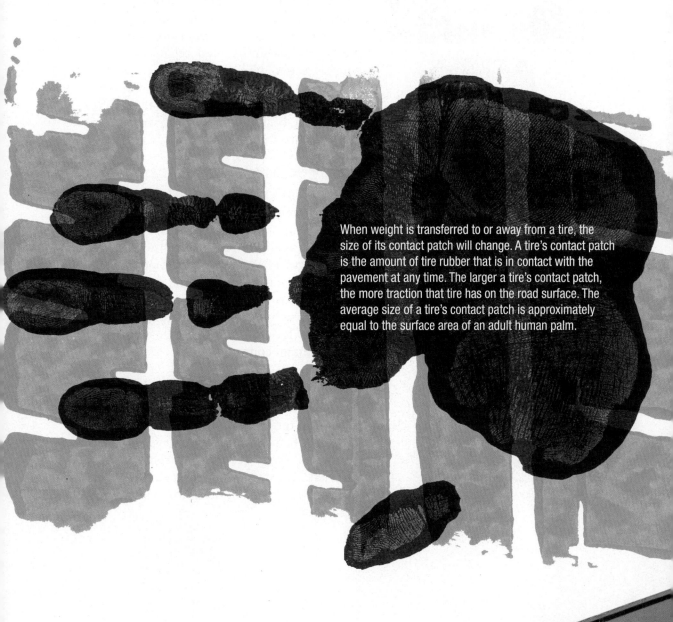

When weight is transferred to or away from a tire, the size of its contact patch will change. A tire's contact patch is the amount of tire rubber that is in contact with the pavement at any time. The larger a tire's contact patch, the more traction that tire has on the road surface. The average size of a tire's contact patch is approximately equal to the surface area of an adult human palm.

HOW *to* **DRIVE**

Changing Vehicle Suspension Load —

Front to Rear. When a vehicle accelerates, its weight shifts to the rear. The rear suspension compresses, and the rear tires' contact patches increase in size, while the front tires' contact patches decrease in size. If acceleration is aggressive, there will be a noticeable rise of the vehicle's front and a drop of the rear. The table on the next page summarizes the effects of acceleration, braking and steering weight transfer and tire contact patches.

Changing Vehicle Suspension Load —

Rear to Front. When the brakes are applied, the vehicle's weight or center of mass is transferred to the front. If braking is hard, there is a noticeable drop of the vehicle's front and a rise of the rear. Occupants will feel forward movement. Apply too little brake pressure, and the vehicle will not stop at the desired point or within the distance available. Apply too much pressure, and the wheels may lock up, resulting in loss of traction and directional control.

Changing Vehicle Suspension Load —

Side to Side. When turning, a vehicle's weight will shift in the direction opposite the turn. For example, when turning right, the vehicle's weight will shift to the left, causing the vehicle to lean to the left. The degree of weight shift depends on speed, traction, and the amount and speed of steering input.

Driver Input	Transfer of Weight	Impact on Tire Contact Patches	Impact on Tire Traction
Accelerating	To the rear	Rear: Increase Front: Decrease	Rear: Increase Front: Decrease
Braking	To the front	Rear: Decrease Front: Increase	Rear: Decrease Front: Increase
Steering Left	To the right side	Right side: Increase Left side: Decrease	Right side: Increase Left side: Decrease
Steering Right	To the left side	Right side: Decrease Left side: Increase	Right side: Decrease Left side: Increase

Maximizing traction. To maximize traction and minimize the chance of traction loss, avoid sudden inputs when accelerating, braking or steering. For example, applying the brakes when cornering too fast will slow the vehicle very little, and may cause a skid because of severe weight shift. Also, focus on executing one input at a time — brake, then steer, then accelerate. Performing smooth inputs one at a time will help maintain maximum traction.

Seating position. To most effectively control vehicle balance, drivers should sit in a comfortable, upright position directly behind the steering wheel. This will also help maximize the driver's view of the driving environment.

Focus on executing one input at a time — brake, then steer, then accelerate. Performing smooth inputs one at a time will help maintain maximum traction.

TEST **3**

Understanding Vehicle Space Needs, Natural Laws and Balance

Study and respond to each of the following questions. Then review the chapter to see if your responses are correct.

Multiple Choice:

1. To allow enough distance to stop in response to threatening objects or conditions, you should identify a planned path of travel _____ seconds ahead.
   a. 2–4
   b. 12–15
   c. 20–30
   d. 50–60

2. Under most conditions a minimum following interval of _____ will enable you to adjust speed or position appropriately.
   a. 2 seconds
   b. 3–4 seconds
   c. 8 seconds
   d. Three car lengths

3. If a vehicle's speed doubles from 20 mph to 40 mph, the distance needed to stop the vehicle increases by _____ times.
   a. 2
   b. 3
   c. 4
   d. 8

4. When braking hard, the weight of the vehicle noticeably shifts _____.
   a. To the rear of the vehicle
   b. To the front of the vehicle
   c. To the left of the vehicle
   d. To the right of the vehicle

5. When turning to the right, the contact patches of the _____ will increase in size.
   a. Front tires
   b. Rear tires
   c. Right side tires
   d. Left side tires

Short Answer:

1. Define "hydroplaning" and how drivers can prevent its occurrence.

2. List and explain the factors that affect traction between a vehicle's tires and the roadway surface.

3. List four substances that can reduce traction between a vehicle's tires and the roadway.

4. Explain the relationship between inertia and traction.

5. Explain the effects of uphill and downhill roadway sections on (a) traveling speed, (b) acceleration ability, and (c) braking ability.

HOW *to* **DRIVE**

CHAPTER 4

Starting, Steering and Stopping the Vehicle

Chapter Objectives

◆ Demonstrate the proper sequence for starting an engine.

◆ Describe proper hand position on the steering wheel.

◆ Explain effective steering techniques.

◆ Describe proper foot position for optimal accelerator/brake pedal control.

◆ Describe the proper sequence for putting the vehicle in motion.

◆ Identify the proper technique for slowing and braking.

◆ Describe proper procedures for safe backing.

◆ Explain the proper procedure for stopping and securing a vehicle.

Forming good habits. There are certain habits you should develop when starting a vehicle engine:

1. Always place your foot on the brake pedal before starting the engine. (If you have trouble reaching the brake or accelerator pedal and you do not have adjustable pedals, obtain pedal extensions.)

2. Check to ensure the parking brake is set.

3. Check to ensure the gear selector lever is in Park.*

4. Turn the key clockwise to start the engine. Note that instead of key-turn starting, some vehicles feature a push-to-start button.

   NOTE: Check your owner's manual for specific instructions on starting your particular vehicle.

5. As soon as the engine starts, release the key (or button). Failure to release the ignition switch can damage the starter system.

6. Let the engine idle for at least 15 to 20 seconds before you start driving. Do not race the engine by pressing hard on the accelerator.

7. Check to make sure all gauges are working and that all indicate normal functioning of vehicle systems.

8. If the vehicle is not equipped with daytime running lights (DRLs), turn on the low-beam headlights.

9. Drive at a moderate speed for the first few blocks to allow the engine and fluids to warm up to operating temperatures.

* See Chapter 10 for recommended habits for operating a vehicle equipped with a manual transmission.

Effective Steering

Enhancing steering control. To maximize vehicle control, position both your hands on the steering wheel. This helps prevent the need to make sudden steering movements or correct for too much steering input. Grip the steering wheel using the hand positions described in Chapter 2. Allow your arms to relax so that your elbows are pointed downward. This can improve stability and help reduce unintended steering wheel movements and fatigue.

Steering Techniques

Three techniques. Turning the steering wheel clockwise will cause the vehicle to change direction to the right. Turning the steering wheel counter-clockwise will cause the vehicle to change direction to the left. Three steering techniques are available to drivers:

- Hand-to-hand steering
- Hand-over-hand steering
- One-hand steering

Hand-to-hand steering. When turning through a slight curve using hand-to-hand steering — sometimes referred to as push-pull or feed steering (it is not "shuffle" steering) — both hands will typically retain their original grip on the wheel, requiring only slight finger or wrist movements to maintain the path of travel. However, in tighter turns, your hands may move as much as 165 degrees up and down the sides of the wheel. (Neither hand crosses the 6 or 12 o'clock positions.) While one hand pushes up or pulls down, the opposite hand slides up or down along the wheel to provide additional steering input or stabilize steering. Reverse the process to return to a straight path — or allow the wheel to slide through your hands to its original position. In either case, both hands are always in contact with the steering wheel.

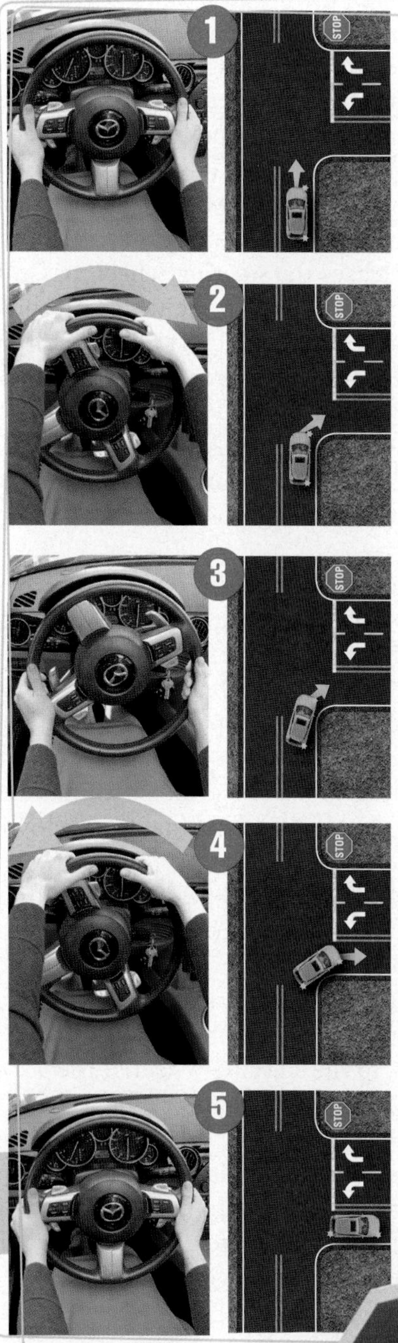

Hand-to-hand steering is shown (turning right).

Hand-over-hand steering. To steer hand-over-hand, grasp the steering wheel with your right hand between 2 and 3 o'clock and your left hand between 9 and 10 o'clock. Use one hand to push the steering wheel up and over the other hand, past the 12 o'clock position, then down toward 9 or 3 o'clock. (Push with your left hand for a right turn, or with your right hand for a left turn.) At the same time, your bottom hand releases the steering wheel, passing across your forearm, to grip the wheel on the far side. The same hand, which is now on top, then pulls the wheel up and over, past 12 o'clock and down. Continue as necessary to complete the turn. Reverse the process to return to the straight-ahead position and then return your hands to their original position.

One-handed steering. One-handed steering is not recommended. Steering with one hand should be used only when backing up in a straight line or only briefly when adjusting dashboard controls. Keep both hands on the wheel when you must turn while backing. Since it is more difficult to maintain steering control when backing, drive slowly.

Steering while backing. Backing and steering with one hand requires shifting your hip and seat position so you can see past the head restraint. To improve balance, your right arm may be braced over the back of the front passenger seat. Grip the steering wheel at the 12 o'clock position with your left hand and move the wheel left or right in the direction you want the rear of the vehicle to go. Make visual checks to the front when you start to back up and continue to do so as you back to ensure that the front of the vehicle is not swinging out of line or about to strike anything.

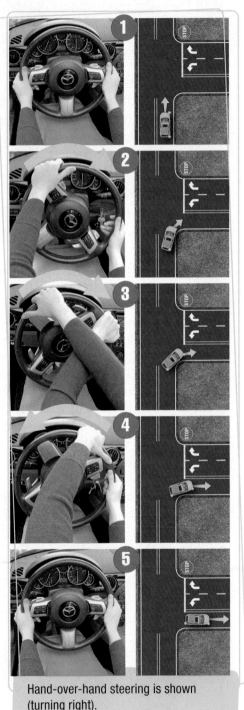

Hand-over-hand steering is shown (turning right).

Improper steering. As stated in Chapter 1, research shows that a substantial percentage of crashes involving 16-year old drivers result from failure to make a quick turn or from improper evasive steering. Whether performed at low or high speed, a quick turn results in a shift of weight (or center of mass) from one side of the vehicle to the other. Speed and steering input have a direct influence on the weight transferred to the front corner of the vehicle opposite the direction of the turn. An increase in weight to the front is accompanied by a reduction in the weight to the rear, particularly on the side in the direction of the turn.

Sudden steering input. If an error has been committed and you are approaching another object at high speed, the quickness of steering input needed to make a 10- to 12-foot lane change increases. Sudden steering input, coupled with a high speed — unless dampened by a smooth, rapid countersteer — can generate enough weight transfer to overcome the tires' traction and result in a skid.

Following an intended path. To steer a vehicle smoothly and precisely, you need a visual target to use as a reference. Beginning drivers frequently use the middle of the hood, the edge of the road, the center line or the fenders to steer by, but such a low aim requires constant adjustments to the steering wheel to maintain lane position. Since we tend to steer where we look, the best approach is to visualize an imaginary line down the middle of your intended path of travel (12–15 seconds or one to one and one-half blocks in the city, or 20–30 seconds on the open road). Directing your visual search back and forth along the center of your travel path provides the best point of reference.

Sudden steering input can generate enough weight transfer to overcome the tires' traction and result in a skid.

HOW to DRIVE

Passing stationary objects. When you pass close to objects on your right side — such as parked vehicles, posts or bridge abutments — look past the object but glance quickly at your right front fender to judge the distance. When space is limited on both sides, position the vehicle closer to the object on the left side, where operating space is easier to judge.

When space is limited on both sides, keep your vehicle as close as possible to objects on the left side.

Steering corrections. Steering corrections must be smooth and made as soon as the vehicle starts to wander from the planned path of travel. New drivers frequently wait too long to make corrections, allowing the vehicle to wander from one side of the lane to the other. When making a correction too late, the driver frequently turns the steering wheel too far, causing the vehicle to move back toward the opposite side of the lane, requiring a constant sequence of countersteers. Learning to search 20 to 30 seconds ahead, identifying a target area along the intended path of travel and making slight, timely steering corrections will help reduce the tendency to wander within the lane. Crosswinds, uneven road surfaces, steering-wheel play and road slope also can cause a vehicle to wander within or between lanes, but slight steering adjustments can overcome such problems.

Searching 20 to 30 seconds ahead will help reduce the tendency to wander within the lane.

Road feel. Assuming you are gripping the steering wheel firmly with your fingers and the tires are properly inflated, you should experience a certain level of "road feel" through the steering wheel. This feedback can tell you if the road surface has changed or if your vehicle is operating properly. For instance, a vibration in the steering wheel could indicate a problem with wheel alignment or tire balance, or it could just be an indication of a rough road.

Power steering. Most modern vehicles feature power steering, which makes it much easier to turn the steering wheel, especially when maneuvering in tight spaces or trying to parallel park. The first time you drive any vehicle, drive with extra care until you become familiar with the steering response. Otherwise, you might not steer enough, or you might steer too much. You also should be aware of the changes in steering systems in recent years that reduce the amount of steering needed to change your direction of travel. When you change from a vehicle with power steering to one with manual steering, you must adjust to the additional effort needed to steer.

Positioning Your Foot to Operate Accelerator and Brake Pedals

Using the right foot. Most drivers brake with the right foot, which ensures that pressure is completely off the accelerator when braking. To operate the accelerator and brake pedals smoothly, rest the heel of your right foot on the floor, centered in front of the brake pedal. This position allows you to pivot easily between the accelerator and brake and offers better braking control.

HOW to DRIVE

Placement of the left foot. Place the heel of your left foot on the floor to the left of the brake pedal, resting on the "dead pedal," a small flat footrest on the left front-wheel housing in many cars.

Using both feet. It is recommended that new drivers use only their right foot to operate both the accelerator and brake pedals. However, some drivers prefer to use the left foot for braking and the right foot for accelerating in vehicles with automatic transmissions. If you do use your left foot to brake, never drive with your left foot poised over the brake pedal except while trail braking, as described on page 77. When you use left foot braking, your right foot must come off the accelerator as your left foot pivots to the brake pedal.

Accelerating the Vehicle

Before shifting gear. Always make sure the parking brake is set and step firmly on the brake pedal before moving the gear selector lever to Drive or Reverse. After shifting, check to make sure the parking brake is completely released before you release the brake pedal. Driving with the parking brake partially on can damage the brakes.

Moving Forward

1. Keep your foot on the brake.
2. Shift to Drive.
3. Release the parking brake.
4. Signal.
5. Check your rearview and side-view mirrors.
6. Check over your shoulder for a safe gap.
7. Pivot your foot from brake to accelerator.
8. Accelerate gently.
9. Steer into the proper lane.

Accelerating. The ability to control speed depends upon good accelerator technique. Resting the right side of the foot against the console or transmission tunnel makes it much easier to control the accelerator to attain and maintain a desired speed. However, no two vehicles accelerate exactly alike, so drivers must develop a sensitivity for each vehicle they drive.

Four levels of acceleration. Basically there are four levels of acceleration:

1. Idling acceleration, where simply releasing pressure from the brake pedal can result in slow forward movement (on vehicles equipped with an automatic transmission). Keeping the accelerator covered with the right foot can help provide a smooth transition from brake release to progressive acceleration.
2. Light acceleration, the purpose of which is to maintain slow forward motion or allowing speed to increase gradually with minimum weight shift.
3. Progressive acceleration, with firm pressure on the accelerator to increase speed.
4. Thrust acceleration, a firm push or thrust of the accelerator for increased acceleration, to shift more weight to the rear wheels for traction, or for passing in higher-speed traffic.

Braking and Deceleration

Stopping smoothly. Braking a vehicle to a stop is a relatively simple task. However, like many actions, braking requires practice if it is to be performed smoothly and precisely. The most difficult task is learning when and how much pressure to apply to bring the vehicle to a smooth, controlled stop at the desired point.

Practice is key. From a speed of 20 to 30 mph, safely practice controlled braking in an area free of children and other pedestrians, and with few vehicles. Select a spot ahead where you want to stop, such as a shadow or the edge of a driveway. You may overshoot or stop short of the target the first few times, but practice will help you judge the distance and amount of brake pressure you need to stop at the desired point. As you experience success, gradually increase your speed — and continue practicing when you have an opportunity to do so safely.

When braking, pressure should be smooth and even, not sudden and hard.

Effective braking. The key to effective braking is to stabilize the foot and control brake pressure with the ankle and toe rather than with the larger, less precise thigh muscles. Place your heel on the floor in front of the brake pedal so the area forward of the ball of the foot is on the pedal. This position will enable you to use your toes for fine pedal-pressure adjustments and makes it easy to pivot your foot smoothly between the brake and accelerator.

Four levels of deceleration. Basically there are four levels of speed reduction or braking:

1. Releasing the accelerator stops the vehicle's forward propulsion. Although the vehicle will continue moving forward, it will be coasting forward rather than being propelled by the engine. This transition from acceleration to deceleration tends to be more noticeable in vehicles with manual transmissions.

2. Controlled or "squeeze" braking is done with sufficient pressure to slow the vehicle while avoiding abrupt weight transfer that could lead to traction loss by the front or rear wheels.

3. Threshold braking is the application of brake pressure to a point just short of locking up the brakes. Resulting in maximum braking capability, this procedure tends to be used during emergency situations where the driver is responding to an unanticipated situation. Too much pressure on the brake pedal can cause brake lockup on vehicles not equipped with an anti-lock braking system (ABS). If this occurs, reducing brake pressure slightly will help the driver regain steering control.

4. Trail braking, or "squeeze off" braking, is used to smoothly and gradually reduce brake pedal pressure at the end of a braking maneuver. This helps to avoid abrupt weight transfer when turning at an intersection or into a curve. This technique is often used in combination with, or at the end of, controlled or threshold braking.

Stopping time. Total stopping time consists of perception, reaction and braking distance. Perception of distance is the most difficult to estimate. However, assuming the driver is not distracted and is paying reasonable attention to task, the average driver will generally take one-half to three-quarters of a second to recognize that something is wrong and requires a response. Executing the necessary response takes another one-half to three-quarters of a second — which is identified as reaction time. Both perception and reaction time estimates are based on the assumption that the driver is in good physical health, has had sufficient sleep, is not impaired by alcohol or other drugs, and is attentive to driving.

To minimize stopping distances and maintain vehicle balance, always strive to brake in a straight line.

Road friction or grip. When pressure is applied to the brake pedal, the rotation of the wheels is slowed. This slowing causes increased friction — or grip — between the tires and the road surface. Since road surface conditions affect this friction, any substance on the road surface such as water, gravel, oil, ice or snow will reduce the tires' gripping efficiency and result in longer stopping distances. To minimize stopping distances and maintain vehicle balance, always strive to brake in a straight line. This helps maximize the tires' contact patches, resulting in the greatest possible traction during braking.

Sudden stops without an anti-lock braking system. Brake pressure control is the key to maintaining steering control when making a sudden stop in a vehicle not equipped with ABS. Maximum braking occurs just before the wheels stop rotating and start to slide. If any wheel locks and starts to slide, it will be difficult, if not impossible, to control the vehicle's direction.

Press the brake pedal firmly to the point just short of wheel lock.

Vehicles Equipped with an Anti-Lock Braking System (ABS)

How ABS works. Most new vehicles are equipped with anti-lock brakes. In an ABS-equipped vehicle, a sensor located in each wheel detects when that wheel stops turning, or locks up. When a sensor detects wheel lockup, the system automatically reduces pressure on the brake slightly, and immediately applies it again, pulsing on and off very rapidly, many times per second. The pulsing action is repeated automatically until you reduce pressure on the brake pedal or the vehicle comes to a stop. When the ABS is engaged, you may feel the brake pedal pulsing against your foot — this is normal.

Emergency braking with ABS. In the event of an emergency when hard braking or a combination of steering and hard braking is needed, apply maximum pressure to the brake pedal. Do not pump the brake pedal or remove your foot from the brake pedal, as this could prevent the system from working properly. Keep in mind that ABS does not result in shorter stopping distances. Rather, it is designed to help drivers maintain steering control during hard braking maneuvers. ABS is a safety feature, and drivers of ABS-equipped vehicles should not drive at higher speeds, brake harder or reduce following distances.

Your vehicle is equipped with ABS if you see this symbol when starting the vehicle.

Drivers of ABS-equipped vehicles should not drive at higher speeds or reduce following distances.

Vehicles Not Equipped with an Anti-Lock Brake System

Braking without ABS. The procedure for braking in an emergency in a vehicle without ABS is a bit different. Since there is no electronic system to monitor whether the wheels are locked, you must rely on your senses to determine the optimal amount of brake pressure. To maintain braking control:

1. With your heel on the floor, pivot your foot from the accelerator to the brake pedal and press firmly with your toes, stopping at a point just before the wheels lock.

2. If the wheels start to lock, relax your toes slightly to release brake pressure just a bit, then squeeze the brake pedal again to just short of lockup.

3. Continue the squeezing to the point just before the wheels lock, a technique referred to as "threshold braking."

Power Brakes and Signaling Before Braking

Power brakes. Most vehicles are equipped with power brakes. Power-assist brakes do not stop a vehicle more quickly, but they do substantially reduce the amount of pressure needed to brake to a stop. Even though power brakes reduce the pressure needed for braking, they work even if the engine stops or the power-assist unit fails. However, if the system should fail, you will have to apply more pressure on the brakes to stop the vehicle.

Changing vehicles. Be careful when changing from one vehicle to another. Braking sensitivity can vary among vehicles. You may lengthen the stopping distance by applying too little pressure.

Signaling a stop. Nearly 30 percent of all reported collisions are rear-end crashes. To reduce the chance of being struck from behind, always check to the rear and tap the brake pedal several times before actually slowing the vehicle to alert any following driver of your intentions.

Hand signals. You also can indicate your intentions to stop by giving a hand signal. To give a hand signal, hold the steering wheel with your right hand, and extend your left arm out the window and down, palm facing to the rear. Hand signals provide an additional safety measure when there is an increased chance of being struck from behind, such as when you are in a line of moving traffic.

Early warnings. Whatever the situation, always check to the rear and warn others through the use of brake lights or hand signals before braking to a stop. Give an early warning whenever possible.

To reduce the chance of being struck from behind, check to the rear and tap the brake pedal several times before stopping.

Left Turn   Right Turn   Stop

Backing

When backing, check traffic conditions in all directions —and check all blind areas carefully.

Take your time. When backing a vehicle, take your time and always back slowly. Check traffic conditions in all directions — **and check all blind areas carefully**. Look in the direction you are moving but never concentrate on any one thing to such a degree that you neglect your surroundings.

Remember, when you back and turn a vehicle, the front of the vehicle swings out in the direction opposite the direction in which the rear of the vehicle is moving. You cannot see objects close to the rear or sides when looking out the windows. Do not forget — your vehicle's response to steering inputs while backing will be much sharper than when driving forward. Be sure to adjust for this, and drive slowly when backing to allow time for steering corrections.

Maintaining control. To maintain control when backing, it is important to move the vehicle slowly and be prepared to stop quickly. Difficulty in steering usually develops as a result of having to look backward, frequently with a limited line of sight. To reduce risk, follow these steps:

◆ Before entering the vehicle, check to make sure the path to the rear and sides is clear. Children and objects are often difficult to see from the driver's seat.

◆ Keep your foot firmly on the brake pedal while shifting to Reverse.

◆ Since you cannot see objects close to the rear or sides when looking out the window, you will have to use both front and rear windows and inside and outside mirrors. Also check to the front to determine whether the front of the vehicle is tracking in the direction you want it to go.

◆ Back slowly. Your vehicle is much harder to control and stop when backing.

- When moving backward, the rear of the vehicle turns in the direction you turn the steering wheel. If you become confused or disoriented while backing, stop and begin again.

- Check traffic conditions to make sure you have time to complete the backing maneuver. Avoid backing into a busy street, highway or pedestrian walkway.

- When the maneuver is complete, bring the vehicle to a full stop before shifting into a forward gear or into Park.

Backing straight or to the right. Place your left hand at the top of the steering wheel. Turn your head and body to the right so you can see out the rear and right-rear side windows. How much your body can be turned is limited by your ability to reach the brake and accelerator pedals. To improve balance, brace your right arm over the back of the front passenger seat. Make visual checks to the front at the start of the backing movement and periodically while backing to make sure the front of your vehicle is not swinging out of line or in danger of hitting something.

Backing straight or to the right.

When backing to the right, turn the wheel clockwise.

When backing to the left, turn the wheel counter-clockwise.

Backing to the left. Look over your left shoulder and grip the steering wheel with your right hand at the 12 o'clock position. Always look in the direction the vehicle is moving and turn the steering wheel in the direction you want the rear of the vehicle to go. Do not open the door to look out, but be sure to make visual checks to the front periodically while backing.

When backing to the left, remember that the front of your vehicle will swing out to the right.

Backing to the left.

When backing, always look in the direction the vehicle is moving and turn the steering wheel in the direction you want the rear of the vehicle to go.

Be sure to make visual checks to the front periodically while backing.

Stopping and Securing the Vehicle

Good habits. It is very important that you learn and use the following sequence for stopping and securing a vehicle every time you arrive at your destination and leave the vehicle.

1. Come to a complete stop with the wheels turned toward or away from the roadway as appropriate.
2. Keep your foot on the brake pedal and set the parking brake.
3. Shift the gear-selector lever to the Park position.
4. Turn off all accessories and lights.
5. Make sure all windows are closed.
6. Turn off the ignition and remove the key.
7. Unfasten your seat belt.
8. Check mirrors and over your shoulder for traffic.
9. Exit the vehicle, keys in hand.
10. Lock all doors.

Always check for traffic before you exit your vehicle.

HOW *to* **DRIVE**

TEST 4

Starting, Steering and Stopping the Vehicle

Study and respond to each of the following questions. Then review the chapter to see if your responses are correct.

Multiple Choice:

1. When starting the engine, you should release the key:
    a. After you check over your left shoulder.
    b. As you release the parking brake.
    c. When you hear a grinding sound.
    d. As soon as the engine starts.

2. When backing:
    a. Brace your right arm over the back of the front passenger seat.
    b. Grip the steering wheel at the 12 o'clock position with your left hand.
    c. Move the wheel left or right in the direction you want the rear of the vehicle to go.
    d. All of the above

3. _____ acceleration is used to maintain slow forward motion or allowing speed to increase gradually with minimum weight shift.
    a. Idle
    b. Light
    c. Threshold
    d. Squeeze

4. Total stopping time is made up of:
    a. Reaction time
    b. Braking time
    c. Perception time
    d. All of the above

5. Anti-lock braking systems (ABS):
    a. Help drivers maintain steering control under hard braking.
    b. Allow shorter following distances.
    c. Result in shorter stopping distances.
    d. Allow higher traveling speeds.

Short Answer:

1. List five habits you should develop when starting a vehicle engine.

2. Explain how to perform the three steering techniques.

3. List and explain the four levels of acceleration.

4. List and explain the four levels of deceleration.

5. Explain the benefits of braking in a straight line.

CHAPTER**5**

Traffic Control Devices

Chapter Objectives:

- Understand the purpose and value of traffic control devices.
- Explain the role of color in the use of traffic control devices.
- Identify and explain the meaning of the three basic types of traffic signs.
- Identify and explain the role and meaning of traffic control signal lights.
- Identify and explain the role and meaning of pavement markings.

HOW *to* **DRIVE**

Traffic Control Devices

Definition and purpose. Traffic control devices include traffic signs, signal lights and pavement markings. The purpose of these devices is to help ensure highway safety by providing for the orderly and predictable movement of all traffic, motorized and non-motorized, throughout the highway transportation system. These devices tell drivers where they are, where they are going and how to get there. They provide information about laws, dangers and the roadway.

Communication modes. Traffic control devices communicate their message in several ways, by using color, shape, words and placement to provide information. Through their messages, they direct drivers' actions and provide a framework of uniform guidance.

Colors communicate meaning.
The color of traffic control devices communicates substantial information, regardless of their shape, words or graphics. The table below summarizes ten colors designated to convey traffic control information.

Colors

YELLOW — General warning/caution

FLUORESCENT YELLOW-GREEN — Warning

ORANGE — Temporary work zone

 **GREEN** — Directional guidance; indicates movement is permitted

 BROWN — Recreational and cultural-interest guidance

 BLUE — Motorist services guidance

 RED — Stop or prohibition

 **BLACK** — Regulatory information
WHITE — Regulatory information

FLUORESCENT PINK — Incident management

General meaning. Designed to be easily understood, traffic signs have uniform shapes, colors and legends. Once drivers learn the general meaning, they can quickly identify the intended message.

Symbols and words. In addition to color and shape, signs may display symbols, words or a combination of symbols and words. Word messages are read from left to right or from top to bottom. However, with few exceptions, symbol-only signs are interpreted from the bottom upward. As signs' shapes and colors can generally be identified well before their symbols and words become clear when approaching, it is important to understand the information signs' shapes and colors communicate.

HOW to DRIVE

Sign Types

Three types. There are three basic types of signs: regulatory, warning and guide. Each conveys a different type of information.

Regulatory Signs

Regulatory signs. These signs tell drivers what they may or may not do. Such signs inform drivers of laws that apply at a given time and/or place.

STOP SIGNS
are eight-sided and red and white. They tell drivers they have to come to a complete stop.

YIELD SIGNS
are inverted triangles with a red border. They require a driver to yield the right of way to vehicles approaching on an intersecting street if close enough to cause a conflict or a collision.

DO-NOT-ENTER SIGNS
are red circles with a white bar on a square background. They prohibit travel on certain sections of roadway.

Other regulatory signs. Most other regulatory signs are vertical rectangles (taller than they are wide). Such signs show turning restrictions, lane use, speed limits or pedestrian or parking controls. A red circle with a red slash through it on any of these signs means "Prohibited."

Warning Signs

Yellow and orange signs. Warning signs and non-motorized highway users' signs are yellow. These signs warn drivers of specific road, environmental and traffic conditions a short distance ahead. Exception: construction-zone warning signs (orange) and pedestrian signs, which may be fluorescent yellow-green.

Diamond-shaped warning signs. Below are examples of diamond-shaped warning signs. These signs are read from the bottom up.

INTERSECTIONS

Crossroad   T-Intersection   Y-Intersection

CHANGES IN WIDTH OR LANE

Lane Reduction   Narrow Bridge   Lane Added

TRAFFIC

Two-way Traffic

Divided Highway Begins

Clearance

CROSSING

Pedestrian Crossing

Deer Crossing

Farm Machinery Crossing

CONDITIONS

Pavement Ends

Slippery When Wet

Steep Hill Ahead

HOW *to* **DRIVE**

CURVES

Right Curve   S-Curve   Reverse Turn

MERGE

Merge signs. A merge sign is a special type of warning sign. When posted at freeway-entrance ramps, a merge sign serves as a warning to drivers on the freeway and those merging from the ramp. To maintain a safe, smooth flow of traffic, drivers already on the freeway and drivers merging onto the freeway should adjust speed and or position as appropriate.

Other warning signs. Whereas most warning signs are black on yellow and diamond shaped, there are a number of exceptions. For instance:

1. **Railroad advanced** — warning signs are round.
2. **Railroad-crossing signs** (crossbuck, located at the tracks) are black on white in the shape of an X. They normally serve as caution signs but become regulatory when a train approaches.

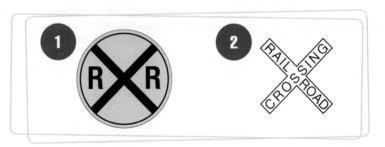

3. **Pedestrian signs can take several forms.** The five-sided, fluorescent yellow-green sign shaped like a house warns of a school zone. Lines representing a sidewalk added to the sign warn drivers of a school crossing. A diamond-shaped, fluorescent yellow-green sign warns of a general pedestrian crossing.

4. **No-passing zone** signs are pennant-shaped signs that indicate stretches of road where vehicles may not pass. For better visibility, these signs are located on the left side of the roadway.

5. **Rectangular signs with arrowhead-shaped symbols** are known as *chevron alignment signs*. These signs warn of dangerous curves and the need to slow to, or below, the recommended speed limit, particularly if the roadway is wet or traction is reduced.

6. **Temporary work zone signs** are orange and nearly always diamond-shaped. They warn drivers to slow down, be alert for construction workers and be prepared to stop.

7. **Slow-moving vehicle sign.** This is a special warning sign that is not located along the roadway. Rather, it is seen on slow-moving vehicles such as horse-drawn carriages, tractors and other equipment to warn motorists of their presence and slower speed. Slow-moving vehicle signs are yellow-orange and triangle-shaped, with a dark red border. These signs mark vehicles that generally move at 25 mph or slower.

HOW *to* **DRIVE**

Guide signs. Guide signs come in several shapes and colors and provide drivers with information about routes, exits and distances. They also indicate points of interest, recreational and medical facilities, and roadside services such as gasoline stations, lodging and restaurants. Here are some examples of guide signs:

DESTINATION AND MILEAGE

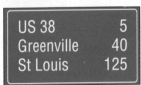

ROUTE MARKERS

ROADSIDE SERVICES

RECREATIONAL AREAS

International symbols. Because so many U.S. citizens travel abroad and foreign residents travel to the U.S., more traffic control signs are beginning to use graphic symbols for quick recognition. Below are illustrations of several such signs:

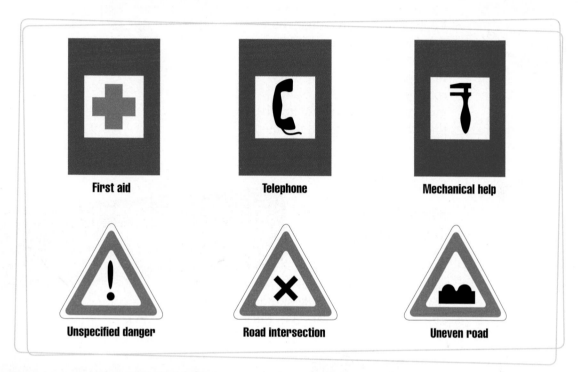

First aid	Telephone	Mechanical help
Unspecified danger	**Road intersection**	**Uneven road**

Route Numbering

Route numbering. Many signs feature route numbers that aid drivers in navigation. The interstate system features unique shield-shaped signs, which are blue on the bottom with a red band across the top. The primary route number is either a single or double digit number. East-west routes have even numbers and north-south routes have odd numbers. Many non-interstate route systems use a similar system of communicating route direction.

HOW *to* **DRIVE**

Interstate spurs and loops.

Loop sign

A loop usually bypasses cities or congested areas and meets the primary route at both ends. Loops feature three-digit route numbers that begin with an even number. A spur is a short route that connects with a primary route at only one end. Spurs feature three-digit route numbers that begin with an odd number.

Spur sign

Traffic Signals

Indicate right-of-way.

Traffic signals are used to control traffic by indicating who has the right of way. It is critical that highway users understand the meaning of each color and symbol, and respond in the appropriate manner.

RED Stop prior to the pedestrian crosswalk, stop bar or roadway-edge line. Do not enter the intersection.

YELLOW Right of way is expiring. Clear the intersection. (Red light will follow immediately.)

GREEN When traffic has cleared and it is safe to do so, you may enter the intersection.

Signal sequence. The standard signal sequence is green → yellow → red → green. To assist drivers who may be color blind or whose view may be partially blocked, signal colors are always in the same order.

Light positions. When signals are in a vertical position, the red light is on the top, the yellow light is in the middle and the green light is at the bottom. Horizontally mounted lights display the red light on the left, the yellow light in the center and the green light on the right.

Additional signals. Here are additional signals that every driver needs to recognize and understand:

FLASHING RED
You must stop. Proceed only when safe to do so.

FLASHING YELLOW
Slow; proceed with caution; be prepared to stop.

RED ARROW
Indicates traffic direction. Movement is not allowed in the direction of the arrow.

YELLOW ARROW
Appears after a green arrow to indicate the light is about to change to red.

GREEN ARROW
Traffic moving in the direction of the arrow may proceed if clear.

HOW *to* **DRIVE**

GRA
N

Countdown timers. Some pedestrian signal systems feature countdown timers, which indicate how much time is left for pedestrians to cross the street. To assist the sight-impaired, many of these emit audible beeps that correspond with the countdown.

"WALK"
Pedestrians may proceed across street.

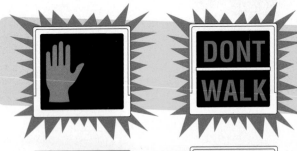

FLASHING "DON'T WALK"
Pedestrians already in the street may proceed across the street. Others should not start.

STEADY "DON'T WALK"
Pedestrians should not enter the street.

Markings on the pavement. Lines, symbols and lettering on the pavement may be used, along with highway signs and signals, to guide drivers. Pavement markings are usually white or yellow and may be reflective. Examples include traffic lane markings, pedestrian crosswalks, vehicle stop lines, parking spaces and directional arrows.

Yellow Markings

Yellow lines are used to separate traffic traveling in opposite directions and to indicate the left edge of multiple-lane divided highways. Yellow center lines may be single, double, solid or dashed (broken). A single broken yellow lane line — or a broken yellow lane line to the right of a solid-yellow lane line — means that a driver can pass, if it is safe to do so. A solid yellow lane line to the right of a broken yellow lane line means that passing is prohibited.

A double solid-yellow lane line means that passing is prohibited in both directions.

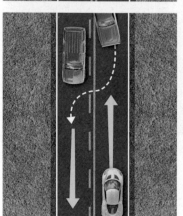
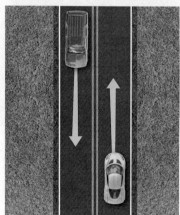

You may pass when there is a broken line on your side of the road and there are no oncoming cars in the passing lane.

You may not pass when there is a solid line on your side of the road.

HOW *to* **DRIVE**

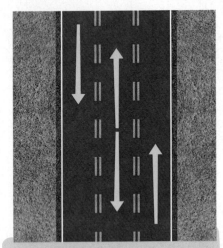

Double-yellow broken lines indicate reversible lanes. You may not cross the lines except at certain times.

Reversible lanes. Marked with double-dashed yellow lines, reversible lanes can improve the flow of traffic by changing the direction of travel within lanes. On multiple-lane streets, special signals can reverse travel in all lanes or a number of lanes to either side of the center line. As a result, large volumes of inbound and outbound traffic can move more smoothly during morning and evening rush hours or special events. Reversible lane signals can also be used to ease traffic flow in tunnels and on bridges.

Reversible lanes can be dangerous. To reduce the chance of crashes among vehicles moving in opposite directions, signs, signals and markings are used to inform drivers which lanes they may use during which hours. When you see double dashed lines on the pavement, check both sides of the highway for signs and check overhead for signals that tell you which lanes you can use. When signals are used, there will be one positioned over each traffic lane. Here is how to read reversible-lane signals:

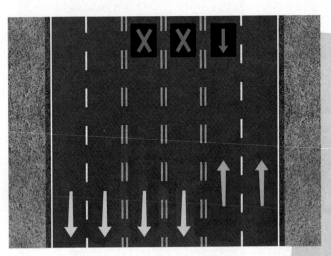

RED X — A red X means the lane is closed to you. Never drive in a lane under a red X signal.

GREEN ARROW — You are permitted to drive in a lane under a green arrow signal.

STEADY YELLOW X — A steady yellow X indicates the driver should safely vacate this lane because it will soon be controlled by a red X.

FLASHING YELLOW X — A flashing yellow X means you can use that lane, but only to turn left. When preparing to turn left, do not move into this lane until you are near your turn. Your turn will not be protected, so be sure oncoming traffic is clear before you turn.

Shared left-turn lanes. The solid and dashed yellow lane markings that identify shared left-turn lanes look similar to those used to indicate a no-passing zone. However, white left-turn arrows on the pavement between the yellow lane markings tell drivers that the lane is to be used for making left turns. Shared left-turn-lane pavement markings are often used where there is a high volume of traffic, and where

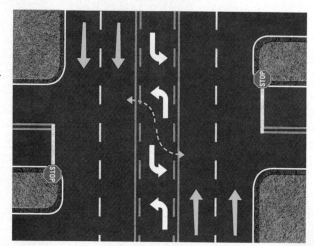

vehicles are turning into and out of businesses on either side of the street. This lane may be used by vehicles traveling in either direction when turning left from the roadway. Using it to enter the roadway from a driveway may also be permitted.

HOW *to* DRIVE

The keys to using shared left-turn lanes safely are:

- **Use the shared left-turn lane only to turn left.** If you do not intend to turn left, stay out of the lane.
- **Do not get in the lane too soon.** The farther you drive in the center lane, the more likely you are to come into conflict with someone coming from the other direction. Give yourself just enough time and space to check traffic in all directions, signal, enter the lane, straighten out your vehicle and, if necessary, bring your vehicle to a stop.
- **Watch for vehicles pulling out of driveways and cross streets.** Drivers may cut across in front of you or turn into the shared lane to wait for a gap in traffic.
- **Yield the right of way to any vehicle that is signaling to enter or that has already entered the lane.** If you need to stop in the left-turn lane, do so with your front tires pointing straight ahead. This will reduce the chance of being pushed into oncoming traffic if you are struck from the rear. (This procedure applies to all left turns to be made across oncoming traffic.)

White Markings

White lines.

Dashed white lines separate two lanes traveling in the same direction. Solid white lines are used to mark the right edge of highways. Solid white lines also are used between lanes to indicate areas where lane changes are discouraged or unlawful due to increased danger associated with such movements. Solid white lines running perpendicular across traffic lanes identify stopping points and pedestrian crosswalks. White lines can also be used to guide traffic around obstructions, mark curbs and control parking spaces.

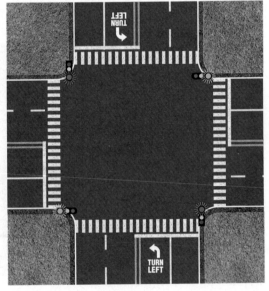

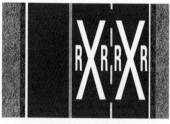

Railroad Crossing

White markings. White symbols and words on the pavement identify movements that may or must be made from or within a lane. They may be used to warn of an upcoming stop sign, signal or school zone, control the direction of travel or mark railroad crossings.

"STOP AHEAD"

"SCHOOL XING"

Left turn arrow

Restricted-lane markings. Restricted-lane pavement markings or signs appear on heavily traveled city streets and expressways. During certain hours of the day traffic in some lanes may be restricted to buses, turning vehicles or high-occupancy vehicles (HOVs — passenger vehicles containing two or more people). HOV signs indicate the minimum number of occupants required to use the restricted lanes, and the times during which the lanes are restricted. Restricted lane pavement markings and signs are designated by a diamond-shaped symbol.

HOW *to* **DRIVE**

TEST 5

Traffic-Control Devices

Study and respond to each of the following questions. Then review the chapter to see if your responses are correct.

Multiple Choice:

1. Signs communicate meaning using:
   a. Color
   b. Shape
   c. Words
   d. All of the above

2. Railroad advance warning signs are:
   a. Red and triangular
   b. Black on white in the shape of an X
   c. Orange and diamond-shaped
   d. Yellow and round

3. An odd-numbered Interstate using a single or double digit number indicates a route that:
   a. Runs in a loop around a city
   b. Extends outward from a loop around a city
   c. Runs east and west
   d. Runs north and south

4. A solid yellow line on your side of the road means:
   a. You may not pass
   b. You may pass, if safe to do so
   c. Oncoming vehicles may pass
   d. You are approaching reversible lanes

5. Solid white lines are used to
   a. Mark the right edge of highways
   b. Between lanes to indicate areas where lane changes are discouraged or unlawful due to increased danger associated with such movements
   c. Mark shared left turn lanes
   d. Both A and B

Short Answer:

1. Explain the key steps in safely using shared left turn lanes.

2. Explain the meaning of a signal light's three colors.

3. Explain the type(s) of information communicated by the following sign colors:

   a. Green

   b. Yellow

   c. Red

4. Explain the type(s) of information communicated by the following sign colors:

   a. Blue

   b. Brown

   c. Orange

5. Identify four signs or roadway markings used with reversible lanes.

HOW to **DRIVE**

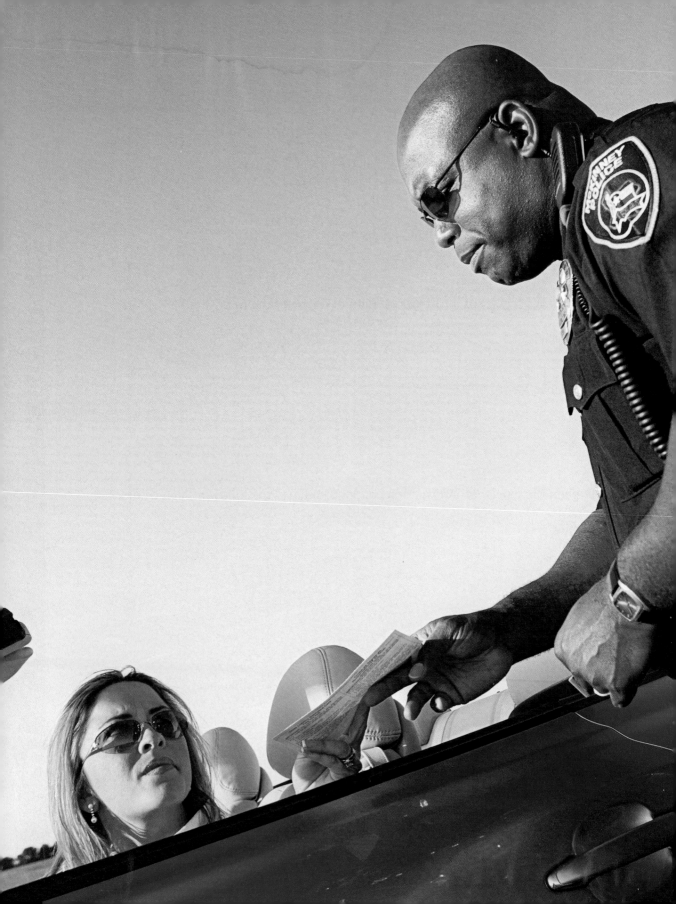

CHAPTER 6

Traffic Laws

Chapter Objectives

- Identify and discuss administrative laws concerning driver behavior.
- Describe the purpose of state-issued driver's licenses.
- Explain vehicle ownership issues, including vehicle registration and financial responsibility.
- Describe the role that traffic rules play in maintaining a safe driving environment.
- Explain issues related to right-of-way.
- Explain traffic rules regarding aggressive driving, impaired driving, drowsy driving and racing on public roadways.

HOW *to* **DRIVE**

Traffic Laws

For safe and efficient traffic movement, drivers must know what is expected of them and be able to predict the behavior of other highway users. The purpose of traffic laws and rules of the road is to prevent traffic crashes and promote the orderly flow of traffic by:

◆ Ensuring that drivers are qualified to operate a motor vehicle on public roadways.

◆ Providing rules for highway-user behavior.

◆ Helping highway users better predict what other highway users will do.

◆ Serving as guides to law enforcement personnel and courts.

The traffic control laws discussed in this book are based on the Uniform Vehicle Code. As such, they generally apply in all states. These include laws governing:

◆ Licensing

◆ Financial responsibility

◆ Vehicle ownership

◆ Rules of the road

◆ Vehicle operation

◆ Driver condition

Administrative Laws

State laws. Each state has laws that enable state officials to control its highway transportation system. These laws set up procedures for driver licensing, motor vehicle registration, financial responsibility and vehicle equipment standards. For more specific information about your state's laws, visit *www.AAA.com/PublicAffairs.*

Licensing

Driver's licenses. Granted by the state, a driver's license gives an individual permission to operate a motor vehicle on public highways. Licensing provides legal identification of drivers. Licensing also provides a structure to verify each driver's knowledge of the laws that govern the use of motor vehicles on public roadways, and for the overall safe operation of his or her vehicle.

The first license. People who apply for their first license must demonstrate that they understand traffic laws. They must pass a written test on the rules of the road as well as a vision test. Applicants also must demonstrate a basic ability to operate a motor vehicle. Demonstrating basic ability does not guarantee that the license applicant is a safe driver. On average, it takes about five years to reach the ability of the average driver on the highway (see Graduated Driver Licensing, Chapter 1).

Licenses can be taken away. Since the state grants a person the license to operate a motor vehicle on a public roadway, the state also can — for cause — take the license away. The courts may suspend or revoke a person's driver's license because of a traffic offense. In addition, the state can take administrative action to suspend or revoke a license.

Suspension/revocation. Depending upon the severity of the driving offense, a driver's license may be either suspended or revoked. A suspension is a temporary removal of a person's license for a specific period, generally less than a year, after which the license is returned. A revocation is a more serious penalty that withdraws the driving privilege completely, generally for a period of at least one year, after which the individual can re-apply for a license.

Since most people depend on their vehicles for everyday activities such as work and school, suspension or revocation of a license is a serious penalty. Additionally, being convicted of driving while a license is suspended or revoked is a serious offense, a misdemeanor that can result in a mandatory jail sentence.

Point system. Most states have a point system for guidance in actions against drivers who have been convicted of traffic offenses or involved in crashes. Each conviction for a traffic violation has a point value, and the number of points on a driver's record governs the type of action to be taken. Point systems help state officials to be more consistent in penalizing drivers when necessary.

HOW to DRIVE

National Driver Register. To help state licensing officials identify problem drivers, the U.S. Department of Transportation has established a system called the National Driver Register. The register is a record of chronic problem drivers reported by state licensing agencies across the country. Licensing officials may check the register when an individual applies for a new license or is suspected of having a poor driving record.

Financial Responsibility

Financial responsibility. All drivers must show proof of financial responsibility — the ability to pay for any damages resulting from a collision, regardless of who is at fault. Failure to show proof may lead to the suspension of one's driver's license. Vehicle owners who fail to show proof of financial responsibility also may have their vehicle registrations suspended. The driver's license or registration will generally remain suspended until the person demonstrates proof of financial responsibility. If a vehicle was driven without the owner's permission (was stolen) and involved in a collision, the owner does not have to prove financial responsibility.

The amount of money or security needed to satisfy the financial responsibility requirement will be based on the damages that result from the collision. The law usually limits the amount to no more than $25,000 for any one collision. However, a judgment against a driver in a court of law may be for a much greater amount.

Showing proof of financial responsibility. There are at least three ways drivers and vehicle owners can demonstrate proof of financial responsibility. They can:

◆ Possess automobile liability-insurance coverage.

◆ Deposit money in the amount required by the state.

◆ Deposit bonds or other securities (title to property, stock certificates) sufficient to meet the state's requirements.

Some states do not require insurance. Not all states require motor vehicle operators or owners to carry liability insurance. However, since few people have the money or other securities immediately available to meet the requirements for financial responsibility, most drivers carry automobile liability insurance.

Proof of financial responsibility for the future. There are two conditions under which a driver or vehicle owner must file proof of financial responsibility for the future (proof of ability to pay $25,000 or more, depending on the requirements of the state, for a period of three years):

1. The driver's license has been revoked.
2. The driver or vehicle owner has failed to provide proof of financial responsibility or pay a judgment after having been found responsible for damages in a crash.

Insuring high-risk drivers. Drivers who are required to show proof of financial responsibility for the future are considered poor risks by insurance companies. As a result, insurance companies often turn down such drivers when they apply for liability insurance protection.

To provide coverage for high-risk drivers, most states offer an assigned-risk insurance plan. Under such plans, each insurance company doing business in a state is required to accept a share of the high-risk drivers. Due to the increased likelihood that such drivers will be involved in crashes, insurance companies tend to charge them much higher premiums and are required to provide only the minimum coverage required by law. For more information about motor vehicle insurance, see Chapter 15.

Vehicle Ownership and Registration

Certificate of title. A certificate of motor vehicle title is required to demonstrate proof of ownership. The state issues a certificate of title when a motor vehicle is purchased. A title document shows the owner's name and address, the vehicle body style, number of cylinders, serial number and vehicle identification number (VIN). If the owner has purchased the vehicle on a time-payment plan (loan), the title also will indicate that there is a lien (debt owed) against the vehicle.

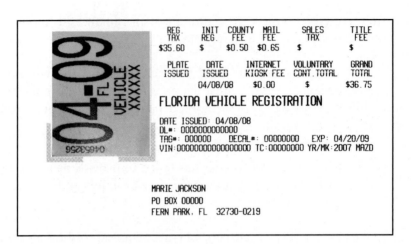

Vehicle registration. A motor vehicle must be re-registered periodically — typically every one to four years — with the appropriate state agency. In states with mandatory liability insurance laws, the name of the insurance company that insures the driver must be provided. At the time of registration, the owner, depending on the state, receives one or two license plates or tags and a registration card.

Rules of the Road

Motor vehicle code. Every state has a motor vehicle code that contains a section on rules of the road. These rules are in effect regardless of whether signs, signals or markings are posted. Some of these laws regulate legal driving speed, lane usage, passing and turning. Other laws address issues such as right of way and signaling intentions when preparing to stop or change direction. Still others address driver responsibilities in a collision and issues such as aggressive driving, distractions and driving under the influence of alcohol or other drugs.

Right-of-way

Right-of-way laws are designed to help drivers understand who should be granted the privilege of proceeding first when more than one vehicle approaches an intersection at about the same time. A driver can never "take" the right-of-way; it is always "given" by one driver to another. Just because the law states that Driver A shall yield to Driver B, the privilege to proceed first is not automatic.

Drivers cannot assume that another driver will yield the right-of-way to them. For instance, a Federal Highway Administration study of 40,000 drivers at intersections controlled by stop signs revealed that two-thirds of drivers failed to stop. Thus, instead of assuming that other drivers will automatically yield the right-of-way, you should pay careful attention to the other driver's intentions and actions.

Exercising due caution. All drivers are required to exercise due care to avoid a collision. Consequently, when two or more drivers approach a situation where someone is supposed to yield the right-of-way, all drivers should be prepared to yield.

Principles of right-of-way. Since they frequently require personal judgment, right-of-way laws are sometimes difficult to understand or apply. The following principles can help you better understand and apply right-of-way laws:

◆ The purpose of right-of-way laws is to prevent conflicts resulting from one driver failing to yield to another.

◆ The right-of-way is always given; it is not something a highway user should take for granted.

◆ To be granted right-of-way, a driver must be driving in a lawful manner. In other words, a driver cannot take the right-of-way by breaking another law.

◆ A driver has not yielded the right-of-way if he or she forces other highway users to slow or wait.

◆ Whoever has the last clear chance to avoid a collision has an obligation to do so.

Pedestrians' right-of-way in crosswalks. When traffic-control signals are not in place or not in operation, the driver of a vehicle shall yield the right-of-way to a pedestrian crossing the roadway within a crosswalk on the same side of the road, or when the pedestrian is approaching so closely from the opposite half of the roadway as to be in danger.

Examples of right-of-way. The following graphics provide examples of common right-of-way situations and how to negotiate them safely.

Entering an unmarked or open intersection

When two vehicles approach or enter an intersection from different roads at about the same time, the driver of the vehicle on the left should yield the right-of-way to the vehicle on the right.

Gold car yields to green car

Gold car yields to green car

Lane ends or is obstructed

When a lane ends or there is an object in the lane, the driver of a vehicle using the lane should yield the right-of-way to oncoming or following vehicles in the adjacent lane.

Blue truck yields right-of-way

Blue car yields right-of-way

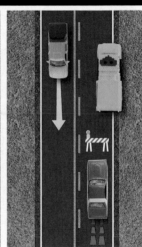

Blue car yields right-of-way

Entering a roadway from driveways, alleys and parked position

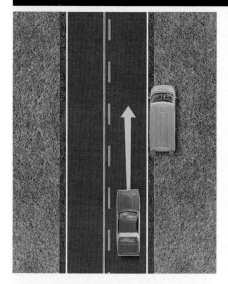

Gray van yields to blue car

Red car yields to blue car and gray van

Gold car yields to blue car

The driver entering a road from a parked position, parking lot, shopping area, alley or private drive should yield to motor vehicles approaching on the road to be entered and to pedestrians on the sidewalk.

HOW *to* **DRIVE**

Entering intersections with sign or flashing red lights

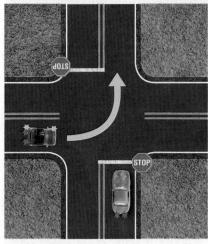

Green car yields right-of-way

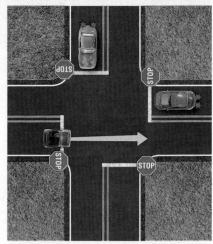

Green and red car yield right-of-way to car in intersection

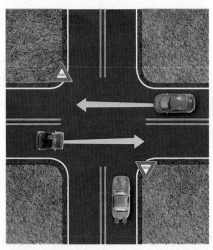

Green car yields right-of-way

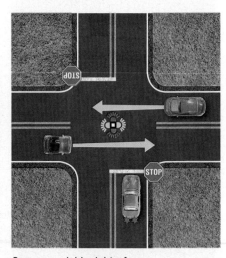

Green car yields right-of-way

A driver entering an intersection controlled by a stop sign, yield sign or red flashing signal light should yield the right-of-way to any vehicle in the intersection or approaching from a cross road. Coming to a complete stop does not relieve a driver of the duty to yield before entering.

Intersections with traffic signal lights

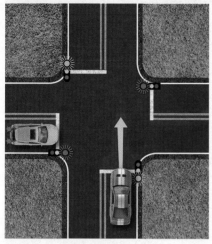

Gold car yields right-of-way

Red car yields right-of-way to car in intersection

Drivers who face the steady green signal light, with or without arrows, should yield the right of way to other vehicles and to pedestrians lawfully within the intersection at the time such signal is lighted.

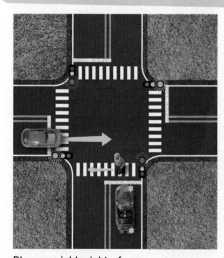

Blue car yields right-of-way

Blue car yields right-of-way

Drivers who face the steady red signal light and turn right, when permitted, should yield the right-of-way to other vehicles and to pedestrians lawfully within the intersection.

HOW to **DRIVE**

Freeway merge

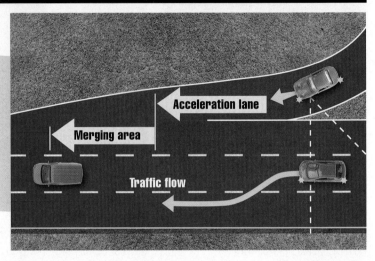

Merging is defined as a coming together or blending of vehicles to maintain a smooth flow of traffic. On freeways, merging requires that both the driver on the freeway and the driver who wishes to enter adjust speed and position to avoid a collision.

Acceleration lane

Merging area

Traffic flow

Entering and passing through traffic circles

The driver of a vehicle entering the circle should yield the right-of-way to vehicles already in the circle. The driver within the circle should yield to other vehicles within the circle when they are attempting to leave the circle.

Authorized emergency vehicles

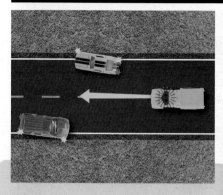 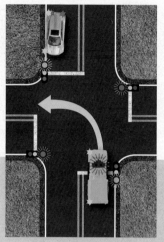 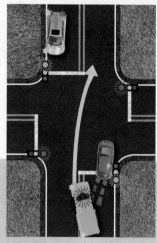

When an authorized emergency vehicle approaches using its lights and siren, all other drivers should — except when otherwise directed by a police officer — drive to a position parallel to, and as close as possible to, the right-hand edge of the road clear of an intersection and should stop and remain in such position until the authorized emergency vehicle has passed.

Funeral processions

The driver of a vehicle should not drive between moving vehicles that are part of a funeral procession. However, the lead vehicle of the procession will obey stop signs and signals when first approaching them.

HOW to **DRIVE**

Pedestrian crossing situation

The driver of a vehicle should yield to a pedestrian crossing the road at a marked crosswalk. Pedestrians crossing the road other than in a crosswalk should yield to any vehicle on the road. A blind person with a white cane or service animal is an exception to this rule.

Stopping for school buses.

Generally, drivers are required to stop when they meet or pass a school bus loading or unloading children. However, laws vary from state to state, so you could find yourself involved in a school bus stop violation. For example, some states require drivers to stop for a school bus only outside a business or residential area when the red stoplights

on the bus are flashing. Other states require drivers to stop for a school bus stopped on any roadway. It is important to learn the school bus stop laws in the state where you will be driving. When in doubt, slow down when you meet or pass a school bus. And stop if the bus is loading or unloading children, or if its red stoplights are flashing.

Traffic Control Laws

Obedience to Traffic Control Devices

All drivers must obey all traffic control devices, unless otherwise directed by a police officer or other person of authority.

Obedience to Authorized Persons Directing Traffic

No driver should willfully fail or refuse to comply with any lawful order or direction of any police officer, firefighter or flagger at a construction or maintenance site, or uniformed adult school crossing guard invested by law with the authority to direct, control or regulate traffic.

Traffic Control Signals

Green light. A green light signals to drivers that vehicular traffic may proceed straight through or turn right or left, unless a sign prohibits either such turn. But vehicular traffic, including vehicles turning right or left, is required to yield the right-of-way to other vehicles and pedestrians lawfully within the intersection or an adjacent crosswalk at the time the green light is illuminated.

Steady yellow light. A steady yellow light signals to drivers that movements allowed under the immediately preceding green light conditions should be safely completed and that a red light will be illuminated immediately thereafter.

Pedestrians facing a steady yellow or yellow-arrow signal, unless otherwise directed by a pedestrian-control signal, are thereby advised that there is insufficient time to cross the roadway before a red light is illuminated, and no pedestrian shall then start to cross the roadway.

Steady red light. A steady red light signals to drivers that vehicular traffic should stop behind a clearly-marked crosswalk on the near side of the intersection. If there is no crosswalk, vehicles should stop behind a clearly-marked stop line. If there is no stop line, vehicles should stop before entering the intersection and remain stopped until an indication to proceed is shown. Be sure to check your state's laws regarding where to stop at intersections.

Stop Signs

Except when directed by a police officer, every driver of a vehicle approaching a stop sign shall stop behind the crosswalk on the near side of the intersection. If there is no crosswalk, the vehicle must stop behind a clearly marked stop line. If there is no stop line, vehicles must stop at the point nearest the intersection where the driver has a view of approaching traffic on the intersecting roadway before entering it.

After stopping, the driver shall yield the right-of-way to any vehicle in the intersection or any vehicle approaching on another roadway so closely as to constitute an immediate hazard while the driver is moving across or within the intersection or junction of roadways. All drivers shall yield the right of way to pedestrians within an adjacent crosswalk.

HOW *to* **DRIVE**

Vehicle Operation Laws

Drivers to exercise due care. Notwithstanding other provisions of this chapter or the provisions of any local ordinance, every driver of a vehicle shall exercise due care to avoid colliding with any pedestrian or bicyclist, give an audible signal when necessary, and exercise proper precaution upon observing any child or any obviously confused, incapacitated or otherwise impaired person.

Use of occupant protection system. Whenever a vehicle is equipped with a safety belt system, the person occupying the seating position shall keep the seat belt properly adjusted and fastened around his or her body at all times while the vehicle is being operated. All children riding in the vehicle must be in the appropriate child safety restraint and in compliance with state child-passenger safety laws.

Moving a vehicle from a parked position. No person shall move a vehicle that is stopped, standing or parked until such movement can be made with reasonable safety.

Emerging from driveway, parking area, alley or building. The driver of a vehicle emerging from a parking area, alley, building, private road or driveway within a business or residential district shall stop the vehicle immediately prior to entering the sidewalk area across such alley, building entrance, private road or driveway. In the event that there is no sidewalk area, the vehicle shall stop at the point nearest the street to be entered where the driver has a view of approaching traffic.

Vehicle entering roadway. The driver of a vehicle about to enter or cross a roadway from any place other than another roadway shall yield the right-of-way to all vehicles approaching on the roadway to be entered or crossed.

Vehicle approaching or entering intersection. When two vehicles approach or enter an intersection from different roadways at approximately the same time, the vehicle on the left shall yield the right-of-way to the vehicle on the right.

Speed laws. The most important requirements for safe driving are time, visibility and space, all of which are related to vehicle speed. What is a good speed? What is a safe speed? Traffic laws provide general guidelines.

Speed limits are set to reflect traffic density, road conditions, sight distance, visual field and type of vehicles. These limits are called fixed maximum or minimum posted speed laws. Under such laws, drivers may not drive faster than the maximum posted speed. Nor may they drive slower than the minimum, unless conditions make it dangerous to travel at the minimum speed.

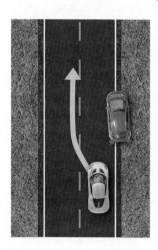

Drive on right side of roadway. Upon all roadways of sufficient width, a vehicle shall be driven on the right half of the roadway, except as follows:

1. When overtaking and passing another vehicle proceeding in the same direction under the rules governing such movement.

2. When an obstruction exists, making it necessary to drive to the left of the center of the highway. Any person would then yield the right-of-way to all vehicles traveling in the proper direction upon the unobstructed portion of the highway.

HOW *to* **DRIVE**

Space and time near emergency vehicles. Many states have laws designed to help protect operators of emergency vehicles, including law enforcement vehicles, roadside service vehicles, fire trucks and emergency medical vehicles. Commonly referred to as "Slow Down-Move Over" laws, they generally require drivers approaching emergency vehicles to take action to reduce the risk to emergency personnel. The required action depends on the speed and position of the approaching vehicle:

1. If the emergency vehicle is on the right side of the road and you are approaching in the right lane:

   ◆ You should safely change at least one lane to the left.

   ◆ If it is unsafe to change lanes, you should reduce your speed to at least 20 mph below the speed limit.

   ◆ Be sure to warn drivers behind you of your change in speed.

2. If the emergency vehicle is on the left side of the road and you are approaching in the left lane:

   ◆ You should safely change at least one lane to the right.

   ◆ If it is unsafe to change lanes, you should reduce your speed to at least 20 mph below the speed limit.

   ◆ Be sure to warn drivers behind you of your change in speed.

Whether required by law or not, these maneuvers can help protect the operators of emergency vehicles. Keep in mind that it may be you stopped on the roadside needing help in the future.

Following too closely. Drivers should not follow another vehicle more closely than is reasonable and prudent, having due regard for the speed of such vehicles and the condition of the highway.

Signals.

- **Signals by hand and arm or signal lights.** Any stop or turn signal is to be given either by means of the hand and arm or by signal lights.

- **Method of giving hand and arm signals.** All signals given by hand and arm are to be given from the left side of the vehicle in the following manner. Such signals should be indicated as follows:

  - **Left turn.** Hand and arm extended horizontally.

  - **Right turn.** Hand and arm extended upward.

  - **Stop or decrease speed.** Hand and arm extended downward.

Left Turn   Right Turn   Stop

Turning movements and required signals.

- No person shall turn a vehicle or move right or left upon a roadway without giving an appropriate signal and until the movement can be made safely.

- A signal of intention to turn or move right or left when required shall be given continuously during not less than the last 100 feet traveled by the vehicle before turning.

- No person shall stop or suddenly decrease the speed of a vehicle without first giving an appropriate signal in the manner provided herein to the driver of any vehicle to the rear when there is opportunity to give such signal.

Position and method.
The driver of a vehicle intending to turn shall do as follows:

- **Right turns.** The approach for a right turn shall be made as close as practical to the right-hand edge of the roadway.

- **Left turns.** The driver of a vehicle intending to turn left shall approach the turn in the extreme left-hand lane. The driver of a vehicle intending to turn left shall yield the right of way to any vehicle approaching from the opposite direction so close as to constitute an immediate hazard.

- **Two-way left turn lane.** Where a special lane for making left turns by drivers proceeding in opposite directions has been indicated by official traffic control devices:
  - A left turn shall not be made from any other lane.
  - A vehicle shall not be driven in the lane except when preparing for or making a U-turn when otherwise permitted by law.

Stopping when traffic obstructed. No driver shall enter an intersection or a marked crosswalk or drive onto any railroad grade crossing unless there is sufficient space on the other side of the intersection, crosswalk or railroad grade crossing to accommodate the vehicle without obstructing the passage of other vehicles, pedestrians or railroad trains, notwithstanding any traffic-control signal indication to proceed.

Limitation on backing. The driver of a vehicle shall not back the vehicle unless such movement can be made safely and without interfering with other traffic.

Opening and closing vehicle doors. No person shall open any door on a motor vehicle unless and until it is reasonably safe to do so and it can be done without interfering with the movement of other traffic. No person shall leave a door open on a side of a vehicle available to moving traffic for a period of time longer than necessary to load or unload passengers.

Unattended motor vehicle. No person driving or in charge of a motor vehicle shall permit it to stand unattended without first stopping the engine, locking the ignition, removing the key from the ignition, effectively setting the parking brake and turning the front wheels appropriately on a grade.

Aggressive and Reckless Driving Laws

Reckless Driving

Reckless driving behaviors. Reckless driving involves an improper driving act such as speeding, failure to yield right of way or turning from the wrong lane. However, it is the conditions that prevail when the act is committed that make the act reckless rather than an ordinary violation of a traffic law. For instance, driving 20–25 mph over the posted speed limit — or speeding through a school zone when children are present — may bring a charge of reckless driving.

Three conditions to uphold a charge. Whether improper driving is considered reckless depends on the behavior of the driver and the conditions under which the behavior occurred. There are at least three conditions that generally must be shown to exist to uphold a charge of reckless driving. They are:

Following too closely

1. The driver consciously and intentionally drives in a dangerous manner.
2. The driver knows, or should know, that the behavior places other persons at increased risk.
3. The conditions make the increase in risk obvious and serious. Important factors include the time and place of occurrence, weather, traffic volume, vehicle condition and driver condition.

Willful and wanton. The key terms in a charge of reckless driving are "willful" and "wanton." These terms imply a purpose or willingness to commit an act without regard for the rights or safety of others. Both words suggest that the person knows what he or she is doing, and that his or her intent is to commit an act even though there may be no intent or desire to do harm.

Aggressive Driving and Road Rage

A number of states have passed or are considering legislation to address these issues as criminal offenses. Most proposed legislation specifies that more than one dangerous act justifies a charge of aggressive driving and/or road rage, such as speeding and tailgating in heavy traffic, cutting into and across lanes of traffic and passing on the shoulder. All of the elements necessary for a charge of reckless driving are typically present in aggressive driving and road rage offenses.

Aggressive driving is generally defined as behaviors indicative of an aggressive mind set but not necessarily directed to another specific driver, including speeding, running red lights, changing lanes suddenly or without signaling and following too closely. By contrast, road rage is more often defined as behaviors directed at specific vehicles or occupants with malicious intent. These could include ramming, sideswiping, throwing objects, verbal attacks, battery, rude or obscene gestures, discharging firearms and more.

Racing on Public Roads

Racing on public highways is extremely dangerous and places all road users at greatly increased risk. Never engage in any sort of race while on public roads. State laws address street racing very clearly:

◆ No person shall drive any vehicle in any race, speed competition or contest, drag race or acceleration contest, test of physical endurance, exhibition of speed or acceleration or for the purpose of making a speed record, and no person shall in any manner participate in any such race, competition, contest, test or exhibition.

◆ Drag racing is defined as the operation of two or more vehicles from a point side-by-side at accelerating speeds in a competitive attempt to outdistance each other, or the operation of one or more vehicles over a common selected course, from the same point to the same point, for the purpose of comparing the relative speeds or power of acceleration of such vehicle or vehicles within a certain distance or time limit.

◆ Racing is defined as the use of one or more vehicles in an attempt to out-gain, out-distance or prevent another vehicle from passing, to arrive at a given destination ahead of another vehicle or vehicles, or to test the physical stamina or endurance of drivers over long-distance driving routes.

Homicide by Vehicle

Vehicular homicide. Whoever shall unlawfully and unintentionally cause the death of another person while engaged in the violation of any state law or municipal ordinance applying to the operation or use of a vehicle or to the regulation of traffic shall be guilty of homicide when such violation is the proximate cause of death.

Driver Condition Laws

Physical or mental condition. Drivers' physical and mental conditions can affect their ability to drive safely. Individuals who are unable to drive safely — due to their mental states, ingestion of drugs or physical conditions that render them incapable of properly controlling a motor vehicle — increase the chance of causing property damage, injury or death.

Driving After Consuming Alcohol or Other Drugs

Driving while impaired by alcohol or other drugs. Alcohol contributes to more than 40 percent of traffic fatalities. Most people agree that no one under the influence of alcohol or other drugs should be allowed to drive a motor vehicle.

Depending on the state, when a driver is stopped for cause and his or her blood alcohol concentration (BAC) tests at or above .08 percent, that person can be charged with driving while intoxicated (DWI), driving under the influence (DUI) or a similarly named charge. Courts generally accept tests of blood, breath or urine to determine BAC. The results of Standardized Field Sobriety Tests may also be accepted as evidence in such cases. In addition, a driver can be charged at any BAC level if he or she exhibits loss of normal use of mental or physical faculties because of alcohol or other drugs.

Drivers under age 21. Many states have much stricter laws related to alcohol-impaired driving by drivers under age 21. So called "zero tolerance" laws feature maximum BAC limits ranging from .00 to .02 percent.

Commercial drivers. A driver who holds a commercial driver's license (CDL) is considered DWI at a BAC of .04 percent.

Implied consent and administrative license revocation (ALR). All states have implied consent laws. Under such laws, by driving on public roads, drivers agree to submit to a test for the presence of alcohol or other drugs if stopped for cause and charged with the offense of impaired driving. Drivers who refuse to take such a test may have their licenses immediately suspended for up to 90 days or longer. Under a procedure known as administrative license revocation, an arresting officer may be authorized to immediately take away the license of a driver who refuses to submit to a test or who tests above the BAC limit established by law. Drivers who refuse to submit to a breath or blood test may still be charged with DUI/DWI based on other evidence such as observed erratic driving and physical behavior.

Additional Laws

Distracted driving. Due to the risks of being distracted while driving, many states have passed laws prohibiting certain behaviors. Some states forbid the use of cell phones while driving, others ban on-board video screens that are visible to the driver. Some states ban the use of any mobile device by drivers under age 18. Other states ban text messaging while driving. Some states prohibit drivers from using headphones on, or ear buds in both ears. Drivers convicted of these offenses can be fined.

Drowsy driving. Because driving drowsy can be as dangerous as driving while impaired by alcohol, some states are considering laws to punish offenders. New Jersey passed legislation allowing drivers who go more than 24 consecutive hours without sleep and are involved in a crash to be fined and/or jailed.

Littering. Litter is a major environmental issue, harming animals, people and waterways and costing millions of dollars each year to clean up. Unfortunately, a primary source of litter is motorists discarding garbage out of vehicle windows. The most common trash discarded by motorists is cigarette butts, which take decades to degrade. Fast-food containers are also commonly discarded. Penalties for littering can be stiff and could include fines, community service and jail time.

Preventing littering. Instead of tossing trash out of your vehicle, place it in a vehicle litter bag and empty it at home or in a trash receptacle. Rather than throwing cigarette butts out of car windows, use a portable ashtray, car ashtray or a container with a secure top. Consider participating in a community clean-up program to help keep roadways and your neighborhoods clean.

Check your state's laws. This chapter is not intended to cover every one of your state's traffic laws. Be sure to check you state's driver handbook and laws for complete information.

TEST **6**

Traffic Laws

Study and respond to each of the following questions. Then review the chapter to see if your responses are correct.

Multiple Choice:

1. A driver's license:
   a. Gives an individual permission to operate a motor vehicle on public highways
   b. Serves to verify each driver's knowledge of the laws that govern the use of motor vehicles on public roadways
   c. Can be taken away by the state
   d. All of the above

2. _____ laws are designed to help drivers understand who should be granted the privilege of proceeding first when more than one vehicle approaches an intersection at about the same time.
   a. Right-of-space
   b. Right-of-way
   c. Emergency vehicle
   d. Reckless driving

3. A certificate of motor vehicle title:
   a. Demonstrates proof of vehicle registration
   b. Gives an individual permission to operate a motor vehicle on public highways
   c. Demonstrates proof of financial responsibility
   d. Demonstrates proof of ownership

4. Which of the following is related to reckless driving behavior?
   a. A driver intentionally drives recklessly.
   b. A driver knows his or her actions will create a significant risk.
   c. Conditions make the risk obvious and serious.
   d. All of the above.

5. Most states have blood-alcohol concentration limits of _____ percent for drivers under age 21.
   a. .04 to .08
   b. .08 to .10
   c. .00 to .02
   d. .02 to .08

1. Explain three ways drivers and vehicle owners can demonstrate proof of financial responsibility.

2. List four principles of right-of-way.

3. Explain the procedure for responding to an approaching emergency vehicle.

4. Explain the difference(s) between aggressive driving and road rage.

5. Explain the conditions under which a driver can be charged with driving under the influence of alcohol or other drugs.

CHAPTER 7

Managing Risk: Vision and Perception

Chapter Objectives

◆ Describe how effective visual habits help to manage risk when driving.

◆ Explain and apply the 20- to 30-second visual lead and 12- to 15-second visual-control zone.

◆ Describe the benefits of good visual habits, including ground viewing, mirror and blind-area checks, and searching ahead, behind and to the sides.

◆ Explain the process by which you would select a safe travel path using effective searching techniques.

◆ Describe the four categories into which information should be classified.

◆ Explain the relationships among time, space and stopping distance.

OBJECTS IN MIRROR ARE CLOSER THAN THEY APPEAR

HOW to DRIVE

SEMI

141

In Chapter 1, you learned that risk can be managed, with the goal of minimizing risk to you and other roadway users. To accomplish this, drivers must develop effective perceptual skills, make good decisions based on the traffic scene, and take accurate action. In sum, drivers must manage vision, time and space to minimize risk. This chapter addresses how drivers can develop effective visual techniques that can be used to obtain information needed to respond to potentially dangerous situations.

The main goal of developing and using effective visual techniques is to maintain a safe intended path of travel. To accomplish this, you need to learn how to identify an intended path of travel and how to adjust time and space as needed to maximize safety.

The Importance of Vision

Effective use of vision is critical to safe driving. No human sense is more important to the driving task.

Critical to Safe Driving. Effective use of vision is critical to safe driving. No human sense is more important to the driving task. Thus, it is useful for drivers to know about the different types of vision, the type of information that can be obtained from each, and how to develop effective visual habits.

Visibility. When you drive you must have a clear field of vision to gather information and guide a motor vehicle effectively. Good visibility depends on the distance you can see ahead and to the sides. It consists of your line of sight and field of view. Line of sight is the imaginary line that extends from your eyes to the point of focus. Field of view is the entire area of the highway and surroundings that you can see at any given moment.

Types of Vision

Central Vision

Targeting. Central vision is that five-degree cone that makes up only three percent of a driver's total visual field. It provides detail of objects and conditions and is the primary visual function employed in targeting.

Fringe Vision

Depth and position. Fringe vision is used to judge depth and position. It provides information about objects close to the travel path and lane position.

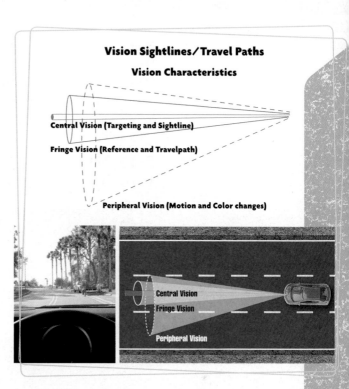

Peripheral Vision

Color and motion. Peripheral vision is conical in shape around the other vision fields. It detects color and motion, providing you with information about moving or stationary objects that could be threats along the intended path of travel. It also gives you a sense of the speed at which you are traveling. Peripheral vision is strongly affected by drugs, fatigue and speed of travel.

Color Blindness

Some drivers have difficulty distinguishing among colors, a condition called color blindness. The most common form of color blindness is the inability to distinguish between red and green. Fortunately, color blind drivers can use cues other than color to help them drive safely, including sign shapes, sequence of lights within a signal light, other drivers' actions, and numbering systems.

HOW to DRIVE

Searching. Searching means moving your eyes in a constant pattern, from near to far and side to side. While your intended travel path is your main area of focus, searching the roadside gives you additional traffic clues. Keeping your eyes active helps you resist distractions, reduces inattention and prevents a fixed stare. Look for:

◆ Vehicles and people that may be in the road by the time you reach them.

◆ Warning signs detailing conditions ahead.

◆ Traffic signs or signals requiring your action.

Using the center of your path of travel as your main point of reference, search from near to far and side to side.

Visual-search patterns. As a driver, you may be forced to respond quickly to traffic events. To control risk in these situations, it is essential that you develop efficient visual search patterns. You will gather information about what is happening ahead along your intended path of travel, as well as to the sides and behind your vehicle. Your goal is to identify anything that might require you to adjust your speed, change your vehicle position or communicate with other road users. In this chapter, we will concentrate on establishing a safe path ahead by searching well ahead of your vehicle and by constantly searching the total traffic scene.

Searching the Total Traffic Scene

Searching Well Ahead

Maintain a visual lead. The distance you look ahead is identified as your *visual lead*. Searching well ahead gives you more time to make decisions about space needs, vehicle positioning, and better control if a situation should arise.

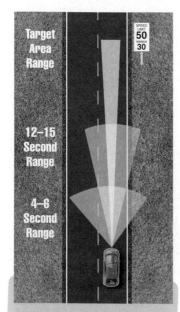

To develop a visual lead, pick out a fixed roadside object well ahead and begin counting.

Search 20 to 30 seconds ahead. How far ahead should you look when driving? Because your visual lead automatically accommodates different speeds, how far you should look ahead is measured in seconds rather than distance. Under normal circumstances, environmental conditions permitting, you should search the highway 20 to 30 seconds ahead. This gives you time to analyze conditions and make speed or position adjustments before problems develop.

Maintain a 12- to 15-second visual-control zone. Searching 20 to 30 seconds ahead gives you time to assess, within the next 12 to 15 seconds, actions you may need to take to control risk. This is known as your *visual control zone*, defined as "a place or places to which I can steer, on or off the road, 12 to 15 seconds ahead if a potential problem situation develops into a threatening situation." Or as an alternative, "If I cannot steer where I intended to go, where can I steer to?" Identifying alternate paths becomes critical if you are in a situation when stopping within your vehicle's stopping zone would result in being struck from behind.

For example, say you must make an emergency stop on a highway. If there are no vehicles behind you, stopping should not be a problem. But suppose there is a tractor-trailer following you, which requires about twice as much stopping distance as a car.

In this circumstance (depending on weather and road conditions), it may be safer to steer off the road and then stop.

HOW to DRIVE

Searching to the Sides

Concentrating on any one object or situation interferes with your ability to detect other potentially dangerous conditions. As you increase speed and concentrate farther ahead along your travel path, you may experience reduced side vision. You must make a conscious effort to maintain wide-ranging eye movements.

Searching ahead along your intended path of travel is an important habit to develop.

Good visibility depends on the distance you can see ahead and to the sides.

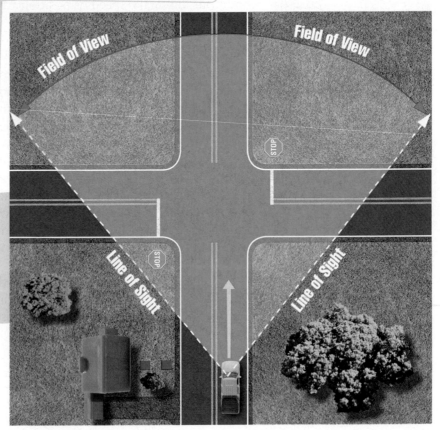

Ground viewing. While your default visual search area should be well in front of the vehicle, searching the visual scene near the ground can help you detect important information to support safe driving. Searching the ground can help you:

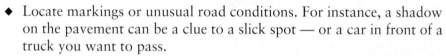

- Judge a vehicle's speed and any changes in speed.

- Determine whether other drivers are maintaining lane position or are about to change direction.

- Locate markings or unusual road conditions. For instance, a shadow on the pavement can be a clue to a slick spot — or a car in front of a truck you want to pass.

- Locate small children or animals behind or between parked cars. This is especially helpful in residential areas.

Directing your search at the ground when you drive near parked cars can help you detect movement and prepare you to respond to actions of other roadway users that could increase the level of risk.

HOW *to* **DRIVE**

SEMI

Looking Behind

Developing skills to check traffic behind you will help avoid collisions when conditions change suddenly:

◆ Check your rearview and side mirrors to see if anyone is following too closely, coming up fast or preparing to pass.

◆ Glance over your left or right shoulder to check blind areas — the areas around the vehicle that you cannot see from the driver's position or any of your mirrors.

Use quick glances in mirrors to check traffic behind you.

Glance over your shoulder to check blind areas.

The frequency of rearview checks depends on traffic conditions. Be sure to check the traffic behind you before changing lanes, when you drive down a long or steep hill, back up, brake abruptly or approach an intersection.

Clearance for braking. To judge clearance for braking, you also need to know what type of vehicle is following you. A large truck or bus may require twice as much stopping distance as your vehicle. Mirror checks also are necessary to judge the type of signals needed and whether others have received them.

Blind area checks. Develop the habit of turning your head slightly in the direction you plan to move to check for vehicles you may not see in your mirrors. Many collisions and near-misses occur when drivers fail to determine if the space into which they want to move is clear.

A better rule for using mirrors. You may have heard you should check your mirrors every few seconds. A better rule is to check your rearview and side mirrors if a situation ahead calls for a possible speed or position adjustment. This helps you judge the position and relative speed of following vehicles. It also helps you find vehicles in your blind areas and the limits on possible escape routes.

Selective Searching

Selecting the right information. Safe driving decisions begin with selecting the right information. Sometimes, there is simply too much information, which leads to distraction and confusion.

There are two steps to developing a selective search pattern:

1. Know where to direct your search.
2. Classify information into major groups.

Directing Your Search

Searching for important factors. The important items to search for are objects, situations or highway conditions

Look for objects or road conditions that may affect your intended path of travel.

that may affect your path of travel. Look for vehicles, pedestrians or other highway users that could move into your path. Identify conditions that may influence traction. Quickly direct your attention away from objects or conditions that do not affect your path of travel.

Gathering information. The more information you gather about other vehicles and highway users, the better you can predict whether they are likely to approach or move across your intended path. A parked car with its front wheels turned toward the street and brake lights on provides a hint that the vehicle may pull in front of you. Suppose the brake lights flash off and the wheels start to roll slightly. This additional information means you need to act quickly to avoid a collision.

Avoid surprises. Surprise is a factor in many collisions. A recent study of more than 11,000 crashes revealed that 37 percent of the drivers involved took no action to avoid a collision. The surprise factor was greater among those who were struck. To prevent being taken by surprise:

◆ Search well in advance for changes in the roadway environment. Road width may suddenly narrow. Curves and hills can cause sight distances to vary. Interchanges and intersections increase the chance for conflict.

◆ Observe the behavior of other highway users.

◆ Watch for drivers who follow too closely, cut in and out of traffic, or travel on the shoulder of the road or in the blind spots of other vehicles.

◆ Be alert for the presence of pedestrians, bicyclists and animals.

Changes in line of sight. Your line of sight changes continuously as you move along the highway. You must be aware of the potential for a limited line of sight well ahead. A limited line of sight is any highway area ahead where the sight distance or field of view is less than that required for safe travel at your current speed. In some places, signs are posted, warning of a "Limited Sight Distance."

Off-road obstacles. Off-road conditions can reduce your line of sight on either side of your intended path of travel. Shrubbery, signs, buildings and parked vehicles may hide intersections, driveways and moving objects. Such obstacles not only reduce your ability to see but prevent other drivers from seeing you. These situations are especially risky, for hidden dangers can appear suddenly in your stopping zone.

Traffic conditions. Traffic conditions also can reduce your line of sight and visual lead time. A fixed or slow-moving object may come into view too late. A van or large truck can reduce your view of the path ahead, particularly if it is stopped at an intersection waiting to make a left turn. Large vehicles or dips in the highway can easily hide compact cars and motorcycles from view. Clues to the direction and rate of movement of an object may be obscured, leaving drivers unaware of a high-risk situation.

Adjusting to changes in visibility. To help identify problem areas, think about your driving environment. Assess factors such as the time of day and the season. For instance, from late August to mid-June, expect to see school buses in the early morning and afternoon hours. There are a number of other solutions you can use to minimize the risk associated with changes in visibility.

Daylight hours. On sunny days, backgrounds such as snow or sand can cause glare, which sharply decreases your ability to see. Driving toward the sun can be a particular problem because your eyes adapt slowly to changes in light intensity. When you face a blinding sun, wear sunglasses and adjust the sun visor.

Obstacles such as trees or signs can reduce your ability to see — and may prevent other drivers from seeing you.

Sunglasses. Speaking of sunglasses, be sure to keep them clean and free of scratches. Polarized sunglasses with neutral gray or green tints are best for reducing glare. Avoid sunglasses with thick temples that create blind areas to the sides. Wearing sunglasses during the day can help protect vision. Never wear sunglasses at dusk or in the dark since they will further reduce your ability to see.

Driving at night. Visibility problems associated with nighttime driving are probably the least understood. In addition to reducing detail, darkness conceals many objects that you can see during daylight. No matter how good they may be, headlights do not show as much of the road as daylight does. You might detect hundreds of details at a certain location during daylight. At night, you might see very little at the same place. Watch for slow-moving or unlighted vehicles, curves, pedestrians and road changes.

Driving at dusk. Be especially alert at dusk. The sky still may be bright, but objects on the road can merge with shadows and fade into the darkness.

Bad weather. A similar effect can occur during snowstorms or rain showers. If the weather becomes too bad, pull off the road to a rest area or parking lot and wait for conditions to improve. If pulling off the road is not possible, pull onto the shoulder, as far away from traffic as possible.

Driving with your low-beam headlights on during daylight hours makes you much more visible to other highway users.

Headlights. Driving with your low-beam headlights on during daylight hours makes you much more visible to other highway users. That is why many of today's automobiles come equipped with automatic daytime running lights (DRLs). During the daylight, on a straight and level road, a vehicle without headlights is visible from about a half mile away. With headlights on, the same vehicle is visible from nearly a mile away. This difference can be critical when you are considering whether to pass another vehicle, in terms of identifying any oncoming traffic.

Lights-on law. A mandatory daylight lights-on law enacted more than 25 years ago in Sweden continues to prove highly effective in reducing frontal crashes between vehicles. The law has even more dramatically reduced fatalities involving pedestrians and bicyclists. Canada is experiencing similar results.

Keep it clean. Dirty headlights and windshields limit visibility. Road grime — dirt, oil, water and other debris — can reduce light output by up to 90 percent. A 30- to 50-percent visibility loss due to dirt or grime is common. To help control this problem, wipe your headlights when you plan to drive at night, and keep both the inside and outside of your windshield clean.

Classifying Information

Classifying information. As you drive, it is important to accurately classify the information you obtain. Regardless of where you drive, classifying information into major groups will help you avoid overlooking a significant event or clue. Traffic elements can be classified into four groups:

1. **Signs, signals and markings.** Signs and signals provide information about the road environment. They warn of curves, hills and other changes in the roadway, and remind drivers of the laws to follow. You should be particularly aware of clues that other drivers may not identify in time, such as a signal light about to change, partially hidden signs or a vehicle in their blind area.

1. Signs, signals and markings

2. Roadway features

3. Motorized vehicles

4. Non-motorized roadway users

2. Roadway features. Roadways have many features that can influence driving decisions, such as lane markings, road width, road surface and available traction, shoulder slope, intersections, interchanges and the general state of repair. Also included are adjacent objects such as light poles, curbs, trees or shrubbery. Any of these can affect your ability to control your vehicle. Some can greatly increase risk. It is important to identify all such elements well in advance. They can affect the movement of your vehicle, as well as those of other drivers, if an emergency arises.

Off-road conditions. You must also be aware of both roadway and shoulder conditions. Always remain alert for off-road objects that obstruct vision, limit choices or adversely affect vehicle control. Vehicles could collide with steep shoulders and ditches, culverts, utility poles, trees, signposts, bridge structures and guardrails. Curbs and potholes could also cause damage or limit your ability to avoid or manage a high-risk situation.

To manage risk effectively, a driver must be aware of both roadway and shoulder conditions.

3. Motorized vehicles. Automobiles, SUVs, vans, pickup trucks, motorcycles, mopeds, recreational vehicles, large trucks and buses have different capabilities, sizes and limitations. It is essential that you become aware of these differences. Here are some clues to possible movements of other vehicles and drivers/actions:

Motor vehicle:

A. Directional control
    a. Turn signals and flashing of headlights
    b. Position on roadway, shoulder or along curb
    c. Direction of front wheels and tire inflation
    d. Load distribution
    e. Backup lights

B. Acceleration and speed
    a. Exhaust smoke
    b. Rear end dipping down or fishtailing
    c. Tire noise

C. Deceleration or stopping
    a. Brake lights steady or flashing
    b. Front end dips down
    c. Tire noise

D. Emergency

    a. Flasher lights, siren or horn

    b. Cloth on door handle or radio antenna

    c. Hood or trunk lid raised

E. Condition

    a. Body damage

    b. Load distribution

    c. Glass areas

    d. Out-of-state license plate

F. Driver Behavior

    1. Behind the wheel

        a. Talking with passengers

        b. Smoking, eating or reading

        c. Eye contact

        d. Posture or position

        e. Talking on cell phone

Clues to motor-vehicle actions

Sudden changes in direction

Sudden acceleration

Sudden deceleration

HOW *to* **DRIVE**

Pay attention to the behavior of other drivers

Out-of-state license plate

Erratic driving

Load distribution

2. **Driving habits**
   a. Use/non-use of signals
   b. Use/non-use of headlights
   c. Following distance and speed
   d. Lane control
   e. Weaving in lane
   f. Sudden lane changes

4. **Non-motorized roadway users.** Pedestrians, bicyclists and animals are the least protected and, in many ways, the least predictable roadway users in terms of giving cues to risky behaviors. Because their vision and hearing are not fully developed, young children — whether on foot or riding a bicycle — have difficulty judging the speed of oncoming vehicles. Nor can they judge the time and space needed to cross a street. Rarely are they aware of what a driver can or cannot do with a motor vehicle. As a result, they may take chances that can cause serious problems for drivers. To reduce danger, watch for clues to predict the actions by pedestrians, bicyclists and animals.

   A. **Pedestrians**
      a. Age and physical impairments
      b. Location on sidewalk, curb or roadway
      c. Standing, walking or running, alone or in a group, talking, eye direction, entering or exiting from a car

   B. **Bicyclists**
      a. Age and body size in relation to bike size
      b. Location on roadway, shoulder or sidewalk
      c. Facing traffic or riding with traffic
      d. Control of movement, waving
      e. Alone or one of a group of riders

C. Animals

   a. Kind of animal — wild or domestic — and size
   b. Location relative to roadway, shoulder, sidewalk
   c. Fenced or loose near road
   d. Standing, running, jumping, being herded or ridden, eating, alone or in a herd or pack

Good Visual Habits

Rewards of good visual habits. Recognizing a dangerous driving situation in advance allows time to plan evasive maneuvers. How can you tell if you are developing good visual habits? It is often easy to identify drivers who do not have good habits!

Drivers with poor visual habits:

- Do not prepare for stops or turns far enough in advance.
- Do not notice traffic tie-ups in advance.
- Become trapped behind large trucks, slow-moving or double-parked vehicles.
- Are often surprised.
- Are unaware of vehicles about to pass.
- Are unaware of their own speed.
- Drive with turn signals flashing although they do not intend to turn.
- Drive with mirrors that are dirty or out of adjustment.
- Drive with fogged, dirty or partially blocked windows.
- Become distracted easily.
- Do not respond to changes in the traffic environment.

HOW *to* **DRIVE**

TEST **7**

Vision and Perception

Study and respond to each of the following questions. Then review the chapter to see if your responses are correct.

Multiple Choice:

1. _____ vision is the five-degree cone that makes up only three percent of a driver's total visual field.
   - a. Central
   - b. Tunnel
   - c. Fringe
   - d. Peripheral

2. The distance you look ahead is identified as your:
   - a. Targeting scope
   - b. Visual scope
   - c. Targeting lead
   - d. Visual lead

3. A driver should search the highway _____ seconds ahead.
   - a. 3–4
   - b. 9–10
   - c. 12–15
   - d. 20–30

4. A driver should maintain a visual-control zone of at least _____ seconds ahead.
   - a. 3–4
   - b. 9–10
   - c. 12–15
   - d. 20–30

5. To effectively search the total traffic scene, drivers should monitor the area _____ of the vehicle.
   - a. To the rear
   - b. To the sides
   - c. To the front
   - d. All of the above

1. Define central vision.

2. Define fringe vision.

3. Define peripheral vision.

4. Explain how to perform ground viewing and how it can help reduce risk.

5. Identify five common errors of drivers with poor visual habits.

159

CHAPTER 8

Managing Risk: Time and Space

Chapter Objectives

◆ Describe the factors to consider in making effective time- and space-management decisions.

◆ Explain how time and space management relate to the selection of a planned path of travel.

◆ Define space margin and how it relates to minimizing risk.

◆ Describe the relationship between space management and safe driving.

◆ Explain the relationship between speed and braking distance.

◆ Describe the risk-management concepts of separating and compromising.

◆ Describe the relationship of speed to time/space management.

◆ Explain factors that affect the choice of a reasonable and proper speed.

HOW to **DRIVE**

Adjusting Your Speed and Position

Speed and position. Now that you know the importance of vision and effective visual habits, the next step is learning how to translate visual information into actions that reduce risk. This involves making good decisions and adjusting your speed and position to your planned travel path and actual driving situation.

Decisions, Decisions, Decisions

Making more accurate, timely decisions. Like most situations in life, driving requires you to make decisions. For every decision you make, you must evaluate your options and consider possible consequences. With practice, you will be able to process information and make critical decisions in a fraction of a second. To make more accurate and timely decisions, you must have an adequate store of information about driving and driving conditions, know the rules, and have experienced a variety of traffic conditions and environments. Driving decisions are many, varied and continuous. The following list gives you an idea of the kinds of decisions you must make:

For every decision you make, you must evaluate your options and consider possible consequences.

WHAT...
- Time to start?
- Route to follow?
- Lane?
- Speed?
- Maneuvers to make?
- Controls to use?
- Methods to communicate?

WHEN AND WHERE TO...

- ◆ Meet other traffic?
- ◆ Yield?
- ◆ Stop?
- ◆ Perform maneuvers?
- ◆ Signal?
- ◆ Change direction?
- ◆ Change speed?

HOW MUCH TO...

- ◆ Accelerate?
- ◆ Slow down or brake?
- ◆ Turn the steering wheel?
- ◆ Communicate?

Deciding your course of action. As soon as you identify an object, condition or area of blocked vision that could cause a problem, you must decide what to do. You should choose the action that involves the lowest possible level of risk. What actions will make the situation more manageable? Perhaps you should change your speed or position, increase your visibility or sound a warning. Or you may combine several of these actions.

Your Range of Choices

Your most important decisions will involve how to manage available time and space.

Critical judgments. Many driving situations offer limited choices, so sometimes deciding what action to take is simple. For example, when encountering highway control devices and design features, you either decide to conform to them or ignore them and accept the consequences.

Your most important decisions. Other more complex traffic situations may call for more difficult decisions that require you to make critical judgments about your speed and travel path. You must decide what to do — and when. Drivers face increased risk because of roadway conditions, their own actions, the actions of other users or vehicle malfunctions. Your most important decisions will involve how to manage available time and space to minimize risk.

HOW to DRIVE

Drivers need to define an intended safe path of travel. One of your tasks as a driver is to identify your *intended path of travel*, defined as the space into which you can safely direct your vehicle with the lowest possible risk. Always select a travel path with the least risk.

Identifying a path of travel. Most roads have marked traffic lanes 10 to 12 feet wide. If lanes are not marked, you might imagine a 12-foot-wide carpet rolled out ahead of your vehicle. Use this imaginary path for steering and control, but be careful to use it only as a point of reference. Never allow your eyes to become fixed on any point or object. It is also important to identify an alternate path of travel in case your intended path becomes blocked or threatened.

Factors Affecting the Selection of a Path of Travel

1. **Roadway conditions.** Many factors influence a driver's ability to manage risk, among them the type of road surface and its state of repair. Items or debris on the roadway are other factors. The condition of the road shoulder also influences risk management.

2. **Off-road conditions.** To manage risk effectively, you must be aware of both roadway and shoulder conditions. You also must be alert to off-road objects that obstruct vision, limit choices or adversely affect vehicle control. Steep shoulders and ditches, culverts, utility poles, trees and signposts all increase risk, as do bridge structures and guardrails. Curbs and potholes could also cause damage or limit your ability to avoid or manage a high-risk situation.

3. **Traffic conditions.** Drivers who have experienced dangerous driving situations most frequently describe scenarios caused by the actions of other drivers, pedestrians, bicyclists or animals. Recognizing others' potential actions is one of the most important and difficult tasks a driver faces. Drivers tend to use expected behaviors such as social custom, courtesy and traffic laws to predict the actions of other users.

4. **The unexpected.** Unfortunately, highway users often direct their attention to something other than traffic, resulting in unpredictable behavior. A study by the Federal Highway Administration revealed that, on average, 67 percent of drivers do not stop for stop signs. The figure reaches 90 percent on residential streets.

Other studies turned up additional disturbing information. It is common during rush hour for several vehicles to enter an intersection after a traffic light changes to red. Observation of driver behavior reveals that few signal their intentions. Many try to pass when it is dangerous to do so. Pedestrians and bicyclists dart into traffic and cross against red lights. Animals running free can suddenly appear in the road. Such dangers make it important for you to have alternate paths — either on or off the road — should your way suddenly be blocked. Always be prepared for the unexpected.

Deciding on options. Selecting a path of travel is a continual process of deciding which options are best. Depending on your circumstances, the shoulder of the roadway may sometimes be the best choice. Here are some questions to ask when selecting your path of travel:

◆ **Which path offers maximum visibility?** Hills, curves, obstructions and other vehicles often limit visibility. Always try to position your vehicle so you have the best view for the situation, which allows others to see you more readily, particularly if you drive with your low-beam headlights on during the daytime.

◆ **Which path provides the most clear space to the sides?** You need enough space to the sides to minimize risk from objects that could enter your path. You also need space to provide an escape path and extra distance for possible errors.

◆ **Which path provides the smoothest flow of traffic?** The path where all vehicles are moving at a reasonable speed for existing conditions provides the smoothest flow of traffic. Furthermore, the path with the smoothest traffic flow usually provides the best space and visibility.

◆ **Which path provides the best roadway surface?** Any rough or slippery road condition will reduce traction, require a reduction in speed and increase chance of error. Rough road surfaces also may alter your vehicle's suspension alignment. Avoid such areas if there is an alternative.

◆ **What traffic laws apply?** In addition to the guides above, certain traffic laws may apply. Most states have laws that require slower-moving traffic to keep to the right. Lane use also is restricted for passing and turning.

Watch out for obstructions that may make the shoulders narrow or unavailable for escape.

A road or highway that narrows ahead should be considered an area of reduced space.

Managing Risk with Adequate Space Margins

A space margin. Efficient, safe drivers maintain a space margin between their vehicles and other objects ahead, behind and to each side. A space margin gives you time to react to changing conditions. It also provides an improved line of sight. Drivers who maintain a proper space margin rarely need to make sudden adjustments in their speed or direction.

Space-margin size. A space margin must be large enough to allow the distance, time and line of sight needed for safe movement at any given time. You need space to accelerate, brake and steer. You also need room to allow for mistakes that you or others make while completing a maneuver. This distance or space also should allow for quick steering or a way out of an emergency situation. The amount of space you need depends on the width and type of your vehicle, your speed and the maneuvers you will perform. Additionally, the size and shape of the space margin will vary with weather, highway and traffic conditions.

Ample space to the front, rear and sides improves visibility and allows time and room to maneuver.

Space Margin to the Front: Stopping Zone and Following Distance

Having already established your 20- to 30-second visual lead and your 12- to 15-second visual control zone, your next step is ensuring that you have plenty of room to bring your vehicle to a stop and enough space between you and the vehicle ahead.

The four- to five-second stopping zone. Under ideal road and weather conditions, it takes four to five seconds to bring an automobile to a stop from highway speeds. In conditions of reduced traction when roads are wet or covered with snow, sand or ice, your stopping time increases dramatically. Thus, for safe travel, you should identify a clear planned path four to five seconds ahead. This time zone represents the absolute minimum distance you should be able to see ahead, regardless of speed. You also need an alternate path where you can steer and brake if your planned path suddenly becomes blocked, or if a vehicle following too closely makes stopping suddenly a risky choice.

Braking distance and speed. For safety, a vehicle must have a clear path ahead equal to the minimum-stopping zone for the speed traveled. The corresponding chart illustrates the minimum stopping distance, in feet, for various speeds. The stopping distances are averages for stopping on smooth, dry pavement and include the typical braking distance. They also allow .5 to .75 seconds for both perception-time and reaction-time distances. These distances will vary, depending on factors such as visual search, attention level, decision-making capabilities, fatigue or use of alcohol or other drugs. Other factors include weather and road conditions.

Speed (MPH)	Perception Distance*	Response Distance*	Braking Distance	Total Stopping Distance	Three-Second Zone	Four-Second Zone
20	15–22	15–22	15	45–59+	90	120
30	22–33	22–33	38	82–104+	135	180
40	29–44	29–44	68	126–156+	180	240
50	37–55	37–55	105	179–215+	225	300
60	44–66	44–66	160	248–292+	270	360

*Perception time and reaction time is ½ to ¾ second.

The three- to four-second following distance. With ideal visibility, dry pavement and a safe alternate path of travel, a three- to four-second following distance is the minimum you should allow between your vehicle and any vehicle you follow. If you are attentive to your driving, this interval will provide you time to stop quickly if it is safe to do so. This space allows you time to stop safely if the other driver brakes suddenly, strikes an object or is struck by another vehicle. If it is not safe to stop, you will have time to steer into your previously identified alternate path of travel. Following closer might restrict your field of vision and limit your ability to take evasive action. New drivers and drivers who are fatigued, ill or more than 55 years old should increase their following distance to four or more seconds.

Higher speeds require greater following distances. The faster you go, the more distance you cover in a second. For instance, if you are traveling at 40 mph, it will take you three seconds to go 180 feet. At 60 mph, you will travel 270 feet in three seconds. The three- to four-second following distance works for speeds up to 50 mph. At speeds of more than 50 mph, you should allow greater following distances. At these higher speeds, it also is important to identify an alternate path into which you can steer if the path ahead is suddenly blocked.

Determine a safe following distance by counting the seconds it takes you to reach a fixed point.

HOW to DRIVE

Adopting a Three- to Four-Second Following Distance.

To put the three- to four-second rule into practice, follow these steps:

1. Pick out a fixed checkpoint: a road sign, light post or other fixed object along the road ahead.

2. As soon as the rear of the vehicle ahead of you passes the checkpoint, start counting, "One one-thousand, two one-thousand, three one-thousand," etc.

3. When the front of your car reaches the checkpoint, stop counting. If you reach the checkpoint before you finish counting three to four seconds, you are following too closely.

Following large vehicles. When following large vehicles that obscure your view of the road ahead, you should increase your following distance to five or more seconds to better monitor the traffic scene in front of the vehicle and to search for an alternate path of travel.

Maintaining a proper following interval and visual control zone, with identified alternate paths of travel, allows you more time to make decisions.

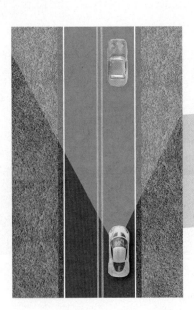

Assuming you are employing an aggressive visual search, a three- to four- second following distance allows you time to respond to situations that develop in the path ahead.

When three- to four-seconds are not enough. The three-second stopping rule works fine when you are following vehicles that are moving at nearly the same speed as you. However, the rule does not provide an adequate stopping zone for stationary objects that suddenly appear in your path or for intersecting traffic. In addition, at higher speeds (50 mph or more), your stopping distance may be greater than the distance you can see ahead. Thus you would be unable to stop in time to avoid hitting intersecting traffic or an object you could not see due to weather, inadequate lighting or other conditions. In these situations, you should increase your stopping zone to at least five seconds. Count off the five seconds as you did the three- to four-seconds.

Space Margin to the Sides

Space to the sides. The space to your sides should be great enough to provide for errors in judgment and an escape path or way out. Therefore, you should have at least one car width of space to one side of your car. When practical, it is best to have space (at least 8 feet) on both sides. Most cars range in width from 5 to 7 feet. Since traffic lanes usually are 9 to 12 feet wide, you should have little trouble identifying an adequate travel path. When lanes are not marked, you must estimate the width of the pathway you need.

If you must drive through areas of reduced space (less than one car width on either side), allow more space in front. When you find yourself in a long line of cars, adjust your speed. Then maneuver out of the situation as soon as practical.

Areas of reduced space. Be alert for areas of the highway where there is less than one car width of safe driving space next to your intended travel path. A road or highway that narrows ahead should be considered an area of reduced space. For instance, the number of lanes may decrease from four to three, or from three to two. Or the width of a two-lane road may change from 24 feet to 18 feet.

HOW to DRIVE

Ample space in front and to the sides, plus an escape path, will help you respond more effectively to problems that suddenly arise.

Extra caution with obstructions.

Watch out for obstructions such as bridges, poles, sides of hills or high curbs. These may make the shoulders narrow or unavailable for escape. A line of oncoming or parked cars, combined with obstructions, also can leave you with no choice but to brake in an emergency. Any changes in driving space require a driver to assess the response options and be prepared to respond quickly.

Space Margin to the Rear

Space behind you. This distance is more difficult to control. When cars follow too closely (tailgate), allow more distance ahead and maintain an escape route to at least one side. Encourage a tailgater to pass by slowing gradually and moving to the right side of the lane or roadway. Avoid driving too slowly for conditions. If you must stop suddenly, make every effort to signal. Move onto the shoulder of the road if you must to avoid a crash.

Try to have at least one car width of space to one side of your car.

Maintaining an adequate space margin. As you drive, you must address objects and conditions close to your intended path of travel. Your main concern should be objects that could come into or stay in your four- to five-second stopping zone. To maintain an adequate space margin, you may have to adjust your path of travel, change speed, or both. Such actions are especially important if an object is closing rapidly or there is more chance of error. For example, a motorist changing a flat tire near the road represents a higher level of risk that calls for a greater space margin.

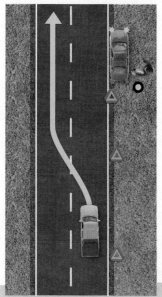

A motorist changing a flat tire near the road calls for a greater space margin.

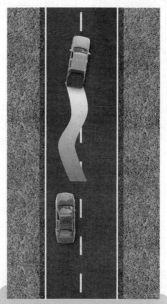

Minimize risk by adjusting your speed and position behind an erratically moving vehicle.

HOW *to* DRIVE

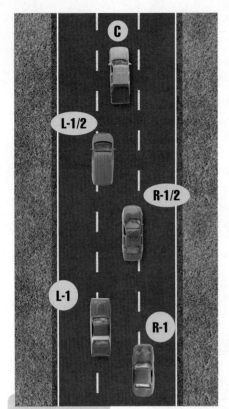

Choice of travel paths. The space margin you maintain will depend on your choice of travel paths. Consider at least five basic positions for each lane. In the illustration at left, the first car (C) is in normal driving position in the center of the lane. The next two cars are positioned to the far right or left of the lane (one-half a car width from your vehicle). The last two cars straddle the lane line (one car width from your vehicle). Taking positions to the right or left of these locations is considered a lane change.

Lane positions. On roadways without marked lanes, visualize these locations at about half a car width apart. This placement will help you to decide how to minimize the level of risk associated with objects or conditions.

Leave space for what you cannot see. Not only should you allow space for dangers that you can see, you should also leave an increased space margin for potential risks or things you cannot see. For example, provide extra space at driveways and intersections where shrubbery, embankments or buildings limit your line of sight. You may see no movement in the area, but vehicles can suddenly pull into your path. If a left lane is available and free of traffic, move over one car width as you approach an area of reduced visibility on the right. If a lane is not available, move over at least half a car width, or as close to the center of the roadway as possible.

Leave space for what you can and cannot see. If a lane change is not possible, position your vehicle one-half to one car width to the left or right.

Increase your space margin for objects you cannot see, but that could be there.

Positioned in the left lane, the driver of Car A has enough space to avoid trouble. This position also makes it easier for the driver to see and be seen. What are the potential threats in this diagram?

CAR A

Stay out of packs. Often, even in light to moderate traffic, vehicles travel in "packs." Vehicles in packs usually travel faster and closer together than normal traffic, greatly increasing risk. One way to stay out of a pack is to move into a lane where vehicles are traveling closest to the speed that you want to drive. Establish a safe following distance from the last car in the pack, reduce your speed by two or three mph, and set the cruise control.

Managing Risk with Effective Time Management

Timing is everything. Proper timing, which may involve adjusting vehicle speed, is key to safe driving. The timing of driver actions, either mental or physical, can be critical. Many collisions happen because drivers are not paying attention to the right thing at the right time. When an object moves into your three- to four-second space zone ahead, you must know how much to decrease or increase speed, or whether any change is needed. Your decision depends on your ability to judge when and where other objects might enter your path of travel.

HOW to DRIVE

Choose the best time and space. You may already know how much time it takes to turn, change lanes and complete other maneuvers. However, many drivers fail to consider the best time or place to perform maneuvers. For example, avoid passing or changing lanes in areas of reduced visibility. Holes, bumps, patches of wet leaves, ice or water on the road can cause you to lose control. Avoid passing a big truck where there may be strong crosswinds. Hedges, billboards and buildings may temporarily block your view of side roads or private drives. A dip in the road may hide a small car. Be especially cautious in such situations and be ready to react.

Avoid passing when traction or visibility is limited.

Timing and traffic conditions. Time a short turn into a narrow side road or driveway so that you avoid meeting another car at the same moment you make a hard steering movement. Do not pass or change lanes when another vehicle is in your blind areas or when you are in theirs. Proper timing of turn signals also is helpful. Timing the execution of maneuvers so you can make them smoothly and gradually gives other roadway users time to adjust.

If you miss a turn. If you miss a turn, do not inconvenience other traffic because of your mistake. Avoid making any sudden turns or quick braking. Continue on to the next intersection and safely return to your route.

One thing at a time. When you are busy with a maneuver, avoid any actions that are not part of the maneuver. The middle of a turn is not the time to adjust the radio, downshift a manual transmission, or adjust the sun visor. You should plan and perform such actions before starting the turning process. If you forget or misjudge an action, wait until you have executed the maneuver before you do anything else. Do not adjust the defroster, wipers, radio, air conditioner or heater while passing another vehicle.

Consider priorities. Critical control actions are top priority. Traffic tie-ups and objects that may enter your path of travel must receive your maximum attention. Do not allow route problems, checking the instruments or reading traffic devices or sign to distract you. Concentrate on searching for, and mentally processing, information that deals with immediate or potential conflicts.

Separating Multiple Risks

Separating. Timing is most important for situations involving multiple risks. This is especially true when you must deal with two or more objects at the same time and place, such as when you are meeting traffic on a narrow bridge. Effective timing allows you to deal with each object separately. It also provides a chance to meet a moving object at a place with better space margins or visibility. Avoid meeting fast-moving vehicles in areas of reduced visibility and space.

Effective timing will help you separate multiple risks.

HOW *to* **DRIVE**

Compromising. Occasionally, two or more objects threaten your travel path at the same time. For example: while driving on a narrow two-lane road, you approach a bicyclist on your side of the road. A long line of cars are approaching in the oncoming lane. If you are faced with two dangerous situations, compromise and give more room to the one with the greater risk. The goal is to reduce the risk posed by each and allow more distance from the object or situation with the most serious consequences or greatest potential for emergency.

If you are unable to separate these two dangers, compromise and give the cyclist more room.

In this situation, since bicyclists may make a sudden move, give the bicyclist more room by moving closer to the oncoming cars. Where possible, give bicyclists at least three feet of clearance when passing. Consider flashing your headlights to help drivers of oncoming cars see you so they will not pull out to pass. You can also adjust your speed to help separate the risks.

Managing Risk by Selecting the Best Speed

Speed and managing time and space. In a perfect world, higher speed would reduce travel time. It may, but higher speeds can also create problems related to managing time and space.

The Basic Speed Law. The key to the Basic Speed Law is to drive at a reasonable and proper speed for conditions. This means a driver should be aware of conditions and drive accordingly. In addition, a driver should have a clear distance ahead to stop if necessary. What is a reasonable and proper speed for conditions? How does a driver go about selecting such a speed?

A reasonable and proper speed. A reasonable and proper speed for any set of conditions is one that provides the driver a safe path of travel. The ideal speed provides time and space to brake or steer to a safe alternate path four to five seconds ahead if an emergency develops. If you drive too fast for conditions, then you will not be able to stay on your intended path of travel or stop in time to avoid crashing. Traveling too fast for conditions also makes it difficult for other drivers and pedestrians to predict your actions.

Adjusting speed to road conditions. A change in road conditions may warrant a speed adjustment. Changes in line of sight (including field of view), traction and space are the three major conditions that require you to adjust speed.

1. **Changes in line of sight.** The distance you can see ahead along your projected path of travel affects your safe speed. For example, imagine you can see only 200 feet ahead of your car because of road or inclement-weather conditions. Assume you are traveling at 55 mph, a speed that requires 235–276 feet to stop. You could not stop your car in time to avoid hitting an object in your path, and should thus reduce your speed.

   Field of view. Your field of view also influences speed selection. You must be able to see both sides of the roadway. You need to check out intersections, driveways and other roadside areas from which objects may move into your path of travel.

HOW to DRIVE

2. **Changes in traction.** Unfavorable weather reduces traction, so you need more time and distance to stop. On snow or ice, you may need eight to 10 seconds or more to stop safely.

3. **Changes in space.** Identification of an adequate stopping zone is important — because the stopping zone provides a valuable guide for how fast you should travel. At highway speeds, always adjust your speed so your stopping zone is less than the distance you can see ahead.

Changes in line of sight, traction and space are the three major conditions that require you to adjust speed.

Collecting information.

Experiments show that the average person can collect five to seven bits of information per glance. A bit of information can be a number, letter, symbol or signal-light flash. It may take several glances to read an overhead sign or a sign along the roadway and then note what other traffic is doing.

Processing information.

In addition, the human brain takes about a half to three-quarters of a second to process information. At 55 mph, your car will travel about 80 feet in one second, or about five to six car lengths.

Gathering information for maneuvers. In many situations — such as changing lanes or accelerating across a gap in traffic — you need to adjust your speed to allow time to complete the maneuver. The number and type of traffic elements and their location relative to your path of travel determine whether a speed adjustment is required. Most control actions require about half a second, while high-risk maneuvers made under stress and severe space limits may take longer.

Adjusting speed. When distance cannot minimize a high-risk situation, speed adjustment is essential. The closer you must pass by an object, the slower your speed should be. This is especially true when you are behind a slow-moving vehicle that might suddenly change direction or stop quickly. Reduce your speed as the risk of a crash increases.

Braking and steering require time, as does accelerating into or across a gap in traffic.

Sometimes, in spite of your efforts, a driver will cut into your space. This type of driver frequently weaves from lane to lane, hoping to reduce travel time. There is little to do but adjust your speed by slowing slightly. Such an adjustment takes just seconds and will not affect your total travel time. Fall back at least three to four seconds behind cars moving erratically — five seconds for large vehicles — and identify alternate escape paths in case of an emergency.

HOW *to* **DRIVE**

TEST **8**

Managing Time and Space

Study and respond to each of the following questions. Then review the chapter to see if your responses are correct.

Multiple Choice:

1. A space into which you can safely direct your vehicle with the lowest possible risk is referred to as your:
   a. Intended path of travel
   b. Intermediate path of travel
   c. Clear path of travel
   d. Expected path of travel

2. The size of your space margin depends on:
   a. Your speed
   b. The width of your vehicle
   c. The maneuvers you expect to perform
   d. All of the above

3. You should always maintain a stopping zone distance of _____ seconds.
   a. 2–3
   b. 4–5
   c. 9–10
   d. 12–15

4. The key to the Basic Speed Law is to drive at a _____ speed for conditions.
   a. Safe and clear
   b. Traffic-matching
   c. Slow and steady
   d. Reasonable and proper

5. Changes in _____ is a major highway condition that requires you to adjust speed.
   a. Traction
   b. Space
   c. Visibility
   d. All of the above

Short Answer:

1. List three factors affecting the selection of a path of travel.

2. Explain how to put the three- to four-second following distance rule into practice.

3. Explain the risk-reduction concept of separating and give an example of its successful use.

4. Explain the risk-reduction concept of compromising and give an example of its successful use.

5. Define "reasonable and proper speed."

CHAPTER 9

Basic Maneuvers in a Low-Risk Environment

Chapter Objectives:

◆ Describe the sequence of actions necessary to safely change lanes.

◆ Describe the sequence of actions and judgments required when approaching and completing left and right turns from and onto one- and two-way streets with single and multiple lanes of travel.

◆ Describe the procedures and level of risk associated with the various methods of reversing your direction of travel.

◆ Describe the procedures for safe angle, perpendicular, and parallel parking.

◆ Explain the procedures for parking safely on hills.

HOW *to* **DRIVE**

Basic Maneuvers

All drivers are required to perform several maneuvers in order to travel from one place to another. A maneuver is defined as changes in the speed you are traveling or the position of your vehicle. Common maneuvers include lane changes, turns, and parking. This chapter will emphasize the skills, procedures and laws that must be developed or applied to these maneuvers.

Changing Lanes

A basic movement. Changing lanes is a basic element in many traffic maneuvers because it involves a movement either to the left or to the right. Like most maneuvers, changing lanes also involves steering actions and generally requires a change in speed. Since you will be changing your vehicle's position on the roadway, you are required to signal in advance to alert other drivers of your intentions.

How to safely change lanes:

1. Check ahead, to the sides and to the rear for a safe gap in traffic.
2. Signal your intention to move left or right.
3. Re-check blind areas to the rear in the direction of your intended lane change.
4. When conditions are safe, steer into the new lane, adjusting your speed to the flow of traffic.
5. Once you reach the new lane, cancel your turn signal and recheck your vehicle's speed and position.

Entering traffic. When you enter traffic from a stopped position, you must yield the right of way to vehicles already in the travel lanes. In the city, approaching vehicles should be at least a half block away before you attempt to enter traffic. Search at least one block ahead along the center of your intended path.

Remember the time-space method of judging distance. If traffic is traveling at faster speeds, then search a greater distance ahead. Steer into the nearest travel lane and accelerate smoothly to the speed of traffic.

Leaving traffic and parking at a curb. Plan well in advance when you decide to leave traffic and park at a curb. Positioning your vehicle parallel to and close to the curb requires time to make space judgments and steer precisely. Signal well in advance and slow gradually. Tap your brake pedal to flash your brake lights. In heavy, slow-moving traffic, giving the "Stop" hand signal may also be appropriate. Lower your window and execute this signal by pointing your hand downward.

Leaving traffic near an intersection. Take special care if you are planning to leave traffic just before or beyond an intersection, because other drivers may misinterpret your intentions. If you intend to park before you reach the intersection, alert drivers behind you by tapping your brake pedal rapidly several times before you signal. If you intend to park beyond the intersection, signal at a time that other drivers will understand you are not intending to turn at the intersection.

Multiple-lane streets. Many situations on multiple-lane streets require a driver to change lanes. For example, a vehicle ahead in your lane may be preparing to turn, or a road sign may indicate that your lane is about to end. Lanes may be restricted for slow-moving vehicles or other obstructions. In all of these situations, right-of-way rules apply. It is the responsibility of the driver traveling in the blocked lane to yield to oncoming vehicles, as well as vehicles in adjacent lanes.

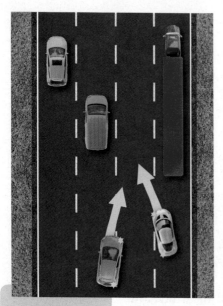

Pay close attention to the actions of other drivers before you change lanes.

Before changing lanes ask yourself:

◆ Will other vehicles, either ahead or behind, be making the same moves I intend?

◆ Is there anyone in the lane I wish to enter?

◆ Will any adjacent vehicle also attempt to enter the same lane I intend to move into?

◆ Is anyone approaching rapidly from the rear?

Common errors. New drivers should be aware of three common mistakes when changing lanes. First, you might neglect to use your turn indicator to signal your intention to change lanes. Be sure to develop the habit of using your turn indicators before changing your vehicle's position. Second, you might decrease your speed before or after steering into a new lane. Unless there is a reason to adjust your speed (a slow-moving vehicle ahead of you, for example), maintain your speed when you change lanes. Third, you might move into the new lane in a position too close to the vehicle ahead of you. The closer your vehicle gets to an object, the less time and space you will have if you need to steer around it. This can affect the precision with which you execute your lane change maneuver.

Turning

What it takes. Turning into the flow of traffic requires spatial judgment, speed control and steering skill. Consider the type of turn you are about to make, plan your steering, adjust your speed as needed and identify the best path of travel to safely complete your turn.

Points to be Aware of Before You Begin to Practice Turning

Your speed. Be aware of your speed when you turn. It is generally best to proceed slowly. When turning from your path onto a perpendicular path, your speed should not exceed 5–15 mph. Before you begin any turn, tap your brake pedal to alert drivers behind you, then apply steady pressure to the brakes. Next, slow to the appropriate speed before you enter the turn, by braking in a straight line. Maintain constant speed while you turn, then accelerate gradually as you complete the turn. Remember, the sharper the turn, the slower you must travel to maintain control of your vehicle.

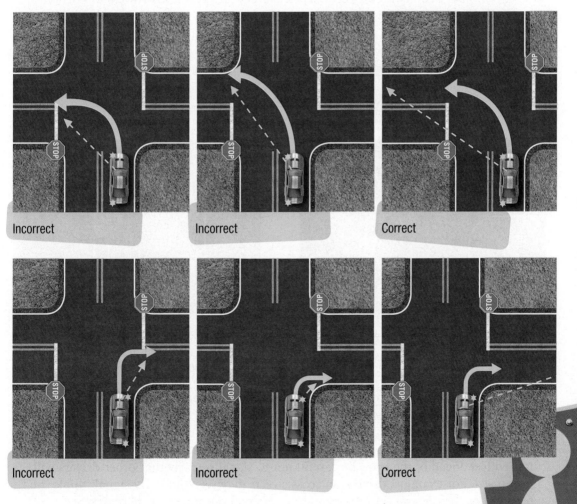

Incorrect   Incorrect   Correct

Incorrect   Incorrect   Correct

Search ahead. Look as far ahead as possible, identify a target area and search ahead continuously to spot any threatening objects. This will also help you keep from wandering from your intended path. As you turn, do not fixate on a specific target or object, because the normal tendency will be to steer toward it. Instead, maintain your focus on your intended path of travel.

Adjust your focus and steering. Always look ahead through the turning path you will be taking. Whether the turn is gradual or sharp, you will be able to look farther ahead and see along the vehicle's pathway to identify any potential obstructions.

Turning radius. Problems can occur when drivers turn too late or too soon or fail to properly control their speed. If you start a left turn too soon, your vehicle will likely cross over the center line of the intersecting street, increasing the risk of a collision. If you begin a right turn too soon, your right rear wheel may strike the curb. Remember that during turning maneuvers, your rear wheels will always turn tighter than your front wheels. Generally, the sharper your turn, the greater the difference in the tracking between the front and rear wheels. If you delay your turn, your vehicle may cross into oncoming traffic as you turn right and go toward the curb as you turn left.

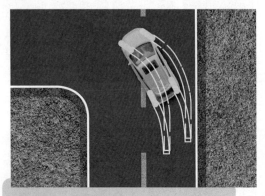

When you start a left turn too soon, you may cut across other lanes.

When you start a right turn too soon, your right rear wheel may strike or run over the curb.

Signal your intentions. Most states require drivers in urban areas to signal a least 100 feet before turning. However, it is recommended that you signal as soon as it can be given without causing confusion, generally 150 to 200 feet before the turn. On rural roadways where vehicles travel at much higher speeds, signal your intentions several hundred feet ahead of the turn. Be careful not to signal so early that other drivers will be confused. For example, drivers on cross streets may see your early signal, think you intend to turn before you actually intend to, and pull out into your path of travel.

Enter the proper lane. At some intersections, arrows on the pavement indicate the actions required of drivers in those lanes. You should position your vehicle in the proper lane before you arrive at the intersection. Many multiple-lane streets have dedicated left turn lanes at intersections. In such an instance, enter the lane as soon as possible to prepare for the turn. If you are driving in the wrong lane, do not block traffic so that you can enter the correct lane. Instead, proceed as directed by the pavement markings or traffic signals. Failure to do so increases risk and can earn you a citation for improper lane use or driving in an unsafe manner.

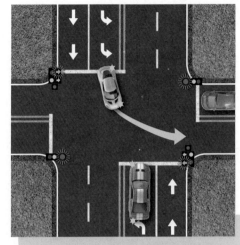

At some intersections, arrows on the pavement indicate the direction drivers must go.

Basic Turning Maneuvers

Turning right:

1. Before you reach your turning point, prepare well in advance — 500 feet, or one city block.

2. Signal at least 150 feet in advance, and when conditions are safe, move into the far right lane.

3. Reduce your speed. If you need to apply the brakes, do so in a straight line before turning the steering wheel.

4. If there is a curb, steer right until the right side of the vehicle is three to five feet from the curb. Make sure there is no bicycle or motorcycle to your right in your blind area.

5. Check traffic ahead to the right, left and rear.

6. Make sure there are no bicycles, motorcycles or pedestrians in your path. Be ready to yield to anyone in the crosswalk.

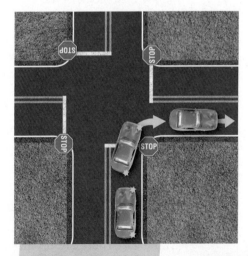

Right Turn. Stay in the right lane by looking ahead as far as possible along your intended path of travel.

HOW to DRIVE

7. If your vision is blocked to the left or right, move forward until the front of your vehicle is in line with the curb or road-edge line.

8. When your front wheels are in line with the point where the curb begins to curve, look through the turn along your intended path of travel.

9. Smoothly turn the steering wheel clockwise through the turn.

10. Stay in the right lane by focusing ahead as far as possible along your intended path of travel.

11. Complete the turn by reversing the steering process, unwinding the steering wheel counter-clockwise.

12. Cancel the turn signal (if necessary) and adjust your speed as appropriate.

Turning left:

1. When making a left turn, yield the right of way to other traffic.

2. Prepare well in advance — 500 feet or one city block — before you reach the turning point.

3. Signal and, when safe move into the far-left lane. (On a one-way street, move into the lane nearest the left curb.)

4. Signal for the turn at least 150 feet in advance of the intersection.

5. Reduce your speed. If you need to apply the brakes, do so in a straight line before turning the steering wheel.

6. Check traffic ahead and to the right, left and rear.

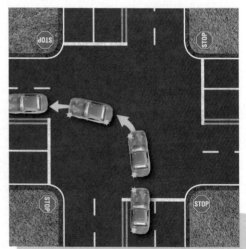

Left Turn. Follow the turning path so that you arrive in the lane that corresponds to the lane you turned from.

7. Make sure there are no bicycles, motorcycles, or pedestrians in your path. Be ready to yield to anyone in the crosswalk.

8. If your vision is blocked to the left or right, move forward until the front of your vehicle is in line with the curb or road-edge line.

9. Look through the turn along your intended path of travel.

10. Begin your turn when the front wheels are in line with the center of the street you are entering. If you are turning from a one-way street into another one-way street, begin your turn when the curb begins to curve.

11. Smoothly turn the steering wheel counter-clockwise through the turn.

12. Follow the turning path so that you turn into the lane that corresponds to the lane you exited. When turning onto a one-way street, enter the extreme left travel lane.

13. Stay in the left lane by focusing ahead as far as possible along your intended path of travel.

14. Complete the turn by reversing the steering process, unwinding the steering wheel clockwise.

15. Cancel the turn signal (if necessary) and adjust your speed as appropriate.

Reversing Direction

Reversing direction. Before turning your vehicle around, consider the advantages, disadvantages and risks involved. Maneuvers you may execute include the following: traveling around the block, a two-point turn, a U-turn, or a three-point turn. Before you make your decision, you must consider traffic density, speed, visibility, street layout and local traffic ordinances.

HOW *to* **DRIVE**

Analyzing the risk. Often, the best choice when you have to turn around is to drive around the block. However, you should consider that you may have to cross the path of oncoming traffic at an uncontrolled intersection. Choose to separate the risks so you can deal with one event at a time. This can be a simple choice of:

1. Turning right, continuing clockwise around the block with a series of right turns, then turning left, crossing traffic and entering your traffic lane at the same time, or

2. Turning left across oncoming traffic, continuing clockwise around the block with a series of right turns, then turning right to enter traffic going the other direction.

Turning left (choice 2) allows you to separate the risks to a greater degree, and requires you to turn left across only one lane of traffic.

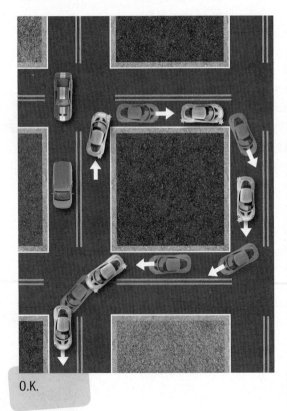

O.K.

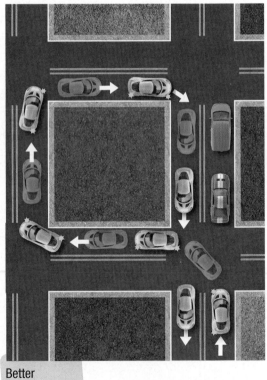

Better

Two-Point Turns

Two-point turns. Two-point turns involve backing or pulling forward into a driveway or a lightly traveled side street. There are at least three types of two-point turns you can make, each involving progressively higher levels of risk.

>   **A. Two-point turn by backing.** This technique involves stopping in your lane, then backing to the right into a driveway or a lightly traveled side street. The advantage of this technique is that you will have full view in both directions as you re-enter traffic.

>   **To make a two-point turnabout by backing:**
>
>   1. Check traffic ahead, to your right, left, behind, and the blind area to your right.
>   2. Tap the brake pedal to alert drivers behind and turn on your right-turn signal.
>   3. Make sure there are no bicycles, motorcycles or pedestrians in your intended path. Be ready to yield to anyone in a crosswalk.

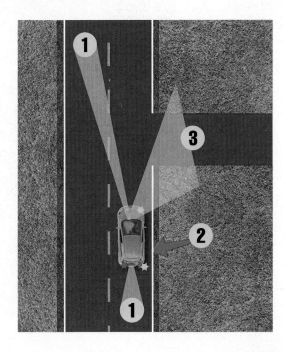

HOW *to* **DRIVE**

4. Stop three feet from the curb, with the rear bumper of your vehicle just beyond the driveway.

5. Keeping your foot on the brake pedal, shift to Reverse and check again for traffic in all directions.

6. When your path is clear, look over your right shoulder and back your vehicle slowly while turning the steering wheel quickly to the right (clockwise). Remember, as you back and turn to the right, you also must check the space to the front, since the front of the vehicle will swing out to the left.

7. As the rear of the vehicle enters the driveway, turn the steering wheel back to the left (counter-clockwise) in order to center the vehicle in the driveway. Stop after the front of the vehicle is in the driveway.

8. Keep your foot on the brake pedal, shift to Drive, check for pedestrian and crossing traffic, and enter traffic when it is safe to do so.

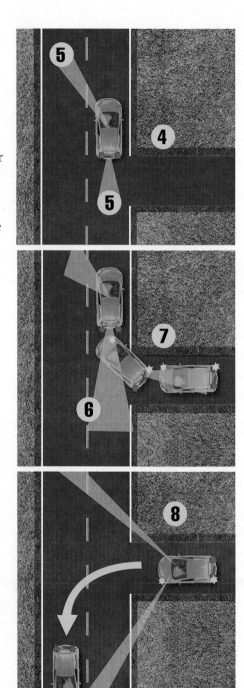

B. Two-point turnabout by turning left. A second but somewhat more risky way to turn around is to make a two-point turnabout by turning into a driveway or alley on the left and then reversing back into the street. To accomplish this, follow these steps:

1. Check traffic ahead, to your right, left, behind, and the blind area to your right.

2. Select a driveway or alley on the left you wish to turn into.

3. Tap the brake pedal to alert drivers behind and turn on your turn signal.

4. Position your vehicle for a left turn.

5. Check for bicycles and pedestrians in your path. Be ready to yield to anyone in the crosswalk.

6. Turn left into the driveway, staying as close as possible to the right side.

7. Stop with the front wheels straight and the rear of the vehicle clear of the roadway.

8. Keeping your foot on the brake pedal, shift to Reverse and turn on your right turn signal.

9. Check again for traffic in all directions.

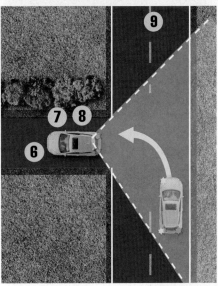

HOW *to* DRIVE

10. When your path is clear, look over your right shoulder and back your vehicle onto the roadway.

11. Steer sharply to the right, keeping your vehicle in the nearest travel lane.

12. When the front wheels are straight, stop and cancel your turn signal.

13. Keeping your foot on the brake pedal, shift to Drive, check for pedestrian and crossing traffic, and enter traffic when it is safe to do so.

C. Two-point turnabout by turning right. A third — but even more risky — way of making a two-point turnabout is to turn into a driveway on the right side of the street. The only turnabouts that are more dangerous are U-turns and three-point turns. When making a two-point turn by turning right, the driver is forced, with limited visibility to either side, to back across the travel lane to the left and stop in the opposing lane. This method of reversing direction should be used only where there is no alternative. However, with slight variations, it is the maneuver performed by many residential drivers when backing out of their driveways.

U-turns

U-turns. This method of turning around can be done in mid-block or at an intersection. Check your local laws and follow road signs to be sure U-turns are permitted. If you make a U-turn at an intersection, you must yield to all other traffic. At busy intersections, this type of U-turn is generally prohibited by a sign. If you decide to make such a turn mid-block, select a spot with little traffic. Be sure that your field of vision is clear and that you are not near a curve, an intersection or the crest of a hill. Be sure other drivers can see you well in advance. Avoid locations where children are playing or pedestrians are present.

Performing a U-turn:

1. Be sure no other vehicles are following you. To alert other drivers that you are slowing, tap your brake pedal lightly and turn on your right signal. Stop as close as possible to the right curb or the edge of the pavement, in order to provide maximum space to execute your turn.

2. Check for traffic to your front and rear. If all is clear, turn on your left-turn signal.

3. Before you proceed, check a second time for traffic over your left shoulder and to your rear.

4. Steer sharply to the left, moving your vehicle slowly until it faces in the opposite direction. If the roadway is narrow and without curbs, your right wheels may move onto the shoulder of the road.

5. When the turn is nearly complete, straighten the wheels, position your vehicle properly in the traffic lane and adjust your speed as appropriate.

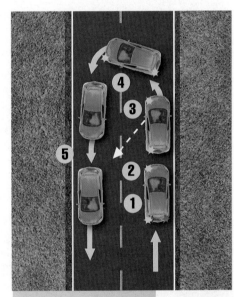

Making a U-turn

HOW to DRIVE

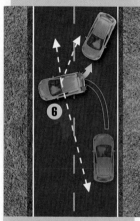

Making a
three-point turn.

Three-point Turnabout

Three-point turnabout. This maneuver, which results in your vehicle being stopped and blocking a complete lane, should only be used during the lightest traffic and when no other option is available. Never attempt this maneuver if you are near a hill or curve, or if your sight distance is limited.

Performing a three-point turnabout:

1. After checking to be sure that there is no rear or oncoming traffic, signal right and stop as close as possible to the right edge of the roadway or curb.

2. This turn will require 15 to 30 seconds to complete, so check once again for traffic in both directions and signal a left turn before you begin.

3. Check your blind area over your left shoulder before you start the turn.

4. While moving slowly forward, steer rapidly all the way to the left.

5. While your vehicle is still moving slowly forward and when the front wheels are about five feet from the curb or pavement edge, slowly roll to a stop just before the right front tire reaches the curb or road edge. At this point you are completely blocking the traffic lane.

6. Quickly check for traffic coming from the left and right. With your foot on the brake pedal, shift to Reverse. Back slowly and steer sharply to the right. When your rear wheels are about five feet from the road edge or curb, look over your left shoulder and keep looking back while rolling slowly and stop just before the left rear tire touches the curb or road edge.

7. Check traffic, shift to Drive and steer into the proper lane, adjusting speed as appropriate. On narrow roadways, it may be necessary to repeat steps four through seven to complete the maneuver.

Parking

Requirements. Although many drivers find it challenging to park in marked parking spaces, it is not difficult once you are able to judge the space available accurately and you have a good understanding and control of steering and speed. As many parking spaces are located in shopping areas, always watch for pedestrians walking to and from their vehicles.

Common types. The most common types of parking are: curb, angled, perpendicular and parallel.

Curb Parking and Reference Points

While parking at a curb is generally not as challenging as other types of parking, there is always the risk of stopping the vehicle too close to or too far from the curb. To aid in positioning the vehicle, reference points can be helpful:

1. **Parking at a curb on the right.** To park your vehicle the correct distance from a curb on the right, project a sight line over your hood, right down the middle. When you match that point of your hood with the road edge, your vehicle is approximately six inches from the curb on the right.

To position your vehicle legally when you stop parallel to a curb or road edge, use the reference points shown above. From the driver's seat, a sight-line projected over the front/center of the hood to the curb will place the vehicle approximately six inches from the road edge.

2. **Parking at a curb on the left.** To park your vehicle the correct distance from a curb on the left, project a sight line over your hood, extending over the left front corner of the vehicle. When you match that point of your hood with the road edge, you vehicle is approximately six inches from the curb on the left.

Angled Parking

The procedure for entering and leaving angled parking spaces, found most often in parking lots and shopping centers, is:

Entering an Angled Parking Space:

1. As you drive the parking lot lane, monitor the vehicles to the left and right to be sure no one is backing out of a nearby space.

2. Signal your intentions by tapping your brake pedal and activating your turn signal.

3. Position your vehicle at least five feet from the rear of the adjacent parked vehicles.

4. When you can look straight down the painted line that marks the near side of the space you plan to enter, steer sharply left or right as appropriate. As you move slowly forward into the space, straighten your wheels to center the vehicle in the space. Also monitor the front and rear of your vehicle to make sure you do not strike vehicles parked to either side.

Entering an angled parking space.

5. As you straighten the wheels, move your vehicle slowly forward, stopping just before the curb or the front of the parking space.

6. Cancel your signal, if necessary.

Leaving an Angled Parking Space:

1. Check carefully for pedestrians and vehicles. Remember you must yield the right of way when you are backing.

2. Signal left or right, as appropriate.

3. With your foot on the brake, shift to Reverse, check traffic in all directions and look over your shoulder in the direction you intend to turn. Remember to check both outside mirrors.

4. Slowly back out until you can see past the vehicle parked to your right or left. Check again for traffic.

5. When there is space enough for the front fender of your vehicle to clear the rear of the vehicle on the side opposite the direction you will be turning, turn the steering wheel rapidly in the direction you wish to turn. Continue backing into the travel lane and start to straighten the wheels.

6. Stop, shift to Drive, straighten the wheels and adjust your speed as appropriate.

7. Cancel your signal, if necessary.

Leaving an angled parking space.

Perpendicular Parking

Because these parking spaces are marked at 90-degree angles, you need to allow more room to maneuver than with angled parking. Whether your turn is to the left or right, as you approach the empty space, position your vehicle at least eight to nine feet away from the rear of the other parked vehicles.

HOW *to* **DRIVE**

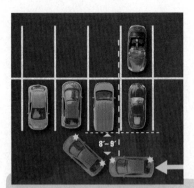

Entering a perpendicular parking space.

Entering a Perpendicular Parking Space:

1. As you drive the parking lot lane, monitor the vehicles to the left and right to be sure no one is backing out of a nearby space.

2. Signal your intentions, using your brake lights and turn signal. Check for nearby pedestrians.

3. Position your vehicle at least eight to nine feet from the rear of parked vehicles on the side to which you will turn.

4. When you can look down the near side of the vehicle parked in the space next to the one you intend to occupy, start turning the steering wheel rapidly to enter the parking space.

5. As you move slowly forward, allow your wheels to straighten, centering the vehicle in the space. Monitor the front and rear of your vehicle to make sure you do not strike vehicles parked to either side.

6. As you straighten the wheels, move your vehicle slowly forward, stopping just before the curb or the front of the parking space. (HINT: To better control risk, select a parking space that allows you to drive through the parking space directly ahead and re-enter traffic by driving forward rather than having to back into traffic.)

7. Cancel your signal, if necessary.

Using a reference point when entering a perpendicular parking space. To help you determine how far forward to pull into a perpendicular parking space, use a reference point. You can know where the front of your vehicle is by projecting a sight line just under the driver or passenger side-view mirror ahead to the ground. The front of your vehicle will be at that point. Always leave enough room between your vehicle and any vehicle parked directly in front of you. Note that this technique can also be useful when approaching intersections where you must stop.

Using left mirror

Pull forward until you see the perpendicular parking stripe just under your left side mirror.

Exiting a Perpendicular Parking Space:

1. Check carefully for pedestrians and vehicles. Remember you must yield the right-of-way when you are backing.

2. Signal left or right, as appropriate.

3. With your foot on the brake pedal, shift to Reverse, check traffic in all directions, and look over your right shoulder in the direction you intend to turn. Remember to check both outside mirrors.

4. Keeping your foot on the brake pedal, slowly back straight out until the windshield of your vehicle is in line with the rear of the vehicles parked to either side. Check again for traffic.

5. Continue backing and slowly turn your steering wheel to the left or right, depending on the direction you are going to travel.

6. Continue to monitor the position of the front of your vehicle so it does not swing into the vehicle parked at your side. When the front of your vehicle clears the rear bumper of the vehicle on the side opposite which you are turning, turn the steering wheel rapidly all the way left or right as appropriate.

7. Continue backing and start to straighten your wheels as your vehicle centers in the travel lane.

8. Stop, shift to Drive, straighten your wheels and adjust your speed, as appropriate.

9. Cancel your signal, if necessary.

Look down and to the right, and locate the perpendicular parking stripe.

Exiting a perpendicular parking space.

HOW to DRIVE

Parallel Parking

Think of parallel parking as nothing more than a lane change in reverse. As you manage your steering and speed, be aware of two areas of your vehicle to aid in using reference points — the center of your vehicle and the rear edge of your vehicle. You will also need to confirm that your intended parking space is at least one and a half times as long as your vehicle.

1. Check traffic to the rear. Signal your intentions, using your brake lights and right turn signal.

2. Position your vehicle (A) two to three feet from and parallel to vehicle B, which is parked.

3. Stop when the center-point of your vehicle is in line with the center point of vehicle B (see Illustration 1). This is your first reference point check.

4. Slowly back your vehicle, steering sharply to the right. Continue backing until the center point of your vehicle is in line with the rear of vehicle B (see Illustration 2). This is your second reference point check. Stop here temporarily while you are learning to park using this maneuver.

5. Continue backing slowly while straightening the wheels. Make quick glances forward to ensure the front wheels are straight. Continue backing until the right front corner of your vehicle is in line with the rear of vehicle B (see Illustration 3). This is your third reference point check. Stop here temporarily while you are learning to park using this maneuver.

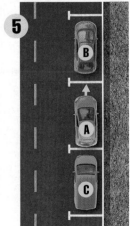

With practice, parallel parking will become easier.

6. Looking to your rear, back up slowly, turning the steering wheel sharply to the left as far as it will go. Check your left side view mirror and stop in front of vehicle C, parked behind you (see Illustration 4).

7. Move slowly forward as you straighten your wheels and stop when your vehicle is positioned an equal distance from vehicles B and C (see Illustration 5).

Continue using reference points. As you gain experience parallel parking, you may continue to use your reference points (the center of your vehicle and the rear edge of your vehicle), but do not stop at each. It is critical, however, that you do not turn your steering wheel while your vehicle is stopped — this could damage the power steering system.

Entering a parallel parking space on the left. Flip the procedure just described in order to parallel park on the left side. You may find that parallel parking to your left easier since the reference points are easier to see.

Exiting a Parallel Parking Space on the Right:

1. Check for traffic coming from the rear. As you back slowly, turn your steering wheel to the right and stop as close as possible to the front of vehicle C, which is parked behind you. (See illustration on previous page).

2. Shift to Drive and check your inside and outside mirrors as well as over your left shoulder for approaching traffic.

3. Turn on your left-turn signal to alert approaching drivers of your intention.

4. When conditions are safe, move slowly forward, steering rapidly as far to the left as possible.

5. When the front of your vehicle clears the rear of vehicle B, straighten your wheels.

6. Move slowly forward until the center point of your vehicle is in line with the rear of vehicle B. While continuing to move slowly forward, start turning the steering wheel to the right. Check the right outside mirror to make sure the rear of your vehicle does not make contact with the rear of vehicle B.

7. When you are clear of vehicle B, search well ahead and steer into the nearest travel lane, adjusting your speed as appropriate. Be alert for traffic approaching from the rear.

Exiting a parallel parking space on the left. The procedures for exiting a parallel parking space on the left side are the same as for the right side. You simply flip all left and right directions.

General Parking Information

Maximum distance from a curb. Parking regulations usually specify a maximum distance a vehicle may legally be parallel parked from a curb. The distance generally varies from 6 to 18 inches. Make sure you are aware of the requirements in your state and city.

Parking rules. Although regulations vary from state to state, do not stop, park or leave your vehicle on the paved portion of a highway when it is possible to do otherwise. If you must stop on the roadway, parking regulations typically require that you maintain an unobstructed lane on the highway opposite your vehicle. Further, there should be a clear view of the stopped vehicle for at least 200 feet in each direction.

Parking laws. Double-parking (parking in a traffic lane) is illegal in most states, as is parking in mid-block pedestrian crosswalks, loading zones and at bus stops. Signs, signals or pavement markings usually identify these locations. Learn your state and community laws on distances you must park from intersections, fire stations, fire hydrants and railroad crossings.

Parking on Hills

When you park on a hill, take precautions to prevent your vehicle from rolling downhill. Always set your parking brake firmly. Put your car in Park. If you have a manual shift vehicle and are parking downhill, set your parking brake and leave your transmission in Reverse. If you are parking uphill, leave your vehicle in Low Gear.

Turn your front wheels toward the curb when parking downhill.

Parking on a downgrade with a curb:

1. Bring your vehicle to a position parallel to the curb. Move slowly forward and turn the steering wheel slightly away from the curb. This provides the curbside front tire enough clearance to accomplish the next step.

2. Move forward very slowly and turn the steering wheel rapidly toward the curb.

3. Stop the vehicle when the front curbside tire just touches the curb.

To move the vehicle out of the parking position, back up two to three feet so you can turn the wheels away from the curb as you move forward. Check for traffic approaching from the rear. Signal your intention and when safe, steer into the nearest travel lane and adjust speed as appropriate.

Turn your front wheels away from the curb when parking uphill.

Parking on an upgrade with a curb:

1. Position your vehicle parallel to the curb.

2. Moving slowly forward about three feet, turn your wheels sharply away from the curb as far as they will go. Stop.

3. Allow your vehicle to roll backward slowly, until your front curbside tire is resting against the curb.

Parking on a grade without a curb.

If there is no curb, the same rules apply whether you park up or downhill. In either situation, always position your vehicle with your wheels turned toward the edge of the pavement. That way, if your vehicle should move, it will not roll into traffic.

The same rules apply when there is no curb. Always position your vehicle so it will run off the road if it rolls.

HOW *to* **DRIVE**

TEST 9

Basic Maneuvers in a Low-Risk Environment

Study and respond to each of the following questions. Then review the chapter to see if your responses are correct.

Multiple Choice:

1. Before making a turn in an urban area most states' laws require a driver to signal at least _____ feet before the turn.
   a. 50
   b. 100
   c. 250
   d. 500

2. When preparing to turn, you should:
   a. Brake as you begin turning the steering wheel
   b. Not brake, but instead coast down to the appropriate cornering speed
   c. Shift to Neutral to help balance the car
   d. Complete your braking before turning the steering wheel

3. When reversing direction, you should consider:
   a. Traffic density
   b. Your speed
   c. Visibility
   d. All of the above

4. Parking in a traffic lane is called _____ and is illegal in most states.
   a. Double-blocking
   b. Double-parking
   c. Double-stopping
   d. Block-parking

5. When parking uphill with a curb, you should turn the front wheels:
   a. Straight
   b. Toward the curb
   c. Away from the curb
   d. None of the above

1. Outline the general procedures for changing lanes.

2. List three common errors made by new drivers when changing lanes.

3. Outline the procedure for making a two-point turn when backing into a driveway.

4. Outline the procedure for entering and leaving a perpendicular parking space.

5. Explain how to use a reference point to help you determine how far to pull forward when entering a perpendicular parking space.

CHAPTER 10

Manual-Shift Vehicles

Chapter Objectives:

- ◆ Describe the sequence of actions needed to shift to a higher or lower gear.
- ◆ Describe the function and operation of the clutch pedal and clutch.
- ◆ Explain the purpose of each gear in a manual transmission.
- ◆ Describe the procedures for starting, downshifting, stopping and securing a vehicle with a manual transmission.

Basic shifting pattern. Today, most passenger vehicles equipped with manual transmissions provide either five or six forward speeds. The gearshift lever is usually mounted on the floor directly above the transmission, and is operated with the right hand. Regardless of the number of gears, the basic shifting pattern is the same: a variation of the letter "H."

The friction point. Learning to shift a car with a manual transmission is not difficult. It is simply a matter of coordinating the actions of the clutch pedal, accelerator and shift lever. The primary challenge is learning to release the clutch smoothly to move forward. This is done by finding the friction point — the point at which the engine begins to move the car as the clutch is released, when the engine and transmission begin to reconnect.

Planning maneuvers. Shifting takes time and coordination, and it demands attention. As a result, you must plan maneuvers — such as cornering — further in advance. Besides the normal turning procedures and checks, you generally must also shift into a lower gear before you start a turn.

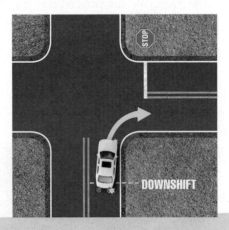

Automatic transmission	Manual-shift transmission
1. Search for obstacles.	1. Search for obstacles.
2. Alert rear traffic.	2. Alert rear traffic.
3. Brake.	3. Brake and downshift.
4. Steer.	4. Steer.

Listen up. When driving under 35 to 40 mph, pay attention to the tachometer, speedometer, sound of the engine and vehicle vibrations. These can tell you if you need to shift to a lower or higher gear. A frequent mistake is shifting into a higher gear at too low a speed, which overloads the engine.

Eyes on the road. While driving, your attention should be directed toward the road and traffic, not at your feet or the gearshift lever. For this reason, you should know how to find and control the friction point of the clutch, accelerate properly and shift smoothly before you begin driving a manual-transmission vehicle in traffic.

The clutch. The purpose of the clutch pedal is to interrupt the connection between the engine and the transmission. The transmission is connected to the engine driveshaft by a gear arrangement that transmits power to the drive wheels. The clutch disengages the connection between the engine and transmission to allow gear changes.

Learning to use the clutch pedal. Pressing the clutch all the way to the floor disengages the transmission from the engine. When the clutch pedal is up and the gearshift is in gear, the transmission is engaged. Never move the shift lever until you have pressed the clutch pedal all the way to the floor.

When you shift gears, look along your intended path of travel, not at your feet or hands.

Pressing the clutch all the way to the floor disengages the transmission from the engine.

1. Find a flat road surface, such as an empty parking lot, on which to begin practicing. (Since you must disengage the clutch when you come to a stop, your vehicle may roll backward as you try to get moving again while driving uphill. So it is better to learn on a flat surface.)

2. Press the clutch pedal all the way to the floor.

3. Place the shift lever in the first gear position and look ahead.

4. With the heel of your left foot on the floor, slowly release the clutch pedal up to the friction point (the point at which the engine speed decreases slightly).

5. Once you locate the friction point, practice adjusting the speed at which you let out the clutch pedal to control the rate of acceleration.

6. Once you master this procedure, switch to reverse gear, look backward through the rear window and follow the same procedure to find the friction point.

HOW to DRIVE

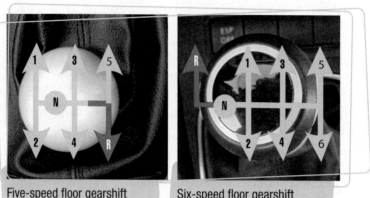

Five-speed floor gearshift | Six-speed floor gearshift

Selecting Gears

Gears provide a range of power and speed. The purpose of the various gears is to provide the range of power and speed demanded by traffic conditions or engine power. Practice placing the shift lever in various positions until you know all the locations. Remember, always press the clutch pedal to the floor before you attempt to move the shift lever from one gear to another.

The Gears and Their Functions

Gear	Description
Neutral	Neutral is used when starting the vehicle, and when coming to a stop.
First	First gear is used for getting the car under way. It provides maximum power and is used at slow speeds (up to 15 mph for most vehicles).
Second	Second gear is an intermediate gear. Its primary purpose is acceleration and power at moderately slow speeds (up to 25–30 mph). It is often used to accelerate when the vehicle is already rolling. It is also used when turning corners in urban driving environments.
Third	Third gear is used at speeds between 30–40 mph.
Fourth	Fourth gear is used at steady driving speeds between 40–50 mph.
Fifth	For vehicles with five speed transmissions, fifth gear is the top cruising gear, used to maximize fuel mileage when driving on expressways.
Sixth	For vehicles equipped with a sixth gear, it is the top cruising gear, used to maximize fuel mileage when driving on expressways.
Reverse	Reverse gear is used to back up.

Neutral. This position means the vehicle is not in gear. The engine is not connected to the drive shaft. Neutral is used when you start the engine or when the car is stopped with the engine running. A vehicle in Neutral rolls easily. You should not park, shut off the engine or leave the vehicle when it is in Neutral. Instead, when you park and leave your vehicle, make sure it is in low or reverse gear with the parking brake set.

Forward gears. The forward gears are used to match the vehicle's speed for optimum engine performance and to maximize fuel mileage. There are generally five to six forward gears, but some vehicles have fewer. The table on the previous page summarizes the gears in a manual transmission vehicle.

Placing the Car in Motion

Getting started. Develop the habit of starting the engine with the shift lever in Neutral, your right foot on the brake pedal, and your left foot pressing the clutch pedal to the floor. Failure to shift to Neutral or press the clutch pedal to the floor will cause the vehicle to move suddenly when you start the engine. In newer vehicles, the engine will not start until the clutch pedal is fully depressed.

To move forward:

1. Press the brake pedal with your right foot.

2. With your left foot, press the clutch pedal to the floor.

3. Shift into first gear.

4. Release the parking brake.

5. Switch on your turn signal to indicate the direction in which you plan to move.

6. Check for traffic in your rear- and side-view mirrors. Look over your shoulder to check blind areas.

7. With your right foot on the brake, slowly let the clutch pedal up to the friction point with your left foot. Remember to look at the roadway, not down at your feet or hands.

8. Move your right foot from the brake to the accelerator.

9. As you press down gently on the accelerator, slowly let up the clutch pedal all the way. Remove your foot from the clutch pedal while under way. Place your left foot on the "dead pedal," the flat area just to the left of the clutch pedal.

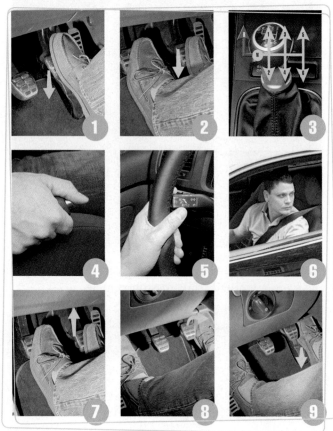

Accelerating and shifting. As your vehicle gains speed — 5 to 15 mph — press the clutch pedal to the floor. At the same time, lift your right foot from the accelerator a little and move the shift lever into second gear. Release the clutch pedal smoothly as you accelerate. As the car gains speed to approximately 30 mph, shift into third gear, following the procedure outlined for second gear. Continue upshifting as needed to reach the optimal gear for your chosen speed. When selecting your speed, be sure to take into consideration the speed limit, the terrain and traffic conditions.

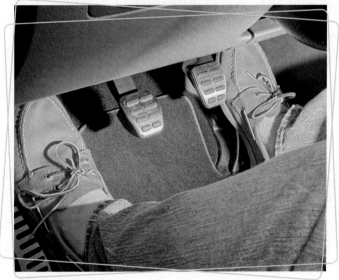

CAUTION: Do not leave your foot on the clutch pedal after you have shifted gears when the vehicle is in motion. Such a habit, called "riding the clutch," rapidly wears the clutch surface and causes slippage. Rest your left foot on the "dead pedal" to the left of the clutch pedal until it is time to shift again.

Easy does it. Always press the accelerator pedal slowly. If you accelerate too quickly as you let the clutch up — especially in first or second gear — the vehicle will jerk when the clutch reaches the friction point. If you continue to accelerate, a series of slow, bumpy jerks may result, or the engine may stall.

HOW to DRIVE

Downshifting

Shifting to a lower gear. For better power and control when turning, downshift from higher gears to a lower gear. Second gear is generally the most appropriate gear when turning in city areas. Downshifting also may be necessary to go up or down hills, around curves, or to pull a trailer. To downshift, press the clutch pedal to the floor while you release some of the pressure on the accelerator. Shift the vehicle into the next lower gear and smoothly release the clutch pedal. Continue downshifting until you reach the desired gear. Be sure to complete your downshifting prior to entering a turn.

Stopping the Vehicle

Do not apply the clutch too soon. When you bring a manual-shift car to a stop from more than 30 mph, press the brake pedal, and when your speed safely matches the next lowest gear's shifting point, downshift into that gear. Continue to brake and downshift through the gears consecutively until you reach second gear. Smooth, full release of the clutch pedal upon completion of each shift is required to maintain control over acceleration. To avoid stalling the engine, when you have slowed to about 15 mph or less, press the clutch down and brake your vehicle to a stop. Check your owner's manual for recommended shifting and downshifting speeds. Be careful to not release the clutch too quickly. This can slow or stop the drive wheels abruptly, reducing traction, disrupting the vehicle's balance, and possibly cause a skid.

Securing the Vehicle

The sequence discussed for stopping and securing your vehicle in Chapter 4 is basically the same for a vehicle equipped with a manual transmission. It is very important to develop the habit of following the sequence:

◆ Come to a complete stop with the wheels straight or turned toward or away from the curb, as appropriate. (See Chapter 9.)

◆ Keep the clutch pedal depressed.

◆ Shift to first gear or reverse, as appropriate.

◆ Set parking brake.

◆ Turn off all accessories and lights.

◆ Make sure all windows are closed.

◆ Turn of the ignition and remove the key.

◆ Check mirrors and over your shoulder for traffic.

◆ Exit your vehicle, with keys in hand.

◆ Lock all doors.

Backing. If your vehicle is equipped with a manual transmission, your backing speed will depend largely on your use of the friction point of the clutch. Maintain control by holding the clutch pedal at the friction point. This enables you to closely control your speed and stop quickly by depressing the clutch and applying the brakes.

HOW to DRIVE

TEST **10**

Manual-Shift Vehicles

Study and respond to each of the following questions. Then review the chapter to see if your responses are correct.

Multiple Choice:

1. The primary challenge in driving a manual transmission vehicle is learning to:
   a. Release the clutch smoothly to move forward
   b. Press the accelerator to increase engine speed appropriately
   c. Depress the clutch when coming to a stop
   d. Downshift before entering a turn

2. The point at which the engine begins to move the car as the clutch is released is called the _____.
   a. Matching point
   b. Blending point
   c. Friction point
   d. Friction cuff

3. A frequent mistake is:
   a. Shifting into a higher gear at too high a speed
   b. Shifting into a higher gear at too low a speed
   c. Shifting into a lower gear at too low a speed
   d. Shifting into a lower gear at too high a speed

4. When shifting gears, you should look:
   a. At the dash gauges
   b. At the gear lever
   c. At the side of the highway
   d. Along your intended path of travel

5. When shifting gears, you should press the clutch:
   a. Down about an inch.
   b. About half-way down
   c. Not at all.
   d. All the way to the floor.

1. Explain the purpose of the clutch.

2. Explain the purpose of (a) the forward gears and (b) neutral gear.

3. Explain why a driver should not leave his or her foot on the clutch pedal after having shifted gears when the vehicle is in motion.

4. Outline the basic procedure for stopping a vehicle that is going more than 30 mph.

5. Explain the process of securing a manual transmission vehicle.

CHAPTER 11

Sharing the Road with Other Users

Chapter Objectives:

- Describe how relating to other drivers can help you avoid becoming involved in a collision.
- Identify common traffic conflicts and how they can cause traffic crashes.
- Identify how the actions of highway users can cause collisions.
- Identify and explain how specific driver errors help you assess crash probability.
- Explain the importance of communication as a means of preventing crashes.

- Explain the special responsibility drivers have for the safety of pedestrians, bicyclists and animals.
- Describe proper responses to approaching emergency vehicles.
- Explain the importance of understanding the features and limitations of other highway users such as motorcycles and large trucks.
- Describe safe procedures for driving through intersections and interchanges.
- Describe the risks involved in railroad crossings and how to reduce the risk of conflict at railroad crossings.
- Explain the necessary precautions and procedures for passing other vehicles on two-lane roadways.

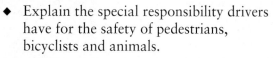

HOW *to* **DRIVE**

Traffic is made up of all types of people and vehicles using the highway system to travel from one place to another. If we all share the responsibility for this system, it will operate more safely and efficiently.

Single-vehicle crashes account for more than 50 percent of all motor vehicle occupant fatalities. However, most collisions occur when two or more objects try to occupy the same space at the same time. As a driver, you must learn to look for movements that could lead to conflict. You must judge the chance of two objects closing on each other. Knowing how others commit errors will help you to better evaluate and execute actions to reduce risk.

Closing Probability and Movements

Definition of closing probability. The chance that a vehicle and another object will move closer together as they move along a projected path of travel is called closing probability. You can detect closing movements successfully if you know what to look for. Most pedestrians and animals enter your path from the front or side. Conflicts with vehicles include the potential for side, front and rear-end collisions.

Closing probabilities do not always involve other vehicles. Watch for pedestrians and animals.

Five Common Traffic-Conflict Situations:

1. **Oncoming vehicles.**
Oncoming vehicles may cross the center line or move into your lane. They may pull into your path while turning or passing another vehicle. Even on freeways, vehicles can cross medians or jump guardrails, resulting in side-angle or head-on collisions.

Beware of oncoming cars crossing into your lane.

2. **Merging and exiting vehicles.** Entering, exiting and merging vehicles typically close in on your travel path at an angle from the side. Generally, these vehicles are either slowing or accelerating from a stop. They also may be changing lanes or merging from a parked position along the side of the roadway. On freeways, vehicles merge from ramps and acceleration lanes. Cars or trucks with wide loads can sideswipe your vehicle while passing or being passed.

Be aware of merging vehicles entering from the side.

3. **Cars ahead of you.** Vehicles ahead of you traveling in the same direction can suddenly increase your level of risk in two ways: either the driver of the vehicle ahead may stop suddenly or swerve, or the driver of a vehicle in an adjacent lane may suddenly swerve into your lane. Either driver may be avoiding a vehicle or object in the road or experiencing mechanical failure that causes loss of control. In either event, a collision could result.

If a vehicle ahead stops suddenly, you may have to swerve to avoid a collision.

HOW to DRIVE

4. **Vehicles behind you.** Vehicles following too closely could crash into the rear of your vehicle if you stop suddenly, a serious problem that is even more likely to occur at night. Drivers who follow too closely cause more than two million rear-end collisions annually.

Following too closely can lead to rear-end collisions.

5. **Intersecting vehicles and pedestrians.** Intersecting traffic can be a serious threat. Crashes occur at intersections frequently when drivers run red lights or fail to obey stop signs. Pedestrians, bicycles or animals can also suddenly dart into the roadway along your path of travel.

You must learn to identify the actions of others that can increase closing probability.

Searching for clues to closing actions. In each of the preceding situations, you must learn to identify the actions of others that can increase closing probability. Drivers may change speed, direction or both. Also watch for any stopped vehicle — the driver may be preparing to back up.

Evaluating actions. In most situations, only one or two of these actions would result in someone or something closing in on your path of travel at any one time. In the case of an oncoming car, you must judge whether the driver would turn left or veer into your path. You will need to judge whether the driver of a vehicle traveling in front of you will gradually decrease speed or brake suddenly. Will a vehicle reach an intersection at the same time as you? Will a following vehicle be able to stop quickly if you do? Will a vehicle parked along the road suddenly pull out and accelerate into your path?

The key question is: What action might the other driver take that could increase the probability of closing?

Human error. Few collisions occur that do not involve human error. If you know what types of errors to expect, you will make fewer mistakes and be able to avoid those other road users. Typical errors drivers make include:

Be aware of blind intersections with limited sight distances and drivers whose vision may be obstructed.

1. **Vision errors**
   a. Driver fails to check rearview mirrors or blind areas.
   b. Driver allows vision to be diverted from the path of travel, such as while reading billboards, talking with passengers, smoking, eating, talking on a cellular phone, or text messaging.
   c. Driver allows vision to be blocked, such as by large signs, ice, snow, dirt, packages or other obstructions inside the vehicle.
   d. Driver does not establish eye contact with other drivers as potential conflict situations develop.

2. **Failure to yield right-of-way**
   a. Driver does not obey stop or yield signs.
   b. Driver runs red lights.
   c. Driver does not yield to vehicle on right.

Always obey traffic lights and stop signs, and be extra careful when pedestrians are present.

HOW to DRIVE

3. **Improper speed adjustment**
   a. Driver approaches stop or yield signs too fast.
   b. Driver approaches turns too fast.
   c. Driver drives through turns too fast.
   d. Driver does not adjust speed to compensate for reduced visibility, space or traction.

4. **Poor judgment of distance or space requirements**
   a. Driver tailgates other vehicles.
   b. Driver swings wide or turns too sharply.
   c. Driver passes or overtakes improperly.
   d. Driver selects improper lane or position for a turn.

5. **Inadequate or improper vehicle control**
   a. Driver brakes suddenly or steers too quickly on slippery surfaces.
   b. Driver recovers poorly from a turn.
   c. Driver uses improper seating position when driving.

6. **Improper signals**
   a. Driver does not signal when changing lanes or turning.
   b. Driver improperly uses four-way emergency flashers.
   c. Driver gives a false signal.

Entering curves too fast, especially when traction is reduced, can lead to trouble.

Tailgaters will not have enough space if the car ahead stops suddenly.

Always signal to tell other drivers your intentions.

Communication

Definition of communication. Communication is an exchange of information. It involves sending and receiving information. As a sender, you must choose the best method and time to send a message. As a receiver, you must be able to receive and understand messages sent by others. Too many drivers assume that just because they see and signal another driver or pedestrian, they are seen and understood.

Four common messages:

1. **Intentions**
   I plan to turn left or right.
   I am turning here.
   I am slowing.
   I want to pass; please move over.
   I want to back up.

2. **Warning**
   I must stop suddenly.
   There is danger in your lane.
   Your lights are blinding me.

3. **Presence**
   I am over here.
   Do you see me?
   I am parked.

4. **Feedback**
   I see you.
   I get the message.
   Go ahead.
   I will stay put.
   Thanks for helping me.

Communication involves sending a clear message as well as understanding messages sent by others.

HOW to DRIVE

Methods of communicating. Drivers use signaling devices to send most messages. Lights signal change of direction. The horn sounds warnings. However communication is performed, it should involve eye-to-eye contact for best results.

Here are some methods to use:

1. **Electric signals**
   a. Turn-signal lights
   b. Brake lights
   c. Back-up lights
   d. Four-way emergency flashers

2. **Horn**
   a. Quick taps
   b. Sharp blast
   c. Lasting blast

3. **Headlights**
   a. Flash on and off
   b. Switch from low beams to high beams and back

4. **Body actions**
   a. Hand signals
   b. Nodding
   c. Smiling
   d. Looking puzzled or confused

5. **Vehicle position**
   a. Lane choice
   b. Position within lane
   c. Drifting movement

Horn

Hand Signals

Daytime Running Lights

Center Brake Light

Headlights

Brake Lights, Directional Signals

Drivers can use hand signals or one of the vehicle's signaling devices.

Left Turn

Stop

Right Turn

Pedestrians often take chances. Keep in mind that many people have never driven a motor vehicle. Thus, pedestrians, especially children and elderly people, often do not know what a driver can or cannot do with a motor vehicle. Because of this, they take chances that can cause serious problems.

Responsibility for pedestrian safety. Motorists have a legal and moral responsibility to take every precaution to avoid hitting pedestrians. Never assume anything about a pedestrian, young or old. Most pedestrians overestimate their visibility to drivers. Allow as much — or more — time and space as you would for a motor vehicle or bicycle.

Do your part. When you wait for a traffic signal at an intersection, be sure to stop behind the stop line or crosswalk. Avoid jumping the gun when the light turns green. Always allow pedestrians to finish crossing your lane before you accelerate. When you turn at intersections where there are signals, be alert for crossing pedestrians. Be alert to pedestrian traffic when you make a right turn on red, which requires drivers to stop and yield the right-of-way to cross traffic and pedestrians in either crosswalk.

Stop your vehicle behind the stop line or crosswalk and allow pedestrians to cross before you proceed through the intersection.

High-risk pedestrian areas. Watch for pedestrians at school zones, parks, playgrounds, bus stops, parking lots, college campuses, intersections and mid-block crossings. Be alert to pedestrians wearing headphones, or ear buds, or talking on a cell phone. They may not hear your vehicle or be aware of your presence. Driving in shopping centers also demands particular care because people carrying packages are not always attentive. Be especially watchful for children playing in residential areas.

When children are present. The unexpected behavior of young children can pose a serious problem. Children under the age of 6 are particularly apt to dart into the street without stopping or looking. In many subdivisions, the problem is compounded by the absence of sidewalks.

Overcoming dangers posed by children. To overcome risk associated with young children, you must develop proper visual habits, particularly ground viewing: searching for movement or shadows under and around parked vehicles. Be alert for children walking, running, playing games or riding bicycles. The presence of pets should alert you to the possibility of children in the area. Children also may be attracted to construction sites or vacant lots.

Inattentive pedestrians. In residential or suburban areas, adult pedestrians who frequently cross in the middle of the block may present problems. Watch for meter readers, postal employees, delivery persons, utility workers and trash collectors. They may wander into your path while concentrating on their jobs. Other pedestrians may step into the street while mowing their lawns or sweeping their sidewalks.

Pedestrians in parking lots before and after an event are likely not to pay close attention to vehicle traffic. Also, when it is raining, snowing or foggy, it may be difficult to see pedestrians. Because of umbrellas, hoods and hats, they may not see you. Pedestrians might take extra risks when it is raining, so be prepared.

Children can dart into the street without thinking about traffic dangers.

Ground viewing can reveal the presence of nearby pedestrians.

Watch for pedestrians around work vehicles.

Alcohol and other drugs. Alcohol and other drugs also contribute to collisions with adult pedestrians. Time of day, location and behavior can provide clues about whether a pedestrian is affected by alcohol.

Time/space gap needs. Like drivers, pedestrians must learn to judge gaps in traffic. For example, the typical young adult can cross a two-lane street in about 4 to 6 seconds. In contrast, elderly people and children may need 7 to 10 seconds to cross the same street. This information should help you adjust your speed accordingly to minimize risk.

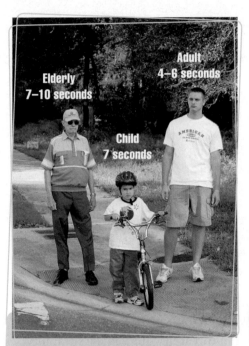

Elderly
7–10 seconds

Adult
4–6 seconds

Child
7 seconds

Depending on their age and physical condition, pedestrians may need as much as 10 seconds to cross a two-lane street.

Emergency Vehicles

Emergency vehicles. Give room to emergency vehicles such as ambulances, fire trucks and police vehicles. These vehicles frequently travel at high speeds and could swerve suddenly. Any time you hear a siren or see flashing red or blue lights, pull over as far as possible and stop, even when you are on a divided highway. Move out of an intersection before pulling over. An emergency vehicle sometimes drives on the wrong side of the road when its path becomes blocked.

HOW to DRIVE

Large trucks. Drivers of large trucks have very limited visibility, and the trucks have large blind areas around them. Do not assume that a truck driver can see you. Avoid traveling alongside or close behind a truck. When a truck is backing, do not pass behind it. The driver may not see you or hear your horn.

A large truck turning right sometimes swings wide so the trailer can clear the curb or other objects in its path. In swinging wide, the truck may move to the left before turning right or swing into the oncoming traffic lane after a turn. It is important to provide trucks ample room to negotiate turns. DO NOT PASS ON THE RIGHT — you could cause a collision.

Because of their size, large trucks create wind currents that can affect nearby vehicles. These currents can threaten your vehicle's stability when you are close. This is an even greater problem when you are riding a motorcycle or towing a trailer or other object. Be sure to allow plenty of clearance between your vehicle and large trucks.

Motorcycles and Scooters

Give motorcycles and scooters as much space as you would a vehicle. When you pass a motorcycle or any other two-wheeled vehicle, give the rider the whole lane. Do not try to squeeze into the same lane. Motorcycles are narrower and harder to see than other vehicles. Keep in mind that riders of two-wheeled vehicles do not have the same occupant protection that you have in your vehicle. If involved in a collision, they are subject to a higher risk of injury.

Motorcycles and scooters can generally stop in a shorter distance, so increase your following distance when driving behind one of these vehicles. A motorcyclist or scooter rider will respond to highway hazards differently than other drivers. An object in the road that is not a problem for a passenger vehicle may require evasive action by the rider. The surface of the roadway may prompt the motorcyclist or scooter rider to reduce speed. It is important to be aware of how traction affects all other vehicles sharing the roadway, not just your own vehicle.

Bicycles

Bicycle riders increasing. The number of bicycles on the road continues to rise as more adults use bikes for transportation and recreation. In addition, child riders present the same dangers as child pedestrians. Unfortunately, parents too often permit their children to ride bicycles on the street when they are too young and lack the necessary training to accurately assess the risks. That is why it is critical for drivers to be very cautious around children, whether they are riding a bicycle or walking as a pedestrian.

Bikes demand increased awareness. Several clues should alert you to the special problems of bicycles. The style of — and equipment on — a bicycle provide some information. A small child on an oversized bike is more likely to behave erratically. Bicycles have limited maneuverability, so you should be aware of — and make adjustments for — roadway conditions hazardous to bicycles. For example, railroad crossings, potholes or gravel on the roadway require major adjustments by bicyclists. Steel bars or gratings on storm drains also can be a serious hazard. Expect bicyclists to steer around these and other objects.

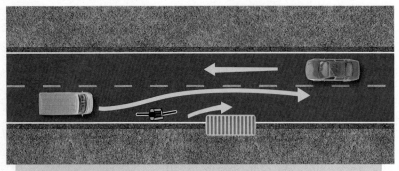

Obstacles such as sewer grates present special problems for bicyclists. Drivers should make adjustments when cyclists are forced to steer around obstacles.

Bicycles are hard to see in traffic. Bicyclists riding in a stream of traffic often are difficult to see. Consequently, you must build into your visual search a special awareness of bicyclists and factors that could influence their paths of travel. In addition, you must allow bicyclists more time and space to respond.

Animals

Pets. Pets present special problems to drivers because of their size and quick movements. Dogs and cats may dart into the roadway when least expected. Drivers may swerve or brake hard in an attempt to avoid hitting these animals. Although no one would want to hurt someone's pet, your safety and the safety of other motorists is more important. Concentrate on slowing down and maintaining directional stability. Aggressive turning maneuvers could result in a dangerous off-road situation, where the chance of injury to you and your passengers increases dramatically.

In rural and forested regions, wild animals are a more serious traffic problem than most people realize. Each year, collisions with wild animals kill approximately 160 people and injure thousands more. It is estimated that 1.5 million deer alone are killed annually in the U.S. by motor vehicles. Wild animals on the roadway are unexpected and their actions are erratic and unpredictable. The size of wild animals varies from as small as a squirrel to as large as a moose. Be alert for wild animals at all times and be especially careful at dusk, dawn and night time when they are likely to be near the road and hard to see.

Horse-drawn vehicles. Special attention needs to be given to animal-drawn wagons or horseback riders on or near the roadway. A sudden noise or movement may cause an animal to shy or bolt. Your best response is to adjust speed and increase your space margin. If you think the horn would be helpful, tap it quickly so you do not frighten the animal, but use it well before you approach the animal and rider.

HOW to DRIVE

Intersections create hazards. Controlled access highways have special ramps that allow entry and exit. All other roadways intersect with cross roadways and private driveways to form intersections. Intersections allow cars or pedestrians to cut across a driver's pathway at various angles.

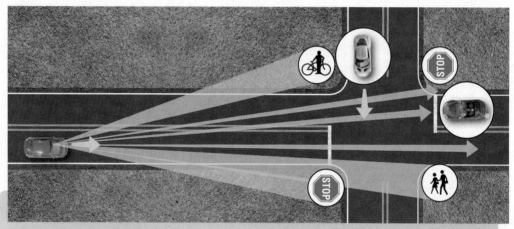

As you approach an intersection, search for traffic control devices, other vehicles and pedestrians who may enter your path.

A safe approach. Whether you drive in the city, on a highway or in an urban area, the safe way to approach an intersection is the same. Be in the correct position, in the proper lane (see page 233). As you approach an intersection, adjust your speed to allow more time to search the area and to smoothly stop if necessary. Remember, many people do not stop for signs and red lights. Also remember that other drivers can see you more easily when you drive with your low-beam headlights on during the daytime.

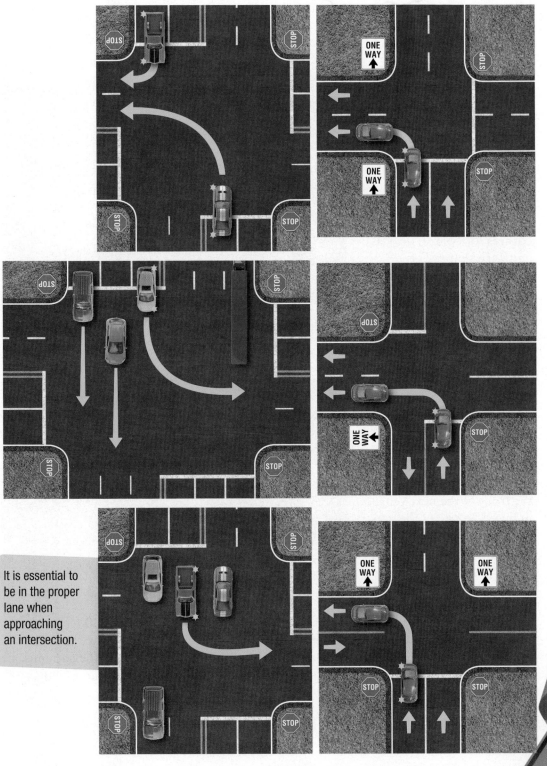

It is essential to be in the proper lane when approaching an intersection.

HOW to DRIVE

ROA
CLOS

Search patterns.

Intersections may differ in design and type of controls, requiring different search patterns. As you approach intersections, search all areas, and be aware of blocked lines of sight. Search all four corners for control devices and curb shape. The shape or sharpness of the curb will provide clues to spacing problems.

Following too closely in an intersection will block your view of potential dangers.

Safe gap. Once you reach an intersection, you will need to decide when it is safe to start across or turn. To do this, you will have to judge a safe gap in traffic. A gap in traffic is the distance or time between the back of one vehicle and the front of the next vehicle in line. The size of the gap needed depends upon the time required to cross the intersection or to turn.

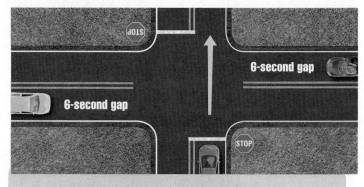

Allow at least 6 seconds to cross a street 30 feet wide.

Correct distances and times.

From a stop, you need about 4 seconds to cross an intersection 30 feet wide. You should wait for a gap of at least 6 seconds to ensure you can cross without interrupting traffic. As the width of a street increases, the size of the traffic gap must be increased. Use the counting method "one-one-thousand, two-one-thousand," etc., to judge correct distances and times.

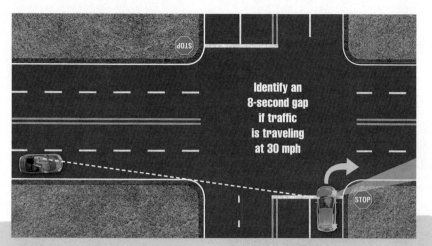

Identify an
8-second gap
if traffic
is traveling
at 30 mph

Turning right onto a road where traffic is moving at 30 mph requires an eight-second gap. When you pull onto a highway where vehicles are traveling at 55 mph, you need a gap of at least 11 seconds.

Turning at Intersections.

1. Depending on the direction you wish to go, turn from the far left or far right lane of traffic moving legally in your direction.

2. Unless otherwise indicated, enter the first traffic lane that goes in the direction you want to go.

3. Where turns are permitted from more than one lane, turn into the lane corresponding to the lane you turned from.

Judging a safe gap. Once you complete a turn, you must accelerate to the speed of traffic. As a result, right and left turns take longer than simply crossing an intersection. In urban areas, you need a time gap of about 8 to 9 seconds to turn right onto a street where traffic is moving at 30 mph. Increase this time to 11 seconds for a left turn. To turn right onto an open highway with traffic moving at 55 mph, you will need a gap of 11 seconds or more. Allow about 14 seconds for a left turn onto the same highway.

Time and space management. Effective time and space management is critical to avoiding collisions at intersections. Timed distances provide an efficient way to judge safe gaps in traffic. With practice, you can easily judge distances without having to count. However, should the need arise, you will have a method for checking how much time you need.

Railroad Crossings

"Always expect a train" is a sound rule to follow when approaching a highway-rail grade crossing. A typical locomotive weighs approximately 200 tons. Add 100 railcars to the locomotive, and the train can weigh approximately 6,000 tons. The weight ratio of a train to an automobile is about 4,000 to 1 and is proportional to an automobile and a soda can. Trains have only one way to go — on the tracks. Trains cannot swerve and can take a mile or more to stop. Pay attention to signs, gates and warning lights at crossings. Use common sense at all times.

How Can You Drive Over a Railroad Crossing Safely?

Despite warning signs, crossing gates and signals, many collisions occur at highway-rail crossings each year. Among the crash causes are driver impatience, driver inattention and errors in judgment.

Never drive over a railroad crossing when a train is approaching. The consequences could be fatal. An approaching train can create an illusion that it is moving slower than you think. Modern trains are quieter than ever, with no telltale "clackety-clack" noise. Remaining patient, paying attention and exercising sound judgment can help prevent you from colliding with a train.

Determine when it is safe to cross. Scanning and searching in both directions will help you safely cross railroad tracks. Here are some basic rules to help you determine when it is safe to cross:

1. Slow down when approaching a highway-rail grade crossing. If gates are down or warning lights are flashing, stop and wait until the gates go up and the warning lights stop flashing. Never rely solely on mechanical warning equipment — take the time to look and listen for an approaching train.

2. Stop no closer than 15 feet from a railroad crossing when a train is approaching. If the crossing is equipped with flashing red lights and they are activated, do not attempt to cross the tracks.

3. If the crossing is not equipped with flashing lights or crossing gates, then use extra caution. Remember, a train could approach at any time. Slow down, look, listen, and if there is no train in sight, proceed to cross the tracks quickly and safely, without stopping.

4. Always wait for the vehicle ahead of you to clear the tracks before you start across. To avoid being trapped at a crossing, never stop on or near the railroad tracks. Be sure to have at least 15 feet between the rear of your vehicle and the tracks on the other side.

5. After a train has passed, check in both directions to see that no other trains are coming. Be careful — a second train could be behind the first or coming from the opposite direction on an adjacent track.

Stay alert. Even if you cross a set of railroad tracks every day at about the same time, do not take familiar crossings for granted. Do not assume the track is clear. Freight trains do not follow set schedules. Trains can run after-hours as well as during scheduled service times. Never attempt to beat a train.

HOW to DRIVE

Stalled vehicle. Never stop your vehicle on railroad tracks for any reason whatsoever. This is a good way to lose your vehicle and possibly your life.

In the rare event that your vehicle stalls on the tracks, do not panic.

◆ Immediately check in both directions for approaching trains.

◆ Get everyone out of the vehicle and a safe distance away from the tracks. Ensure that you and your occupants will not be in the path of flying debris should a train approach and collide with the vehicle.

◆ Call the emergency number that is posted on the crossbuck mast or near the crossing, local law enforcement or 911. Provide the operator with the 6-digit number and letter that identify the crossing. This number is unique to that crossing and may be located on the crossbuck, mast, fence or electrical box. That way, the railroad will know exactly which crossing is blocked and an oncoming train may be stopped by the dispatcher.

Returning to your stalled vehicle could be dangerous and deadly. Trains can approach from any direction on any tracks at any time!

Interchanges

Definition. Highway interchanges connect intersecting sections of roadways. Common on expressways and interstates, interchanges consist of overpasses, underpasses, loops and ramps. Limited access eliminates many hazards by crossing over or under the traffic on other highways. Unlike intersections, interchanges permit vehicles to change from one roadway to another without crossing in front of other traffic. Drivers adjust speed as necessary and merge into or out of moving traffic.

Interchange types. There are several types of interchanges. The cloverleaf and diamond are the most common. Other interchange configurations are variations of these designs.

Cloverleaf

Diamond

On freeways or expressways, you normally will enter and exit from the right lane. Sometimes you will enter or exit from the extreme left or high speed lane. Therefore, you must read the signs and select the proper lane well in advance.

Lanes and ramps. Interchanges consist of through lanes, ramps and speed change lanes. Entrance or exit ramps usually are designed for speeds of 25 to 45 mph. Speed change lanes alongside the main travel lanes are special highway lanes that allow a vehicle to reduce speed to exit or increase speed for merging. Speed-change lanes also are called deceleration and acceleration lanes.

Merging. When you enter an expressway from a ramp, you will merge into high-speed traffic. Merging is a coming together — or blending — of vehicles to maintain a smooth, uninterrupted traffic flow. As they merge, drivers already on — and those entering — the highway need to adjust speed and position to avoid collisions. Both the drivers on the expressway and the drivers on the ramp have a responsibility to cooperate with each other. Some jurisdictions use metered ramps, which use signal lights to control the rate at which vehicles enter the expressway.

ROA
CLOS

Steps to follow for merging:

1. While on the entrance ramp, search the through lane for a safe gap in traffic. A gap of at least four seconds is desirable. Note the length of the acceleration lane ahead.

2. Maintain a proper space margin from cars that are on the ramp with you. Continue searching ahead and in the direction you intend to merge.

3. As you near the acceleration lane, signal and accelerate to the speed of traffic.

4. Keep checking for a gap and any following vehicles.

5. Adjust speed near the end of the ramp or at the beginning of the acceleration lane. You want to be traveling at a speed that matches that of adjacent traffic before you merge from the acceleration lane into the right most lane of travel. This helps you avoid having to adjust speed while steering into the travel lane.

6. Pull into the selected gap and cancel the turn signal.

Avoid entering the freeway at a sharp angle. Adjust to freeway speed in the acceleration lane. Merge carefully into the flow of traffic.

Help entering drivers by either moving into the next lane or adjusting your speed. This is called a "courtesy lane change."

Leaving the expressway. Select the proper lane to leave an expressway well before you approach your exit. Signal and steer into the deceleration lane as soon as you reach it, and reduce speed. If the deceleration lane does not allow for enough space to reduce speed, signal your intention and reduce speed only as much as needed to safely exit the expressway.

Ramp speeds. Posted exit ramp speeds usually are low because of roadway design. It is dangerous to drive onto an exit ramp at expressway speed. After driving at high speed for many miles, you may be going too fast to exit, even though you think you have slowed enough. Some exits that have extreme ramp designs are posted for speeds as low as 5 mph.

Speed-change (weave) lane. At many interchanges, the speed-change lane is used as both an acceleration and deceleration lane. This situation requires a weaving pattern movement, since vehicles must cross one another's paths. Entering or exiting traffic requires skillful use of time and space. A spirit of cooperation is needed among all drivers involved when negotiating weave lanes in heavy traffic. Although right-of-way usually should be granted to exiting traffic, conditions may dictate otherwise.

1. When you are leaving the freeway, enter the lane next to the deceleration lane a mile or more before the intended exit.
2. Avoid slowing down before entering the deceleration lane — but reduce speed to the posted speed for the exit ramp. Avoid sudden, last-second exits.

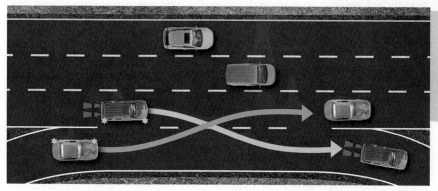

When acceleration and deceleration lanes are shared, watch for conflicting traffic movements.

Older interchanges or expressways. Some interchanges on older expressways have short acceleration lanes. Sometimes, interchanges like this include signs that read "Yield Ahead — No Merge Area." In rare instances, there might be a stop sign that assigns right-of-way at the end of the entrance ramp. In these situations, you must yield to traffic on the expressway. You will need a much larger gap in expressway traffic to accelerate from a very slow speed or from a stopped position.

Passing Other Vehicles

Hill

Three questions. When considering passing another vehicle, you must ask yourself three questions, and the answer to each question must be YES in order to justify passing:

1. Is passing legal?
2. Is passing safe?
3. Is passing worth it?

Only very rarely can a driver honestly answer all three questions with a resounding YES.

These passes are all unsafe and in most states, illegal.

Curve

Intersection

Bridge, tunnel or viaduct

Oncoming vehicle

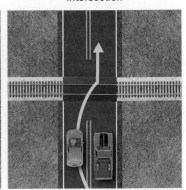

Railroad

Two dangers. Two dangers face the driver who wants to pass: impatience and errors in judgment. Passing calls for critical application of time and space rules. Failure to apply these rules results in thousands of deaths annually from head-on crashes.

When is it illegal to pass? You may not pass when approaching cars are too close. Nor may you pass when a solid yellow line is on your side of the center line, or when a sign indicates a no-passing zone. Usually, it is illegal to pass on two-lane roads when approaching a hill crest, curve or intersection. Most states also prohibit passing on bridges, in tunnels, near railroad crossings, or where traffic is limited to one lane in each direction. It is also illegal to exceed the speed limit even when you pass another vehicle.

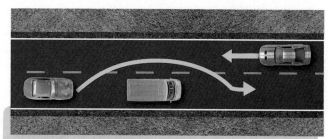

If you are traveling 60 mph and wish to pass a vehicle going 50 mph, you will need at least 19 seconds to pass the other vehicle. The best way to judge this gap is to pass only when any vehicle in the oncoming lane appears to be standing still.

When is it safe to pass?

This question is difficult to answer. You must ask yourself several questions before you try to pass:

◆ Is the road ahead clear?

◆ How far away is the approaching vehicle?

◆ Can I see far enough ahead?

◆ How long will it take to pass and get back into my lane?

◆ Can I make the driver of the vehicle I am planning to pass aware that I am passing?

◆ Is there an intersecting road or driveway that may allow vehicles to enter before I complete my pass?

◆ Am I being passed, or about to be?

When is it worth it to pass? Very rarely is it worth it to pass, as strong as the temptation to pass might be. Usually what happens after one vehicle passes another on a two-lane road is that the two vehicles simply trade places. More often than not, at the next place where stopping is required, as at an intersection, the vehicle that was passed ends up directly behind the vehicle that passed. Passing on a two-lane road is one of the riskiest driving maneuvers there is, and usually there is very little (if any) benefit realized compared to the risk involved.

Use low beams when passing. Driving with your low-beam headlights on can reduce the level of risk when you are passing. You will be much more visible to other roadway users.

Recommended steps for passing another vehicle:

1. **Prepare to pass**

   a. Position yourself approximately three seconds behind the vehicle you want to pass. Check for roadside obstacles and areas of reduced space and visibility ahead.

   b. Check mirrors and oncoming traffic. Be prepared to wait for an adequate, clear distance. At 60 mph, you will need at least 19 seconds to pass a vehicle that is traveling at 50 mph. An effective way to judge this gap is to pass only when a vehicle in the oncoming lane appears to be standing still.

   c. Check ahead for a safe passing distance. Assume that you are traveling 60 mph, approaching a vehicle traveling 50 mph. You are moving approximately 88 feet per second, which is 15 feet per second faster than the vehicle you are overtaking. If you start your pass two seconds — 176 feet — behind the vehicle ahead, it will take you 12 seconds to catch up. You need another second to come parallel with the vehicle you want to pass.

To pull safely back into your lane, check to see that the front of the vehicle you have passed is visible in your inside rearview mirror, a distance of about one second, or 88 feet. It will take you about six seconds to gain this distance. By now, you will have been in the passing maneuver for a total of 19 seconds. During those 19 seconds you have traveled a total distance of 1,672 feet. A vehicle approaching from the opposite direction at 60 mph will also have traveled 1,672 feet. Thus, allow a distance of 3,520 feet (more than a half mile) between you and any oncoming vehicle at the time you begin this pass.

An oncoming vehicle will not be visible to you during the day until it is about 2,500 feet away. If the same vehicle had its headlights turned on it would be visible to you from about 4,700 feet. If you were to complete this pass in 10 seconds, you would have to increase your speed from 60 to 70 mph. If the vehicle was long, like a tractor-trailer you need about 24 seconds to complete this pass at 60 mph. This also assumes that the other driver maintained a steady 50 mph while you were passing.

d. Signal your intention. Use your turn signal and tap your horn or flash your lights.

e. Check your blind spots to your side and rear.

2. **Pass the vehicle ahead.**

a. Signal your intention and accelerate into the passing lane. Check the path ahead. Identify an escape path.

b. Accelerate quickly to an appropriate speed 10 to 20 mph faster than the vehicle you are passing. Remember, if you accelerate to a speed beyond the posted speed limit, you are breaking the law. If you had to accelerate beyond the speed limit to safely pass, the pass was not necessary.

c. Concentrate on the path ahead. Use peripheral vision to monitor the position of the vehicle you passed and the left shoulder of the road. Glance quickly at the front wheels of the vehicle you are passing for any clues of possible movement to the side.

d. Check your mirrors for following cars.

3. **Return to your lane.**

a. Check your rearview mirror for the front of the vehicle you are passing.

b. Signal your intention to move to the right.

c. Change lanes and maintain speed.

d. Cancel your turn signal. Check your speedometer and adjust your speed as needed.

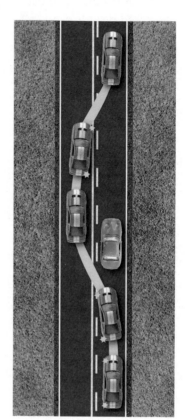

Check your rearview mirror until you can see the front of the vehicle you are passing before you return to the lane.

HOW *to* **DRIVE**

ROA
CLOS

Sharing the Road with Other Users

Study and respond to each of the following questions. Then review the chapter to see if your responses are correct.

Multiple Choice:

1. Single-vehicle crashes account for more than _____ percent of all motor vehicle fatalities.

    a. 20
    b. 35
    c. 50
    d. 75

2. All of the following are common messages communicated by drivers to reduce risk except:

    a. Frustrations
    b. Intentions
    c. Warning
    d. Presence

3. Areas where pedestrian traffic is heavy include:

    a. Parking lots
    b. Bus stops
    c. School zones
    d. All of the above

4. When passing a motorcycle or scooter, _____.

    a. Give the rider the whole lane
    b. Give the rider the right side of the lane
    c. Give the rider the left side of the lane
    d. Do not pass

5. _____ is a coming together or blending of vehicles to maintain a smooth, uninterrupted traffic flow.

    a. Combining
    b. Merging
    c. Weaving
    d. Yielding

Short Answer:

1. Identify five common traffic-conflict situations.

2. Explain the steps you should take when approached by an emergency vehicle.

3. Explain the procedures for safely approaching an intersection.

4. Describe the basic rules to help determine when it is safe to cross a railroad intersection.

5. Describe the three steps in preparing to pass another vehicle.

CHAPTER 12

The Effects of Alcohol and Other Drugs on Driving

Chapter Objectives:

◆ Explain how alcohol and other drugs affect your ability to drive safely.

◆ Identify several drugs that can adversely affect your ability to drive safely.

◆ Explain how, and the rate at which, alcohol is eliminated from the body.

◆ Identify several guidelines for controlling drinking situations.

◆ Explain why new young drivers who consume alcohol are at much greater risk of being involved in crashes.

◆ Identify several alternatives to drinking and driving.

Alcohol and Driving

Drinking and driving. Research shows that at least half of all drivers admit to occasionally driving after drinking alcoholic beverages. There are many reasons people drink and drive. Some people are not aware of the dangers. Others enjoy drinking but ignore the fact that they have to drive home or elsewhere. Whatever your feelings may be about drinking, two things are not open to debate: **First, drinking alcohol is illegal in all 50 states for anyone less than 21 years of age. Second, anyone who has been drinking should not drive.**

The overall picture. If you drink an alcoholic beverage and then drive, you increase the risk of being involved in a traffic crash. Any way you address this issue, drinking and driving is a serious problem. What is the overall picture?

Alcohol is involved in nearly half of all motor vehicle-related deaths. Each year approximately 17,000 people — more than 300 per week — die, and more than 1 million are injured in alcohol-related crashes. About half of those killed were not the ones who had been drinking. In all, about three of every 10 Americans can expect to be involved in an alcohol-related collision at some time in their lives.

Alcohol is involved in nearly half of all motor vehicle-related deaths.

The odds. Compared to sober drivers, the odds of a 150-pound male (over 21 years old) being involved in a crash increase with each drink he consumes before he drives:

◆ One to two drinks — chances nearly double.

◆ Three to four drinks — chances increase three to seven times.

◆ Five to six drinks — chances increase 13 to 20 times.

◆ Seven to eight drinks — chances increase 55 to 85 times.

Added risk for young drivers. Young people who drink and drive take an even greater chance than older drivers do. First, equal amounts of alcohol will usually affect young people more. More importantly, young people have limited experience in both driving and drinking. This combination of inexperience can easily prove fatal. Even a small amount of alcohol impairs a young driver's newly-learned skills.

BAC and risk. The greater the blood alcohol concentration (BAC), the greater the risk of being involved in a fatal crash. Young drivers between the ages of 16 and 19 with a BAC of .02 to .05 percent (one to two drinks) are at least seven times more likely to be killed in a crash than a sober driver of any age. At .085 percent (three to four drinks), young drivers are 40 times more likely to be killed than a sober driver and 20 times more likely to be killed than a 55-year-old driver at the same BAC level. By .12 percent BAC (four to six drinks), a 16- to 19-year-old is 90 times as likely to die in a traffic crash as a sober driver.

How Alcohol Affects the Body and Driving Ability

What is alcohol? Alcohol contained in adult beverages is ethanol, a clear, odorless, depressant drug that slows down and impairs the central nervous system. It is quickly and directly absorbed into the bloodstream without being digested. Absorption can be slowed down a little if there is food in the stomach. Eventually, however, all the alcohol consumed is absorbed into the bloodstream. The bloodstream carries alcohol to all parts of the body, and behavior is affected when alcohol reaches the brain.

Alcohol and the brain. The first part of the body affected by alcohol is the brain, particularly the part of the brain that allows you to think clearly and make good decisions. Its sedative effects impair judgment in a way that is usually not noticed by the drinker. The part of the brain that controls social inhibitions is also affected, causing people to say and do things they normally would not. These effects start with one drink.

HOW *to* **DRIVE**

Alcohol and muscle control. The second part of the body affected by alcohol is muscle control. Due to the small muscles in the eye being very susceptible to the effects of alcohol, vision can be significantly affected, even at low alcohol levels. The following table summarizes the effects of alcohol on vision.

Type of Vision	Effects of Alcohol
Visual acuity, or sharpness of vision	Alcohol can cause vision to become blurry, making it more difficult to perceive the traffic scene and make good driving decisions.
Side, or peripheral vision	When sober, most people have about 180 degrees of side vision. Even while looking straight ahead you can detect objects moving at the side. As BAC rises, side vision decreases.
Color distinction	Color plays an important role in the highway transportation system. Alcohol reduces your ability to distinguish colors, decreasing your ability to perceive the full traffic scene.
Night vision	Alcohol decreases your night vision, reducing your eyes' ability to automatically and quickly regulate the amount of light entering the eyes.
Distance judgment	Alcohol decreases your ability to accurately judge distances. Determining how far objects are from your vehicle is a critical driving skill.
Focus	The eye is able to change focus rapidly from objects close by to objects far away. Alcohol slows this ability, reducing the ability to see things clearly soon enough to respond properly.

Other signs that muscle control has been affected include loss of balance and slurring of speech.

Alcohol's impact on behavior. Here are some of the ways in which different numbers of drinks consumed **in one hour** may affect a 150-pound adult. The beverage in these examples is beer (12 ounces).

After one drink, inhibitions are lowered. A person may be less critical of him– or herself and others, and judgment begins to be affected. Coordination may also be affected. (BAC: .02–.03 percent).

After two drinks, reaction time is slower. A person may appear relaxed and friendly. Reaction time begins to slow. (BAC: .04–.05 percent).

After three drinks, judgment is not sound. A person will not think clearly and may do or say things that are rude or unreasonable, and reasoning is less reliable. Reaction time slows down. (BAC: .06–.07 percent).

After four drinks, hearing, speech, vision and balance are adversely affected. A person may have difficulty pronouncing words. As eye muscles become more relaxed, focusing and tracking becomes more difficult. Although the drinker may not be aware of it, reaction time is greatly slowed. (BAC: .08–.09 percent).

After five drinks, most behaviors are affected. Body parts do not seem to work together. Speech may be slurred. Performing any task that requires the use of hands and feet is difficult. Walking without stumbling also is difficult. (BAC: .10–.11 percent).

After 12 drinks, a 150-pound person's BAC is about .30 percent. At this level, a coma or deep sleep is not unusual. If there is enough alcohol in the stomach when the person passes out, the blood-alcohol level will continue to rise. If the BAC reaches .40 percent, the person will be in a deep coma and near death.

HOW *to* **DRIVE**

Amount of Alcohol in Typical Beverages

It does not matter how you get alcohol into your body. You can drink it in any of a variety of different "delivery systems," each containing pure alcohol. However, the total amount of alcohol per serving will vary with the type and size of alcoholic beverage consumed. Standard-size servings of beer, wine, wine cooler, whiskey and mixed drinks contain different amounts of alcohol.

Beer. Beer, which includes malt beverages, is generally served in 12-ounce portions and is approximately 4.8 percent pure alcohol. If 4.8 percent of a beer is alcohol, then 12 ounces of beer will have .58 ounces of pure alcohol. That is just over one-half an ounce. Here is the math: 4.8% X 12 oz. = .58 oz. of pure alcohol.

Wine. A standard serving of wine is about 4 ounces, yielding approximately six glasses of wine per 750 milliliter bottle. On average, wine is about 12 percent alcohol. If 12 percent of wine is alcohol, then a 4-ounce glass will have .48 ounces of alcohol. That is just under one-half an ounce. The math: .12% X 4 oz. = .48 oz. of pure alcohol.

Whiskey. A standard serving of whiskey is one ounce. This is referred to as a "shot." Whiskey can also be available in larger portions, including a "jigger" (one and one-half ounces) or a "double" (two ounces). As with other liquors, the strength of whiskey is measured using "proof." It is easy to compute the percentage of alcohol from proof: proof is simply twice the alcohol percentage. For example, a 100-proof (100°) beverage would be 50 percent alcohol.

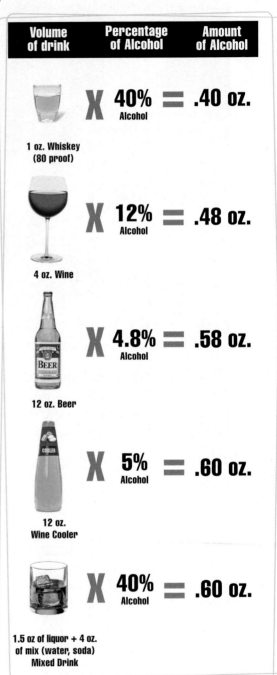

Volume of drink	Percentage of Alcohol	Amount of Alcohol
1 oz. Whiskey (80 proof)	X **40%** Alcohol	= **.40 oz.**
4 oz. Wine	X **12%** Alcohol	= **.48 oz.**
12 oz. Beer	X **4.8%** Alcohol	= **.58 oz.**
12 oz. Wine Cooler	X **5%** Alcohol	= **.60 oz.**
1.5 oz of liquor + 4 oz. of mix (water, soda) Mixed Drink	X **40%** Alcohol	= **.60 oz.**

On average, whiskey is 80 proof, or 40 percent alcohol. If 40 percent of whiskey is alcohol, then a one ounce serving (one shot) will have .40 ounces of alcohol. The math: 40% X 1 oz. = .40 oz. of pure alcohol.

For drinks with multiple alcoholic beverages (mixed drinks), simply compute the amount of pure alcohol for each beverage, then add them together to obtain the total amount of pure alcohol for the total drink.

Wine cooler. Wine coolers are popular alcoholic drinks for some young people. They are generally served in 12-ounce portions and are approximately 5 percent pure alcohol. If 5 percent of a wine cooler is alcohol, then a 12-ounce wine cooler will have .6 ounces of pure alcohol. That is just over one-half an ounce. The math: 5% X 12 oz. = .6 oz. of pure alcohol.

Surprisingly, the wine cooler tops them all. And if you compare the drinks side by side, the beer contains approximately 45 percent more alcohol than the shot of whiskey!

These computations raise several important points. First, beer is certainly strong enough to intoxicate a drinker. In fact, it is the second-strongest beverage in these examples. Second, when you look at the differences among the beverages when having just one or two drinks, the total differences may not be great. However, when a drinker consumes three or more beverages, the differences can become substantial. Thus, what you drink can make a difference in how high your BAC rises.

Keep in mind that these computations are based on standard drink sizes. Depending on who mixes the drinks or what size container is purchased, the actual amount of alcohol in an alcoholic beverage could be even higher. Additionally, some drinks may have a higher concentration of alcohol. Some generally more expensive liquor can be 100, 150 or even 190 proof (50 percent, 75 percent or 95 percent), and some import beers may be 8 or 9 percent alcohol.

HOW *to* **DRIVE**

Factors that Affect BAC Level

It all depends. People may drink the same amount of a beverage, but the percentage of alcohol in the blood depends on gender, body weight, strength of the drink, size of the drink, whether there is food in the stomach, and time spent drinking.

Gender. Alcohol does not affect men and women equally. Research indicates that alcohol's effects on females tend to be stronger and last longer. This is because women produce a smaller amount of *alcohol dehydrogenase*, an enzyme that breaks down alcohol in the stomach. As a result, women reach a peak BAC about 20 percent higher than men do.

Body weight. Your weight affects the percentage of alcohol in your blood. A heavier person has more body fluids with which the alcohol will mix, and thus will have a lower BAC.

Strength of the drink. As discussed above, the stronger the beverage consumed, the higher the BAC will rise.

Women reach a peak BAC about 20 percent higher than men do, all other things being equal.

Lower BAC   Higher BAC

Size of drink. A larger drink will contain more alcohol and result in a higher BAC than a smaller drink of the same alcohol strength. For example, a 24-ounce beer contains twice as much alcohol as a 12-ounce beer of the same brand.

Food. Food in the stomach does not absorb alcohol, but it can slow the rate at which alcohol is absorbed. But all the alcohol consumed gets into the blood eventually. Trying to prevent becoming intoxicated by drinking only on a full stomach may just result in a well-fed drunk!

Time spent drinking. The faster a drinker consumes alcohol, the more quickly BAC will reach its peak. Spreading out drinking over time will result in a lower peak BAC, other factors being equal. For example, the BAC would reach a higher level if a person had three drinks in one hour then if a person had one drink each hour for three hours.

Elimination of Alcohol

Three ways. Once alcohol reaches the bloodstream, the body immediately goes about removing it. It does so in three ways:

◆ **Breath.** Approximately 8 percent of alcohol is eliminated by breathing (exhalation). This is why you might be able to detect the odor of an alcoholic beverage on a drinker's breath.

◆ **Sweat.** About 2 percent of alcohol is eliminated by sweating. It may be possible to detect the odor of an alcoholic beverage on a drinker's body.

◆ **Oxidation.** The majority of alcohol (90 percent) is removed by the liver as it burns up the alcohol through the process of oxidation.

Strength of Drink

BEER

4.8%   12%

Size of Drink

12 oz. Beer   24 oz. Beer

YIELD

BAC and time. Some drinkers try all sorts of things to sober up. In reality, coffee, fresh air, exercise and cold showers will not help. Neither will sleep. Time is the only thing that will sober you up. It takes a lot longer than most people think for the body to eliminate alcohol. In fact, it takes between 1¼ and 1½ hours or longer for the body to eliminate the alcohol contained in one standard-size drink. While some very large males (over 250 pounds) can eliminate this amount of alcohol in about one hour, it takes much longer in everyone else. The figure below depicts a drinking scenario that demonstrates the actual rate of elimination.

Say a person starts drinking at 9 pm and continues to drink until 1:30 am, drinking at a rate of about 2 drinks per hour. This graph depicts the scenario, showing the alcohol level on the left axis and the time of day along the bottom axis.

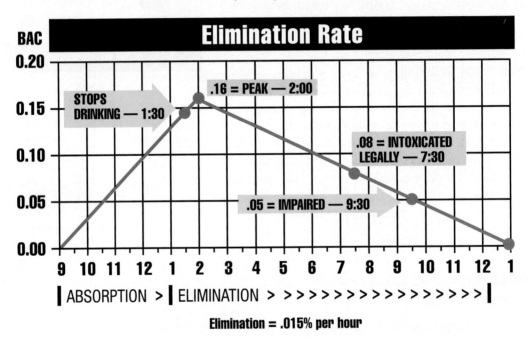

By 1:30 am, the drinker has reached a BAC of about .14 percent. Note that the alcohol level continues to rise for at least 30 minutes after drinking has stopped. This is because it takes a while for alcohol to be fully absorbed into the bloodstream, causing this drinker's BAC to rise even more.

By 2 am, the drinker's BAC has peaked and the body continues its efforts to eliminate the alcohol at an average elimination rate of about .015 percent per hour. At 7:30 am the next morning, this drinker will still have a BAC of .08 percent. This drinker is still legally intoxicated, and this could be of great concern if this person chooses to drive to work, school or elsewhere.

The elimination of alcohol continues, but the drinker is still impaired (.05 percent BAC) at 9:30 am! It is not until 1 o'clock in the afternoon that the drinker's alcohol level is back down to zero. Even at that point, the drinker could still be impaired by the effects of a hangover.

The bottom line is that it takes much longer for the body to eliminate alcohol than most people think. That is one reason it is so important to separate alcohol from driving.

In fast, out slow. As you can see, the body takes in alcohol quickly and gets rid of it slowly. If a person drinks more alcohol in one hour than the body can get rid of in that hour, the person's BAC starts to climb. The greater the BAC, the more intoxicated the person becomes.

How to control the effects of alcohol. As a pedestrian, passenger or driver, you may have to deal with the problem of alcohol and traffic safety, whether you drink or not. There are ways to control alcohol rather than letting it control you or your friends. In fact, *if you are less than 21 years of age, it is illegal in all states for you to buy, possess or consume alcoholic beverages.* But what if circumstances are such that alcohol becomes a factor you have to deal with? For example, suppose you are 21 or traveling with someone who is 21. You attend a wedding reception or other celebration and you or your companion decides to drink. How can you protect yourself from becoming another alcohol-related statistic?

Any amount will impair. First of all, remember that drinking any amount of alcohol will impair driving ability. Your safest option is to not drink and drive, and to not ride with a driver who has been drinking. *Instead, get someone else to drive — someone who is 100 percent sober.*

Limit your drinking. Other than not drinking and driving, the best way to reduce risk is to severely limit and control drinking. As a rule of thumb, no one should consume more than one drink per hour. Some people should drink less. How can you control drinking? Use the key factors of weight, time and amount.

Alcohol is quickly and directly absorbed into the bloodstream without being digested.

Control Drinking

Control drinking is a common way for adults to limit alcohol consumption. Know that this strategy is unreliable, because once you have started drinking, your judgment of "what your limit is" becomes distorted due to alcohol's effects on judgment. The following control drinking techniques can help a drinker minimize his or her BAC and avoid impaired driving.

Know your limit. Adults who choose to drink should know their limit and keep to it.

Drink slowly. If, as an adult, you choose to drink, make a conscious effort to sip drinks rather than drink them quickly. To make a drink last longer, add ice or mix it with soda. Some drinkers make or request half-strength drinks to limit the amount of alcohol.

Alternate between alcoholic and non-alcoholic beverages. By alternating between alcohol and non-alcoholic beverages, your BAC remains lower than it would be if you consumed only alcoholic beverages.

Set a limit in advance. Because alcohol affects judgment, you cannot expect to be able to tell when you have had enough. You need to set a limit in advance.

Avoid pushing impairment. Stay below your limit. It is harder to stop drinking if you become impaired. Being impaired means that self-control is reduced and the ability to make decisions about how to act is impaired.

Stick to the limit. You should not drink more just because you do not feel the effect of the first drink or two. Alcohol is like a sunburn — when you begin to feel it, it is already too late.

Do not try to keep pace with others. If you are drinking, set your own pace rather than drinking to keep up with others. Stop drinking and switch to non-alcoholic beverages when you reach your limit — or sooner. And remember the rule of thumb: no more than one drink per hour.

Watch for signs. Some people recognize signs that they have had too much to drink. These signs may include speaking louder than usual, feeling warm or flushed, being overly relaxed, feeling drowsy, feeling dizzy, or having difficulty walking or talking. Pay attention to the message sent by these signs: stop drinking.

Get a grip. Monitor your condition and feelings. Take into account your mood, your physical health, the situation you are in, any medication you may be taking and other relevant factors. Recognize that getting a grip on yourself becomes more difficult the more you drink. Play it safe by having a non-drinking friend keep an eye on you — and drive you home if necessary.

Drinkers should stop drinking early to allow their bodies time to get rid of the alcohol consumed.

Use time. There is drinking time and there is non-drinking time. You should stop drinking soon enough to allow your body time to get rid of the alcohol consumed. The body can reduce BAC by about .015 percent each hour. In general, you should drink less than one drink an hour, and you should allow at least 1½ hours for each drink to leave your body.

Be a Responsible Host

Hosting. Everyone shares the responsibility for keeping drinkers from driving. However, the person who hosts a party or other social gathering assumes extra responsibility. The host generally knows who is coming, who drinks, who drives and who is most likely to drive after drinking. The host also usually knows the condition of guests when they leave. The host, therefore, shares the blame if a guest is involved in a crash, is arrested or arrives home drunk. It is the host — or the host's family — who will get the angry phone calls, have to talk to the police, be called to appear in court or possibly be sued or charged with an offense. The host is legally responsible for ensuring only those legally old enough are served or consume alcohol.

HOW to DRIVE

Decide in advance. If you are going to try to control the drinking of others, you must recognize that:

◆ You have a responsibility to prevent your friends from drinking to excess.
◆ You must be willing to brave the resistance of the excessive drinker or others in the group.

Be a real friend. In making these decisions, it may be helpful to know that people who drink excessively seldom remember much the next day. Those who do are likely to thank you for sparing them a hangover or worse.

Get help. Before the party starts, enlist a few friends to help with:

◆ Keeping other friends from drinking too much.
◆ Assisting in cutting off people who have had too much.
◆ Helping if somebody tries to drink after being cut off.
◆ Taking charge of serving drinks to prevent others from drinking too much.

Set a limit. To control the drinking of others, set a limit in advance on the number of drinks that anyone may be served. If you know that a particular person is sensitive to alcohol or might cause problems, set a lower limit for him or her.

Know the signs. Remember that one of the first things alcohol affects is judgment, including the ability to determine the effect alcohol is having. People who have had too much to drink generally do not recognize it. If they do, they are not likely to admit it. Therefore, it is important for you to be able to recognize signs of impairment:

◆ Loud talking or slurred speech.
◆ Dropping things or spilling drinks.
◆ Walking unsteadily, using hands for support.
◆ Drowsiness.
◆ Perspiring, or turning pale or red in the face.

Any behavior that is unusual for the person is a possible sign. For example, if a normally loud person becomes quiet, it could be a sign of excessive drinking.

Prevent overdrinking. Preventive efforts may be more effective than trying to influence how much your friends drink. A little preparation can go a long way toward preventing trouble. Preparation tips include:

Control the supply. Do not have a lot of alcohol easily available. Putting the supply out all at once tends to encourage people to drink everything and makes it hard to keep track of how much is consumed. Set out a limited amount of alcohol.

Offer alternative beverages. Offer non-alcoholic beverages. Many people feel more comfortable at a party if they are holding a drink. That drink can just as easily be soda.

Use standard amounts. Help people keep track of how much they drink. Provide a shot glass (1 ounce) to measure standard amounts of liquor. Have small, 4-ounce glasses for wine. This helps everyone keep track of the number of drinks consumed, and whoever is serving will have an easier time controlling the supply of alcohol.

Provide a shot glass (1ounce) to measure standard amounts of liquor.

Space drinks. If you offer alcoholic beverages, try to space drinks out over time to keep consumption down.

Do not pass the bottle. Passing the bottle encourages excessive drinking. Some people might feel they have to take a swig each time the bottle is passed, even if they do not necessarily want to.

Do something else. Involve your friends in activities other than drinking — dancing, games (except drinking games) — anything that will force people to set their drinks down. As long as a person has a drink in hand, it is hard to avoid sipping it.

Additional hosting tips include:

◆ Do not encourage people to drink.

◆ Skip people who are on their way to drinking too much.

◆ Do not serve a drink to someone who already has one. Doing so encourages rapid drinking.

◆ Stop serving alcohol to anyone who has had enough — or too much.

Alternatives to Drinking and Driving

Just don't. The safest alternative to drinking and driving is to not drink. Remember that it is against the law for anyone less than 21 years of age to drink, buy or possess beer, wine or any other alcoholic beverage. Bottom line — do not drive while under the effects of alcohol. Drinking and driving is not worth the risk to you and others.

If you drink, don't drive. Aside from not drinking, the next best alternative for adults who choose to drink is to separate drinking from driving. One way to do this is to let time pass. That is, allow enough time for BAC to decrease so you are no longer under the influence of alcohol. Of course, while waiting for time to pass, you must stop drinking! Here are some other ways to separate drinking and driving:

Stay home. The best way to avoid having to drive home is not to leave home in the first place. If, as an adult, you drink at home, either stay there or let someone sober drive.

Agree on a designated driver. Travel with one or more friends, with the understanding that the person driving will not drink. If no one was chosen in advance to drive, be sure to let a sober person drive home.

Plan to stay overnight. If you are going to drink at someone's home, make it an overnight party so no one has to drive.

Call someone for a ride. If you cannot drive, call a friend, parent, spouse or relative. Even if you have to travel only a mile or two, the risk of drinking and driving is too great. Calling a family member may be awkward, but it is better than crashing or being arrested.

Find a ride. If you are in no condition to drive home from a bar, restaurant or other place, leave your car. Get a ride home from a sober friend, call a taxi, or use public transportation. You can pick up your car the next day.

Temporary Illnesses

Temporary illnesses can complicate driving more than people realize:

◆ A person with one eye may be safer at the wheel than a hay fever sufferer who has both eyes filled with tears.

If you are ill, first determine what effects, if any, your illness will have on your ability to drive.

- A driver whose diabetes is controlled by insulin may be less of a danger than a non-diabetic person who has taken cold medicine.
- A person suffering from a toothache or a splitting headache is probably a greater threat than a person who has recovered from a heart attack.

Effects. Many temporary illnesses affect vision and are often accompanied by dizziness, drowsiness, nausea or pain. Any of these conditions make it difficult to concentrate on driving. In addition, illness can affect your judgment, decision-making abilities, timing and coordination.

What to do. If you are ill, first determine what effects, if any, your illness will have on your ability to drive. Second, decide what steps you can take to minimize the effects. Finally, if the effects are severe or you cannot compensate for them, delay driving.

Other Drugs and Driving

What is a "drug?" A drug is any substance taken by a person to achieve a better physical or mental state, real or imagined. Drug use means taking any amount of drugs under any condition — legal or illegal. Alcohol is a drug, and there are many others. For example, people consume caffeine in coffee and nicotine in tobacco and may not realize that these, too, are drugs.

How will a drug affect you? When using any drug, you should consider the risks and the effects it might have on your ability to perform routine and complex tasks. You should keep your level of risk low and avoid taking drugs that interfere with anything you might do. Remember that in addition to their intended purpose, many drugs have side effects. To complicate matters, drugs can affect various people in different ways, or a drug may affect a person differently each time it is used.

Prescription, Over-the-Counter and Illegal Drugs

Legal drugs. Use of legal drugs is common in the U.S. Generally, they are designed to address causes or symptoms of problems by changing the body's chemistry.

Prescription drugs. A doctor's prescription for these drugs includes directions for use. Be sure to follow directions exactly, not only to accomplish the drug's purpose, but also to limit dangerous and undesirable side effects. Prescription drugs can be helpful when used as directed. But they also can hinder your driving ability by reducing your level of alertness or ability to perform complex tasks. Do not use prescription drugs that are prescribed for other people.

Over-the-counter/non-prescription drugs. Available without a prescription, over-the-counter drugs can include anything from aspirin to cold pills, cough syrup and sleep aids. By law, these drugs must provide adequate directions for use in addition to information about possible side effects.

Whether a drug is prescribed by a doctor or obtained over-the-counter, always read the label carefully, especially if you intend to drive. Some may cause drowsiness or otherwise impair driving ability. If you have a question or concern about a drug's effects, ask your doctor or pharmacist. Ask specifically how the drug could affect driving ability. Always read labels.

Illegal/illicit drugs. Illegal drugs, or street drugs, are sold without a prescription. An obvious danger in buying street drugs is not knowing what is in them. With street drugs, buyers also risk having one drug substituted for another without their knowledge.

Drugs and Their Effects

Drugs vary by type and effect. Most drugs act on the central nervous system, which includes the brain and spinal cord. Stimulants — such as amphetamines — speed up the system, while depressants — such as tranquilizers — slow it down. Another drug family, hallucinogens, affects the way a user sees things. Below is a summary of common types of drugs and their possible effects.

Amphetamines (Benzedrine, Dexedrine, *speed, black beauties, uppers*) can make the user feel more alert and self-confident. However, for drivers, these effects result in a false sense of security. Because amphetamines can keep drivers from realizing how tired they are, drivers may feel extremely confident at a time when driving abilities are actually reduced. Amphetamines also can cause loss of coordination, over-excitability, and lack of concentration.

Barbiturates (Phenobarbital, Nembutal, Seconal, *downers, yellow jackets, yellows*) have an effect similar to that of alcohol. They are usually prescribed to calm nervousness. Barbiturates can make thinking difficult and cause depression, especially when combined with alcohol. They can also cause excitability, blurred vision, reality distortion, drowsiness and even loss of consciousness. The skills important to safe driving — alertness, attention to detail, judgment and reaction time — may be affected for several hours after taking barbiturates.

The biggest danger in using illegal drugs is not knowing what is in them.

Tranquilizers (Valium, Librium, Miltown, *downers*) also slow down the central nervous system. They are used by people with emotional problems, high blood pressure, epilepsy and muscle injuries. Tranquilizers can slow reaction time, impair coordination, hinder judgment and affect vision — all negative effects on driving. Taking a tranquilizer with alcohol combines a downer with a downer. In extreme cases, this combination can reduce blood pressure and cause the heart to stop, preventing oxygen from reaching the brain.

Hallucinogens (marijuana, LSD, PCP, mescaline) are so named because they can distort the user's sense of reality. They can cause confusion and impair judgment and reaction time.

Marijuana (*pot, grass, weed*) is a mild hallucinogen. The effects of marijuana vary widely — it can act as a stimulant or depressant. The effects depend on the drug's strength and the user's mood and experience with the drug. Users often become drowsy and have difficulty judging time, space and speed of movement. Some users report that they concentrate on one object at a time, ignoring all other objects. Marijuana is stored in fat cells and is eliminated very slowly, remaining detectable for up to two weeks after consumption.

In a survey, chronic, infrequent and former marijuana users reported that marijuana decreased their ability to judge time and slowed their reaction time. Chronic users, however, indicated that they were less affected than other users. In the same study, 65 percent of the infrequent and former users reported that marijuana decreased their ability to keep a vehicle under control. Eighteen percent of the chronic users reported the same problem. Seventy-five percent of the infrequent and former users and 48 percent of the chronic users felt their ability to respond to an emergency situation was impaired.

HOW to DRIVE

LSD (*acid, red dragon, white lightning, blue heaven, sugar cubes*) primarily affects the central nervous system but also changes mood and behavior. The effects of LSD and other hallucinogens (STP, peyote) are similar to, but more extreme than, marijuana.

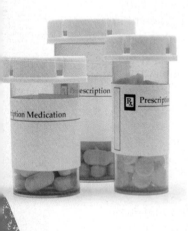

Combining drugs increases the risk of harmful and unexpected effects.

Inhalants are the fumes of paint, markers, nail polish, aerosol sprays, gasoline or other chemical products that some people deliberately inhale to get high. Breathing such fumes — often called *huffing* — distorts perception and impairs judgment. Users may become dizzy or light-headed and lose coordination. They may have hallucinations. Using inhalants is extremely dangerous. Inhalants can permanently damage the brain, kidneys and liver. They can cause unconsciousness and heart failure. They also can kill the user — with only one use.

Stimulants are drugs that temporarily excite or accelerate the function of a vital process or organ — in particular, the central nervous system.

Cocaine (including *crack* and *rock*) is a stimulant and a narcotic. Cocaine impairs judgment, distorts reality and hinders concentration. In small doses, the drug causes feelings of joy and delight. Moderate doses may produce violent stimulation, hallucinations and paranoia. Cocaine can affect a driver's coordination, cause over-excitability and produce a false sense of alertness. Cocaine also hinders vision. Users report increased sensitivity to light, difficulty focusing and blurred vision. Cocaine is addictive and can cause serious, painful withdrawal symptoms when use is discontinued.

Narcotics (morphine, opium, heroin) depress the central nervous system and can produce a wide range of unwanted side effects. The user can become incoherent and dizzy and experience nausea and vomiting.

Narcotics use can lead to both physical and mental drug dependence. Drivers using narcotics may experience a wide range of effects, from hallucinations and confusion to drowsiness and slowed reaction times. As with cocaine, when the supply is cut off, the user usually develops serious and painful withdrawal symptoms.

Combining drugs. What are the effects of taking two or more drugs at the same time? The result may be a synergistic effect: more than just one plus one. This means that the combined effect is greater than the sum of the two effects separately. Synergism is not a rare occurrence. For example, a beer and another depressant may produce a synergistic effect. Anytime another drug is combined with alcohol, the effects may be different from those expected if either drug is taken alone. Combining drugs increases the risk of harmful and unexpected effects. One joint of marijuana + two beers = 6 beers.

Synergism occurs when the combined effects of multiple drugs are greater than the sum of their separate effects.

Drugs and Their Effects on Driving

Alcohol, drugs and crashes.

Numerous studies have shown how alcohol contributes to driving-related injuries and deaths. Less research has been done on the role of prescription, over-the-counter and illegal drugs in traffic crashes. However, there is no doubt that drugs, whether used alone or with alcohol, are a major driving danger.

Testing for drug use. Field-

sobriety tests are used to detect drug-impaired drivers. Like alcohol-use tests, these screening procedures involve assessing a person's balance, coordination, eye movements and concentration. Besides alcohol, the drug most often found in the bodies of crash victims is marijuana.

Besides alcohol, the drug most often found in the bodies of crash victims is marijuana.

Studies of drugs and driving. Research into the link between drug use and motor vehicle crashes has expanded in recent years. Research into drugs and driving indicates that:

◆ At least one out of seven fatally injured drivers has some drug in his or her system at the time of the crash.

◆ About half of fatal crash victims who have drugs in their system also have BACs high enough to impair their driving abilities.

◆ Young driver alcohol-related crashes are more likely to involve another drug than crashes that are not alcohol-related.

Additional research. A Canadian research study offered additional finds. The study involved about 500 car-crash victims who were tested for both illegal and legal drugs, and found that:

◆ Overall, about 41 percent of the victims had been using drugs other than alcohol.

◆ About 25 percent had used at least one drug, but not alcohol.

◆ About 15 percent had been using alcohol in combination with one or more other drugs.

◆ The most often-used drugs (other than alcohol) were marijuana and tranquilizers, followed by cocaine, narcotics and barbiturates. Many of the victims also tested positive for drugs found in common over-the-counter cold medications.

Alcohol and marijuana are the most widely used drugs among young people.

Marijuana and driving. Aside from alcohol, marijuana is the most widely used drug among young people. Studies indicate that marijuana users make more driving errors and are arrested more often for traffic violations than nonusers. More specifically, tests using driving simulators suggest that marijuana's greatest impact is on a driver's ability to recognize and respond to dangerous situations.

Marijuana and new users. Marijuana's impact on driving may be greatest for new users who also are new drivers. These people are unaccustomed to the drug's effects and, at the same time, inexperienced at handling the challenges of driving. As a result, by combining drugs and driving, they sharply increase the likelihood of a collision.

About Drug Use

Take any drug with caution. Pills are produced and used by the ton, and one of every four Americans takes some kind of drug every day. The yearly production of barbiturates alone could supply more than 10 doses for every man, woman and child in the United States. It is in everyone's best interest to think carefully about the use of all drugs, legal and illegal. Prescription medicines and even over-the-counter drugs can cause drowsiness and slow reaction time. They can also impair coordination and concentration. That is why taking any drug requires caution and good sense, especially if you intend to drive. Here are some points to keep in mind:

Read labels and follow directions. Read the label carefully before you use a medicine. If you have a question, ask your doctor or pharmacist. Check the medicine's expiration date, too. Old drugs can be ineffective or even harmful.

Know a drug's effects. Find out from your doctor or pharmacist if a drug is likely to affect your driving ability. Ask about other possible side effects too.

Avoid excessive drug use. Do not take drugs when you do not have to, and never exceed a drug's recommended dosage.

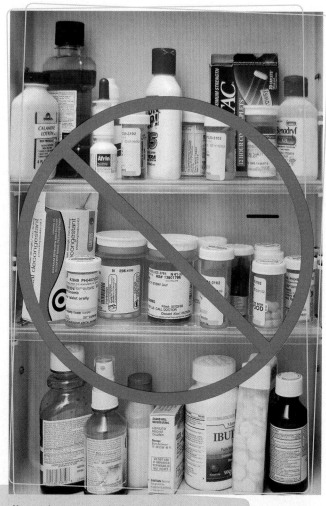

Never take someone else's medicine.

Avoid dangerous drug combinations. Remember the synergistic effect. Check with your doctor or pharmacist before taking more than one drug at a time.

Do not take someone else's medicine. A doctor prescribes a drug for a specific patient under a certain set of conditions. Taking medicine meant for someone else is illegal and can be harmful.

Do not take illegal drugs. Avoid all illegal drugs, and do not underestimate the dangers of "gateway drugs." Research studies show that using drugs such as alcohol, marijuana, tobacco or inhalants may "open the gate" to drug problems. One drug may lead to others or to increased drug use. If you are thinking, "It will not happen to me — I can control it," think again. Everyone with a drug problem started off thinking that way.

It is up to you. As a driver, it is your responsibility to consider how any drug may affect your alertness, judgment, vision, concentration and coordination. If you are going to drive, avoid taking drugs that affect your driving ability.

Alternatives to Mixing Drugs and Driving

Abstaining. You already know that the safest alternative to drinking and driving is abstinence. The same principle applies to other drugs and driving. Here are some other suggestions for protecting yourself and others from the dangers of drugs:

Do not ride with a driver who is using drugs. If you are about to get into someone's vehicle and you see evidence of drug use, stop. Do not get into the vehicle. Find another ride. If a driver begins using drugs while you are already on the road, insist that he or she stop and let you out of the vehicle as soon as safely possible, then call a friend or relative to pick you up.

Do not let your passengers use drugs. Your vehicle, your rules. You do not need to explain, apologize or make excuses. Drug use is dangerous and illegal. Do not allow it in your vehicle.

Do not give in to peer pressure. Do not let the words or actions of others cause you to do something you know you should not. What other people put into their bodies is their choice. What you put into your body is yours. Anyone who pressures you to do something risky or illegal is not acting as a friend.

Do not put yourself in difficult situations. If you know in advance that people will be using drugs at a party or other social occasion, think hard about whether you should attend.

If you know you are in trouble, get help. If you have a drug problem, or think you may be developing one, take action immediately. Talk to your parents, teacher, counselor or doctor. Join a support group. Contact one of the many organizations that help people who are having trouble with alcohol or other drugs. Some of these organizations are listed in the phone book or on the Internet. You can find others through your local library.

TEST 12

The Effects of Alcohol and Other Drugs on Driving

Study and respond to each of the following questions. Then review the chapter to see if your responses are correct.

Multiple Choice:

1. "BAC" stands for _____
   a. Breath alcohol content
   b. Breath alcohol concentration
   c. Blood alcohol content
   d. Blood alcohol concentration

2. Alcohol is a _____ drug.
   a. Stimulant
   b. Narcotic
   c. Depressant
   d. Barbiturate

3. The first ability to be impaired by alcohol or other drugs is _____.
   a. alertness
   b. knowledge
   c. judgment/decision-making
   d. balance

4. A one ounce shot of 80 proof whiskey contains _____ alcohol than/as a 12 ounce can of beer.
   a. more
   b. less
   c. the same amount of

5. It takes the body, on average, approximately _____ to eliminate the alcohol contained in one drink.
   a. ½–1 hour
   b. 1 ¼–1 ½ hours
   c. 2 hours
   d. 4 hours

Short Answer:

1. Define "BAC" and explain its relationship to driving ability.

2. List and explain four factors that can affect a drinker's BAC.

3. List and explain the three ways alcohol is eliminated by the body.

4. Explain how marijuana can affect driving ability.

5. Define "synergism" and explain its impact on behavior.

CHAPTER **13**

The Effects of Distractions, Drowsiness and Emotions on Driving

Chapter Objectives:

- Describe how distractions, drowsiness and emotions can cause traffic crashes.
- Identify distractions that increase risk while driving.
- Describe strategies to reduce driving distractions.
- Identify techniques to reduce the risk of being involved in a drowsy-driving crash.
- Describe actions you can take to control emotional responses to events that occur when driving.

HOW *to* **DRIVE**

Distracted Driving

Driving requires your full attention. Alcohol and other drugs are not the only factors that can cause a driver to be impaired. Driver distraction and inattention are also major causes of impairment, resulting in thousands of collisions and deaths each year. Consider these facts:

◆ An estimated 80 percent of collisions involve some form of driver inattention.

◆ Each year, driver inattention is a factor in more than 1 million crashes in North America.

◆ Looking away from the path of travel for two or more seconds doubles the likelihood of a crash.

◆ Young drivers are especially susceptible to becoming distracted while driving.

◆ Every state has legislation under which drivers can be charged for inattentive driving.

Inattention and distraction. Distraction results when a situation, event or person draws a driver's focus away from driving. Inattention, on the other hand, occurs when a driver's attention drifts away from driving without having been influenced by a situation, event or person. Both can result in the same outcome — a collision. When you drive, you are already multitasking — do not make it more difficult by performing additional tasks while behind the wheel.

Effects of distraction. It does not take long to become distracted, and a lot can happen in a second or two. Distractions can affect driving performance in at least three ways:

1. **Slowed perception.** Distracted driving may cause drivers to be delayed in perceiving or completely fail to perceive an important traffic event. For example, a distracted driver may fail to perceive another vehicle pulling out of a parking lot directly into his or her path of travel.

2. **Delayed decision-making.** Distraction can cause a driver's decision-making process to be delayed, or cause a driver to choose an action inappropriate for the situation at hand. For example, a distracted driver may not decide quickly enough on a specific course of action to avoid a collision.

3. **Improper action.** Once drivers make a decision, they need to execute the chosen action. Distraction can cause drivers to be delayed in taking the intended action, or to make incorrect inputs to the steering, accelerator or brakes. For example, a distracted driver who decides to change direction in response to sudden blockage of the lane ahead may turn the steering wheel too slowly or too late to avoid a collision.

Types of distractions. Some are more obvious than others. When windshield wipers were first introduced on vehicles at the beginning of the last century they were considered a distraction. Today, we would not drive without them. There are many causes of distraction, all with the potential to increase risk.

Distractions can be physical or mental in nature and are often a combination of both. A physical distraction is one that causes a driver to take his or her hands off the wheel or eyes off the road, such as reaching for an object. Mental distractions are activities that take the driver's mind away from the road, such as engaging in conversation with a passenger or thinking about something that happened during the day. Both increase the risk of a collision substantially. When physical and mental distractions are combined, there is an even greater chance a crash could happen.

Distractions inside the vehicle. There are many potential causes of distractions related to events and objects inside the vehicle. Some of these include:

Passengers. Other occupants' behavior can be very distracting to the driver, especially for young drivers. Research shows that for each additional passenger, risk of a collision increases dramatically. Specifically, for teen drivers, the addition of just one teen passenger doubles the likelihood of experiencing a fatal crash. With two or more teen passengers, the risk of a fatal crash jumps by 300 percent.

Teen driver alone

Adjusting the radio. Many young drivers enjoy listening to the radio while driving. However, research shows that each time a driver adjusts the radio, the risk of a collision increases. Adjustments to the radio could include changing a CD, selecting a song from an MP3 player or changing the radio station. All of these functions involve taking hands off the steering wheel, eyes off the road, or both.

Teen driver with one teen passenger – collision risk increases by 100%

Reaching for a moving loose object. Similarly, research shows that teens are especially vulnerable to collisions when reaching for a loose object. This frequently involves taking eyes off the road.

Using a cellular phone. Using a cellular (cell) phone while driving can be extremely risky. While using a cell phone might seem simple, it requires significant concentration that takes attention away from the driving task. It is estimated that cell phone use accounts for approximately 2,600 motor vehicle fatalities and 300,000 collisions each year. Overall risk of a collision while using a cell phone increases by 400 percent.

Teen driver with two teen passengers – collision risk increases by 300%

Young drivers are especially vulnerable to becoming distracted while using a cell phone. Additionally, modern cell phones are capable of far more than spoken communication; many can perform navigational functions, access the Internet, share photos and send and receive text messages. As such, today's cell phones hold even more potential for increased risk while driving.

- **Dialing.** While it may not take long to dial a phone number, doing so may require a driver to remove one hand from the steering wheel and look down at the phone's keypad.

- **Talking and listening.** Holding a conversation requires mental effort, which diverts attention away from driving. One study indicated that talking on a cell phone was over four times more likely to cause a near crash than the next-most frequent cause of distraction. Drivers talking on cell phones frequently vary their speed and weave along the roadway.

- **Hand-held versus hands-free.** Some drivers choose to use a headset that eliminates the need to physically hold a cell phone. While a hands-free device may initially appear to be less distracting, research indicates no differences in risk between the two modes. Both methods of cell phone use are fully capable of diverting a driver's attention so much that a collision results.

- **Text messaging.** Text messaging is the common term for sending short (160 or fewer characters) text messages from cell phones. Faster than email, cell phone users receive incoming text messages almost immediately after they are sent. Evidence suggests that text messaging is even riskier than talking on a cell phone, as text messaging often requires the driver to both look at the phone and manipulate the keypad with one's hands.

HOW *to* **DRIVE**

Navigating. Every driver has a destination, and driving an unfamiliar route can be challenging enough without being distracted. Using a map while driving can cause distraction, not to mention significant reductions in visibility. Even drivers who use an electronic navigation system can become distracted.

Other internal distractions. Additional causes of distractions inside the vehicle include eating, drinking, grooming, adjusting vehicle controls such as climate systems, and attending to pets.

Distractions outside the vehicle. Distractions can also be caused by objects, people and events outside the vehicle. These could include:

Crash scenes. It can be tempting to reduce speed and divert attention to a nearby crash scene. Sometimes this is referred to as "rubbernecking."

Emergency vehicles. Emergency vehicles are often present at crash scenes or to deliver roadside assistance. With their flashing lights and other warning devices, they can easily divert a driver's eyes from the path of travel.

Objects. There are many objects outside the vehicle that could compete for a driver's attention, including other vehicles, pedestrians, road debris, collisions and billboards and other signs. Some signs may electronically alternate among different messages, and thus be even more likely to catch a driver's eye. Construction zones may contain unusual vehicles or machinery that can also divert a driver's attention.

Animals. On certain types of roadways, animals are more likely to cross into the path of travel. Often, animals move very quickly onto the roadway, surprising the unwary driver. Even if there is no risk of colliding with an animal, it may still draw a driver's attention away from the roadway.

Other roadway users. Although full-size motor vehicles are the most common users of the roadway, other users could attract a driver's attention. These could include horse-drawn buggies, motorcycles, scooters, bicycles and pedestrians.

Eyes off the road. Regardless of the cause of distraction, drivers can be tempted to look away from the roadway. While this might appear harmless, it is actually very risky. When a driver looks away from the roadway for two or more seconds, the risk of a collision doubles. The bottom line: regardless of what may be occurring that could draw your attention and vision away from the road, keep your eyes on your intended path of travel.

Preventing and Managing Distractions

Preventing and managing distractions. The key to preventing becoming distracted is to prepare as much as possible before you drive. With a little forethought, you can anticipate potential distractions and address them before getting behind the wheel. Despite your best efforts, distractions can arise while driving. Handling distractions effectively is critical to minimizing your risk. Techniques for preventing and managing distractions include:

- Familiarize yourself with your vehicle's features and equipment, before you get behind the wheel.
- Preset radio stations, MP3 devices, and climate control.
- Secure items that may move around when the car is in motion.
- Do not text message, access the internet, watch video, play video games, search MP3 devices, or use any other distracting technology while driving.
- Avoid smoking, eating, drinking and reading while driving.
- Do your personal grooming at home — not in the car.
- Review maps and driving directions before hitting the road.
- Pull safely off the road and out of traffic to deal with children.
- Monitor traffic conditions before engaging in activities that could divert attention away from driving.
- Ask a passenger to help you with activities that may be distracting.
- Recognize driving requires your full attention. If you find your mind wandering, remind yourself to stay focused on the road.

HOW *to* **DRIVE**

Cell phones. The first tip is: Do not use a cellular phone while driving. But if you must:

◆ Familiarize yourself with the features of your cell phone before you get behind the wheel.

◆ Use message-taking functions and return calls when you are stopped at a safe location.

◆ Use the cell phone only when absolutely necessary. Limit casual conversations to times when you are not operating a motor vehicle.

◆ Plan your conversation in advance, and keep it short — especially in hazardous conditions such as bad weather or heavy traffic.

◆ Let the person you are speaking with know you are driving.

◆ Do not engage in emotional conversations while driving. Pull off the road to a safe spot before continuing this type of conversation.

◆ Do not combine distracting activities such as talking on your cell phone while driving, eating and adjusting the audio system.

◆ Ask a passenger in the car to place the call for you and, if possible, speak in your place.

◆ Secure your phone in the car so that it does not become a projectile in a crash.

Remember, driving is a full-time job. You have learned it involves more than controlling the vehicle and keeping it on the road. Driving involves searching where you plan to go, identifying problems and potential conflicts, making decisions on what you perceive, judging what may occur and carrying out appropriate actions. To do all of this competently and safely you must stay focused and avoid distractions. When you do anything else while you are driving, you increase risk to yourself and others.

Drowsy Driving

Drowsiness. Drowsiness while driving is a condition that affects everyone at one time or another. As drivers become tired, their ability to drive becomes impaired, and the risk of a collision rises. Driving while drowsy is dangerous because your senses and abilities become impaired. You may not see objects clearly, or in a timely manner. You may miss critical information — signs, lights and sounds. It may also take you longer to process the information you take in or to make decisions in potential high-risk situations. You may misjudge speed and distances. In sum, drowsiness can affect every process involved in safe driving.

The risks. Drowsy driving is now recognized as one of the leading causes of traffic collisions. The NHTSA conservatively estimates that 100,000 police-reported crashes each year are the direct result of drowsy driving. This results in an estimated 1,550 deaths, 71,000 injuries, and $125 billion in monetary losses. These figures may be just the tip of the iceberg, because it can be challenging to determine with certainty that drowsiness was involved in any given crash.

Unfortunately, driving while drowsy is not rare. In fact, according to the National Sleep Foundation's *Sleep in America* poll, 60 percent of adult drivers — about 168 million people — say they have driven a vehicle while feeling drowsy in the past year, and more than one third (36 percent, or 103 million people) admit to having actually fallen asleep at the wheel! Drivers may experience short bursts of sleep lasting only a few seconds (microsleeps) or fall asleep for a longer period of time. Either way, the chance of a collision increases dramatically.

HOW to DRIVE

Who is at risk? Many drivers are at increased risk of becoming drowsy behind the wheel, including:

1. **Drivers on long trips.** Drivers could become fatigued while driving on long trips. Some drivers attempt to drive longer than they should on any given day.

2. **Drivers lacking sleep.** Drivers who are sleep-deprived are more likely to fall asleep behind the wheel. According to the AAA Foundation for Traffic Safety, people who sleep only six to seven hours a night are twice as likely to be involved in a drowsy-driving crash as those sleeping eight hours or more. Additionally, people sleeping fewer than five hours increase their risk of a collision by four to five times.

3. **Drivers with undiagnosed or untreated sleep disorders.** Drivers with sleep disorders are more likely to fall asleep while driving. Untreated disorders such as sleep apnea (stoppage of breathing due to soft-tissue blockage of the airway), narcolepsy (the inability to remain awake) and others can cause serious sleep disruption and uncontrolled nodding or falling asleep at the wheel. If you suffer frequent daytime sleepiness, often have difficulty sleeping at night, and/or snore loudly every night, consult your physician or a local sleep disorder center for diagnosis and treatment.

4. **Drivers on the road during the body's natural "low" times.** Each person's alertness, energy and sleep likelihood rises and falls throughout the day. This is referred to as the body's "circadian rhythm," the pattern of energy throughout a 24-hour period. Most people experience "lows" between approximately midnight and 6 am, and again between approximately 2 to 4 pm.

5. **Drivers on the road after extended wakefulness.** Remaining awake for extended periods of time can significantly increase drowsiness and its impact on driving ability. Research shows that being awake for 18 hours produces impairment approximately equal to a blood alcohol concentration (BAC) of .05 percent. After 24 hours awake, the impairment rises to that roughly equal to a BAC of .10 percent. Remember that fatigue can set in after a long day's work, an outing at the beach or any other activity.

6. **Young drivers.** Drivers under age 30 are involved in over two-thirds of all fall-asleep crashes. Additionally, these drivers are four times more likely to experience a sleep-related crash than drivers age 30 and older.

7. **Shift workers.** Drivers who work late-night or early-morning shifts are more likely to fall asleep while driving. Working the night shift increases collision risk by nearly six times. Rotating-shift workers and people working more than 60 hours a week need to be particularly careful.

Other causes of drowsiness. Emotional stress, illness or boredom can cause drowsiness. Sun glare, a major factor in eyestrain, can also contribute to fatigue. Overeating, drinking alcoholic beverages or riding in a warm passenger compartment can all affect the likelihood of becoming drowsy.

Monotony. Driving on an empty, straight road with no signals or billboards may seem like a simple task. Yet there is often not enough stimulation in the environment to keep you mentally alert. Compound this with the engine's constant purr, the hum of the tires, the tendency to fix your eyes on a single point ahead and the general monotony of easy vehicle operation, and mental alertness drops. Under such circumstances, a driver is much more likely to doze off than when on a more difficult and demanding road.

HOW to **DRIVE**

How can you tell if you are at risk of becoming drowsy? There is no guarantee that you will recognize when you are becoming tired behind the wheel. One half of drivers who crashed after falling asleep did not detect *any* signs of drowsiness before the crash. Be aware that there may be no warning before falling asleep, but recognize any warning signs that you may detect, including:

◆ Difficulty focusing, frequent blinking or heavy eyelids.

◆ Yawning repeatedly or rubbing your eyes.

◆ Daydreaming; wandering/disconnected thoughts.

◆ Trouble remembering the last few miles driven; missing exits or traffic signs.

◆ Trouble keeping your head up.

◆ Drifting from your lane, following too closely or hitting a shoulder rumble strip.

◆ Feeling restless and irritable.

Preventing drowsiness. To help prevent becoming drowsy, take the following steps before driving:

◆ Get a good night's sleep. While this varies from individual to individual, sleep experts recommend between 7 to 9 hours of sleep per night for adults and 8½ to 9½ hours for teens.

◆ Prepare your route carefully to identify total distance, stopping points and other logistic considerations.

◆ Plan to drive long trips with a companion. Passengers can help look for early warning signs of fatigue or take over driving when needed. At least one passenger should stay awake to talk to the driver.

◆ Avoid medications (over-the-counter and prescribed) that cause drowsiness or otherwise impair performance.

Once you are on the road. To help maintain your alertness while driving:

◆ Protect yourself from glare and eyestrain with sunglasses.

◆ Avoid heavy foods.

◆ Be aware of your physiological down time during the day (circadian rhythm).

◆ Have another person ride with you, and take turns driving.

◆ Take periodic breaks. A good rule of thumb is to stop every 100 miles or every two hours.

On long trips, stopping periodically can temporarily offset fatigue. You should be able to drive a reasonable distance without difficulty if you stop for at least 10 minutes every two hours or every 100 miles and make regular stops for fuel, food and restrooms. The problem with long-distance driving is that many people do not know, or choose to ignore, how much driving is too much. There is no rule to say how far you should drive at any given time, but no destination is worth gambling with your life. Do not overextend yourself. Determine a reasonable distance in advance and stop driving when you reach it.

Ineffective actions. The following actions will not help prevent drowsiness longer than just a few minutes:

◆ Trying to tough it out.

◆ Playing the radio at high volume.

◆ Driving at a faster or slower speed.

◆ Chewing gum.

◆ Opening the windows.

Rest is the key. Remember, resting is by far the most effective way to counter drowsiness. It usually is not a good idea to sleep in a vehicle at the side of the road. Yet there may be times when it is better to pull off than continue driving. If you must stop along the roadway to rest, follow these practices:

◆ Stop at a roadside area where security is present. If no such facility is available, make sure that you are as far off the highway as possible.

◆ After dark, find a populated, lighted area.

◆ Give yourself a little outside air, but be sure that windows are closed enough to prevent entry from outside.

◆ Lock all doors and turn off your engine.

◆ Turn on parking lights and turn off other electrical equipment.

◆ After you rest, if safe to do so, get out of the vehicle and walk a few minutes to be sure that you are completely awake before you begin to drive again. Keep in mind that sleeping for more than 20 minutes can make you groggy for at least five minutes after awakening.

The winner of the 1990 America's Safest Teen Driver Award was later killed in a crash after falling asleep while driving.

Feelings. It is natural for us to attach meaning and feelings to things we do. Strong emotions such as fear and anger can affect the way we perceive and process information. Therefore, emotions can — and do — affect the way we drive. A major study of driver performance indicates that the most critical factor in a driving record, regardless of training, is an individual's self-awareness and ability to interact with other people.

Causes. Any number of situations may lead to temporary upsets. A person who has just received news of a serious illness or death of a close friend or family member may be too upset to operate a vehicle safely. What about the person who has an argument, jumps into a vehicle and drives off, or the person who is excited or disappointed at the end of a closely played ball game? It is easy to become angry under such circumstances. You also can become frustrated or impatient when you wait in long lines of traffic or follow a slowly-moving vehicle along a winding roadway.

Effects of emotions. When emotionally upset, a driver's normal response to common traffic situations can change. Strong emotions affect our ability to think, reason and make decisions. The upset or emotionally-charged driver may look directly at a traffic light or stop sign and drive through it. That same person also may follow too closely and pass on hills or curves. Emotions can draw a driver's attention away from driving, reduce concentration on the roadway and impair the ability to process information and take necessary actions. While positive emotions can certainly cause impairment, negative emotions such as anger may affect driving safety to an even greater degree.

Aggressive Driving and Road Rage

Aggressive driving. Today, many drivers are operating their vehicles aggressively. Aggressive driving occurs when a driver operates a vehicle in a pushy or bold manner. Exceeding the speed limit, following too closely, failing to obey traffic controls and making improper turns and maneuvers are all examples of aggressive driving.

Road rage. Road rage occurs when a driver uses the vehicle or some other weapon to threaten or cause harm to another roadway user in response to a traffic incident. Road rage is an escalation of emotions generally ignited by aggressive driving behaviors. Drivers who drive aggressively are more likely to allow their emotions to overwhelm self-control and engage in road rage. Examples of road rage include throwing objects at a vehicle, yelling at a specific roadway user and attempting to ram another vehicle.

HOW to DRIVE

Guidelines for Controlling Emotions

Self-control. Since strong emotional responses are learned, you also can learn to control them. The following guidelines may help you keep emotions from unduly affecting your driving abilities:

Understand your own emotional makeup. Limited self-awareness may be the cause of fear or other strong emotional responses. The more you know about yourself and why you act a certain way, the better you can control your actions. If you can predict the emotional responses of other drivers, you can better prepare your responses.

Identify situations that tend to upset you. People tend to become excited, afraid or angry when they are faced with threatening situations. If a situation can be handled easily or does not concern you, it is not likely to lead to your being upset, and you can prepare for it more effectively. Effective trip planning can prevent numerous problems. Many traffic situations are frustrating because we fail to allow enough time for trips. In contrast, the pleasure of driving generally increases when friends are along.

Realize that smiles and courtesy can be spread among drivers just as easily as upsets and anger can.

Expect other drivers to make mistakes. The more you drive, the more you will realize that all drivers make mistakes. They may be distracted or inattentive. Other drivers may not have the skill or knowledge they should have. You need to realize that others' mistakes may be ones that you have made or may make in the future.

Emotions are contagious. Quite often, one emotion leads to another. If you yell at another person, he or she could become angry and take his or her anger out on someone else. That person, in turn, may get mad and take it out on someone else. This same thing can happen in traffic situations. Realize that smiles and courtesy can be spread among drivers just as easily as upsets and anger can. If you know what to expect, you can plan to overcome the errors and upsets of others.

Direct your emotions to actions rather than the individual. It is easy to become angry with another person or driver without knowing exactly why. Drivers have different goals. Sometimes you are in a hurry. Remember, however, that other drivers do not know your goals or have anything against you.

Delay driving when upset. Most emotional upsets are temporary. If you must drive, wait until the strength of the emotion has faded so that you are more likely to drive safely and courteously.

Unwind. When an upset occurs while you are driving, find a place to stop and unwind. Take a short walk. Take a few deep breaths. You might choose such a time to stop for refreshments.

Ask someone else to drive. Emotional upsets such as grief and anxiety may last several days. If you are depressed, it might be wise to have another person drive. In some cases, it might be best to use public transportation.

Preventing Aggressive Driving and Road Rage

One key to preventing aggressive driving and road rage is to avoid engaging in them yourself and trying not to give other roadway users cause to become aggressive. These guidelines can help:

◆ Leave in plenty of time to reach your destination.

◆ Remain calm at all times. Listening to soothing music can help.

◆ Maintain adequate distance between you and the vehicle ahead. Following too closely can easily cause the driver being followed to become angry.

◆ Avoid changing lanes unnecessarily.

◆ Do not block the passing lane. Except when passing, stay out of the far left lane.

◆ Always use your turn signals before changing lanes. Be sure you have plenty of room between you and other vehicles.

◆ Avoid using aggressive or offensive hand gestures when communicating with other drivers.

◆ Use your horn sparingly. A couple of short taps may be perceived as less aggressive than one long blast.

◆ Do not park across multiple parking spaces. Be sure not to touch adjacent vehicles either while parking, or with another vehicle's doors as you enter or exit your vehicle.

◆ When using high-beam headlights, return to using low-beam headlights as soon as you detect an oncoming vehicle. Do not drive behind another vehicle with your high-beam headlights on.

◆ If safe to do so, move out of the right-hand lane to allow vehicles entering the roadway to merge with minimal difficulty.

Unfortunately, sometimes other drivers become aggressive or enraged. If you are confronted by a driver displaying aggressive behaviors toward you, follow these guidelines:

- Do not respond to the other driver. Avoid any escalation of conflict.

- Remain calm, and take a deep breath.

- Avoid eye contact with the other driver or passengers.

- Be tolerant and forgiving — the other driver may be having a really bad day and be looking for a way to vent anger.

- Be polite and courteous, even if the other driver is not. Your behavior may help reduce his or her anger.

- Be sure to allow enough room around your vehicle so that you can pull out or around if someone approaches your vehicle.

- Do not get out of your vehicle — it offers protection.

- If necessary, contact 911 for assistance.

- If necessary, drive to a busy public place where there are witnesses, such as a hospital, fire station or busy convenience store or gas station. Once there, use your horn to attract others' attention if needed.

Avoid conflict. As you drive, your goal is to avoid conflict. Realize that other drivers' mistakes are not directed at you personally, so do not take them personally. Be as polite in your driving as you would be in any other social situation. If another driver challenges you, do not get out of your vehicle. Just as in a crash, your vehicle can give you protection. Do not lose that protection by getting out. You do not control traffic, but you do control your reaction to it.

HOW to **DRIVE**

TEST 13

The Effects of Distractions, Drowsiness and Emotions on Driving

Study and respond to each of the following questions. Then review the chapter to see if your responses are correct.

Multiple Choice:

1. An estimated ___ percent of collisions involve some form of driver inattention.
   a. 20
   b. 50
   c. 70
   d. 80

2. Overall risk of a collision while using a cell phone increases by ____ percent.
   a. 30
   b. 50
   c. 200
   d. 400

3. _____ drivers who crashed after falling asleep did not detect any signs of drowsiness before the crash.
   a. One quarter of
   b. One half of
   c. Three quarters of
   d. All

4. Most people experience dips in energy between approximately midnight and 6 am, and again between approximately _____, during which they are more likely to fall asleep while driving.
   a. 9 to 11 am
   b. Noon to 2 pm
   c. 2 to 4 pm
   d. 5 to 7 pm

5. _____ occurs when a driver uses the vehicle or some other weapon to threaten or cause harm to another roadway user in response to a traffic incident.
   a. Aggressive driving
   b. Circadian rhythm
   c. Road rage
   d. Microsleep

Short Answer:

1. Explain three ways that being distracted can increase driving risk.

2. List five techniques for preventing and managing distractions.

3. List five groups of drivers who are at increased risk of becoming drowsy behind the wheel.

4. Describe three steps to take before driving to help prevent becoming drowsy.

5. List six guidelines to help you avoid driving aggressively or engaging in road rage.

HOW to DRIVE

CHAPTER **14**

Adverse Driving Conditions and Emergencies

Chapter Objectives:

- ◆ Describe how reduced visibility increases the level of risk when driving.
- ◆ Identify factors that reduce traction and how you can safely test for a slippery road surface.
- ◆ Describe evasive steering and braking actions a driver can take under conditions of limited time and space.
- ◆ Identify actions that can cause a skid and how to regain directional control of the vehicle.
- ◆ Identify vehicle failure problems and how to respond to reduce risk.
- ◆ Describe specific steps for reducing the risks of an unavoidable crash.
- ◆ Describe your duties at a collision scene.

HOW *to* **DRIVE**

SCHOO

Emergency Situations

Emergencies happen. Adverse conditions, vehicle failures and driver errors all can create emergency situations. Emergencies happen suddenly — leaving little time for evaluation and decision-making. As a result, emergencies often lead to an incorrect panic response or no response at all. A review of nearly 12,000 reported crashes revealed that more than 37 percent of drivers involved took no action whatsoever to prevent or avoid the incident. Clearly it is critical for drivers to remain attentive to the traffic environment at all times in order to perceive potentially dangerous situations.

Staying in control. Correct responses to most emergencies can be learned by thinking through possible situations and mentally rehearsing appropriate responses. Practicing "what if" responses to simulated emergency situations under safe conditions can reduce the emotional impact and increase the chances of correct performance. Obviously, the driver who knows what to do in an emergency is more likely to stay in control.

Reduced Visibility

Minimizing the effects of reduced visibility. Weather conditions, traffic, your own vehicle or the highway environment can reduce visibility. There are several ways to minimize the effects of these conditions.

Plan to be seen. Driving with your headlights on is recommended any time the vehicle is in motion; however, it is especially important in rain, smoke, fog or snow. Using your headlights in the daytime enables other highway users to see you from twice as far away as vehicles without their lights on.

Using your headlights in the daytime enables other highway users to see you from twice as far away as vehicles without their lights on.

Keep headlights clean. When you drive on wet streets, mud and dirt splashed by other cars can cover your headlights with film. Unless removed, this film can reduce headlight effectiveness by up to 90 percent. Clean them periodically to restore their effectiveness.

Road grime and dirt can build up on your headlights, reducing their effectiveness.

Clear the windshield and rear windows. Snow and sleet can collect and freeze on the windshield, producing wide blocked areas that windshield wipers cannot sweep clear. These areas can restrict vision to the sides and decrease your ability to see other highway users that may move into your path of travel. If you must drive under such conditions, reduce your speed and carefully search road conditions ahead. Make sure your headlights are on so that you are more visible. Also, remember that in extremely cold temperatures your windshield washer fluid may freeze onto the windshield if you attempt to spray fluid while driving.

It is important that you clean the outside and inside of your windshield at least once a week. Frequent cleaning is even more important if you smoke.

A dirty windshield restricts vision.

Clean glass provides better visibility.

Defrosters. Keep your car's windshield and rear-window defrosters in proper working condition. Use an ice scraper to remove snow and ice from your windshield and all windows before you drive. Before you turn on the defroster and blowers, move the heat control to hot and allow the engine to warm up. This will help prevent frost from forming on the inside of the glass. If the windshield and side windows start to fog on the inside, open a window slightly and turn the defroster to a higher speed. If your vehicle has an air conditioner, use it to reduce the humidity level.

If you must leave the roadway. A hard rain or snow can limit vision so much that you cannot see the edges of the roadway. If you must pull off the road, wait for conditions to improve. It is best to pull into a rest area or parking lot. If this is not possible, pull off the road as far as you can, preferably past the end of a guardrail. If possible, back up outside the guardrail, turn your headlights off and turn on your emergency flashers to alert other drivers of your presence. When bad weather makes it hard to see, vehicles on the sides of the road are at risk of being hit by moving traffic. Placing something – like a guardrail – between your vehicle and the traffic approaching from behind you can provide extra protection.

Driving at Night

Driving at night. One of the biggest problems when driving at night is reduced visibility. Your sight distance at night is limited to the distance illuminated by your vehicle's headlights. At night, you do not have the advantage of color and contrast that you have during the daytime.

Low light. Being able to see well during the daytime does not necessarily mean that you will see well at night. Your eyes must adapt to bright lights and dark areas. After driving four or five hours on a bright sunny day, it may take an hour or more for your eyes to adjust to low light at dusk or night. Some people may not adapt well to low light and should avoid night driving. Night driving also reduces your ability to see to the sides. Regardless of how effective your headlights are, they do not adequately light off-road areas.

Glare and recovery time. At night, all drivers are affected temporarily by the glare of headlights and brightly lit signs or buildings. Most people's eyes recover from such glare within three to five seconds. However, recovery times of seven seconds or longer are not uncommon. Typically, the time to recover from glare increases with age.

To minimize the challenges of night driving:

1. **Adjust your speed to the reach of your headlights.** Do not overdrive your headlights. Remember that a blacktop surface does not reflect light as well as concrete and thus reduces the amount of light available. Properly aligned, clean headlights on high beams will light up the roadway 350 to 500 feet ahead. Low beams will light a much shorter distance. Compensate for reduced visibility by increasing your following distance to four or more seconds and decreasing your speed.

2. **Keep your eyes moving.** Do not focus on the middle of the area illuminated by your headlights. Be sure to search the darkened roadway ahead and the edges of the lighted area. Watch for sudden flashes of light at hilltops, around curves or at intersections; these may indicate the presence of an oncoming vehicle. Concentrate on the street-level activities in or near your intended path when signs or brightly lit buildings may distract you.

Your sight distance at night is limited to the distance illuminated by your vehicle's headlights.

All drivers are affected temporarily by the glare of headlights and brightly lit signs or buildings.

HOW to **DRIVE**

3. **Look to the sides of objects.** In dim light, focus on the edges or outlines of objects. Your eyes can pick up images more sharply this way than by looking directly at the object.

4. **Protect your eyes from glare.** Prolonged exposure to glare from sunlight during the day or headlights at night can temporarily affect your night vision. It can also lead to eyestrain and drowsiness. Wear good sunglasses on bright days and take them off as soon as the sun goes down. Look to the center of your pathway and use the painted edge lines to guide your vehicle. After steady daytime driving, rest awhile before you drive at night.

5. **At night, if an oncoming vehicle is using high beams, flash your lights from low to high and back to low.** If the driver fails to dim the lights, look down toward the right side of the road to avoid being blinded. You should be able to see the edge of the lane or the painted edge line and stay on course until the vehicle passes.

6. **Use your headlights wisely.** Use high beams when possible. Switch to low beams when you follow or meet oncoming vehicles. Flash your lights to signal that you are overtaking and passing vehicles. Parking lights are not for driving. Parking lights are designed to protect you when you park in areas where light is limited.

7. **Make it easier for others to see you.** Drive with your lights on during the day. Other drivers can see you at a distance of about 4,700 feet with your lights on, compared to about 2,500 feet without your lights. Also, when you prepare to slow or stop, tap the brake pedal to flash the taillights. This will help alert drivers behind that you are about to decelerate. If you break down, pull completely off the roadway and turn on your emergency flashers. In addition to emergency flashers, use flares, reflective triangles or, if necessary, a flashlight to help other drivers see you better.

8. **Avoid constant-speed driving around your usual bedtime and downtimes.** Your alertness level automatically decreases around your regular bedtime and during your afternoon physiological downtime, which for most people occurs between 2 and 4 pm. Try to avoid driving during these times. If you must drive during these hours, take frequent breaks.

Driving in Fog

Driving in fog. Driving in dense fog can be like driving with sunglasses on at night. Objects such as other vehicles or traffic signals may not be visible until the last moment — sometimes too late to take proper corrective action.

By far the two most important safety measures you can take when you encounter fog while driving are:

1. Slow down.
2. Turn on your low-beam headlights.

Use low headlight beams when driving in fog.

A major cause of crashes in fog is overdriving visibility — driving too fast for the distance you can see ahead of you. By reducing speed, you will increase your available reaction time should you encounter a situation that requires corrective action.

Keep your low beams on. Driving with your low beam headlights on not only helps you to see the roadway ahead more clearly, but also makes you more visible to other vehicles. Remember to keep your headlights on low beams; the additional light from your high beams will be reflected by the fog back into your eyes, reducing visibility. Parking lights will do little to make you more visible to other drivers. If your vehicle is equipped with daytime running lights (DRLs), you may need to manually turn on your headlights so your taillights will also be illuminated.

Use low beams when driving in fog. Using your high beams will reflect more light back into your eyes due to the Tyndall Effect, which describes how water molecules suspended in the air scatter and reflect light.

Additional tips for driving in fog:

◆ Use your windshield wipers to increase your visibility and reduce glare from oncoming vehicles.

◆ Avoid sudden stops and remember that larger vehicles need more distance to slow down or stop.

◆ If you must stop, steer off the roadway as far as safely possible.

◆ In severe fog, emergency flashers may help make you more visible to other drivers. (Check your state law regarding use of flashers while moving.)

Problems associated with driving in fog are magnified during nighttime hours. No trip, no matter how important, is worth gambling your life or the lives of others. By far the safest thing to do if you run into unexpected fog is to move off the highway and wait for the fog to lift.

Driving in smoke and sandstorms. Smoke from forest or brush fires can be dangerous because it can occur suddenly, without warning, and be very dense. Likewise, clouds of sand can significantly reduce visibility. When you approach areas where smoke or sand clouds are present on the roadway, emergency flashers may help make you more visible to other drivers. The best option is to move off the highway and wait for conditions to improve.

Reduced Traction

Testing the surface. Reduced traction always increases the risk of skidding, loss of control and a collision. You should determine how much traction there is and any changes in traction. A quick drop in temperature can freeze rain or wet snow into a slick, icy surface. Judging the amount of traction from inside the vehicle is difficult, but you can test the available traction. First, wait until there is an area free of traffic. Then, after you slow to 15 to 20 mph, quickly press the brake pedal and note if the tires begin to skid or if the anti-lock braking system engages earlier than when in dry conditions.

You can also accelerate to check how much traction is available. Either test should provide guidelines to help you adjust your speed and allow you to brake effectively while maintaining traction. Be sure not to place yourself, your vehicle or anyone else at risk when performing these brief tests.

Hydroplaning

Hydroplaning. In wet conditions, water on the road, excessive speed, under-inflated tires and low tire tread can cause your vehicle to lose contact with the roadway and lose traction. As speed increases, water between the tires and the road can build until the tires begin to ride on a film of water. This is calling hydroplaning or aquaplaning.

Hydroplaning occurs when the tires ride up on a film of water.

HOW to DRIVE

Tire tread. Adequate tire tread allows water to evacuate from under the tires, which prevents hydroplaning at moderate speeds. However, even with good tread, hydroplaning can take place when water is deeper than the tread depth.

Hydroplaning and speed. At 30 mph or less on a wet surface, properly inflated tires with good tread should wipe the road surface and maintain contact with the road. But when a vehicle travels over 30 mph on a wet surface, water may separate the tire from the road, resulting in hydroplaning. Usually a driver has little warning that a critical speed has been reached until a change in road shape or a slight turn causes a skid.

Certain signs can help a driver identify conditions that can lead to hydroplaning:

◆ Water standing on the roadway.

◆ Raindrops that bubble as they hit the surface of the road.

◆ A slushing sound made by tires on the pavement.

◆ A sensation that the steering wheel is loose, or has become disconnected from the front wheels of the vehicle.

Preventing hydroplaning. To prevent hydroplaning, slow down when you see water standing on the surface of the pavement, especially on freeways. Drive in the tracks or wipes left by any vehicle ahead. Use tires with deep, open treads and be sure to inflate them to the vehicle manufacturer's recommended pressure. If hydroplaning does occur, avoid slamming on the brakes; instead, ease your foot off the accelerator to gradually decrease speed until your tires regain traction, and continue to look and steer where you want to go.

Braking in Slick Conditions

Braking with ABS. Braking on slippery roads is tricky business. Sudden, hard or prolonged braking can cause a skid. However, if your vehicle is equipped with anti-lock brakes, all you need do is press the brake pedal and hold it down. The system automatically senses if a wheel begins to lock and quickly releases and reapplies the brakes as many times as necessary to keep the wheel from locking up.

Braking without ABS. If your vehicle is not equipped with anti-lock brakes, the best way to brake under these conditions is to use squeeze (or threshold) braking. To squeeze brake, keep your heel on the floor and use your toes to apply pressure on the brake pedal. If the wheels lock, ease off the brake pedal to a point just before locking. Adjust pedal pressure as necessary. This method gives you the best combination of braking effort and directional control.

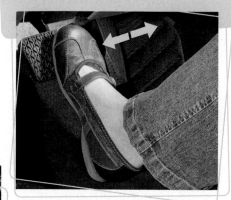

Rest your heel on the floor and squeeze the brake pedal with your toes.

Drive with care on wet or slippery surfaces.

Off-Road Recovery

Off-road recovery. At some point, your vehicle may drift off the roadway onto the shoulder, or you may steer onto the shoulder to avoid a collision. Most shoulders provide less traction than roadway surfaces. Shoulders may be narrow strips of loose gravel, grass or mud, and can be several inches lower than the road surface. In spite of these factors, you can pull off onto the shoulder and return to the roadway safely if you know and practice the proper procedures. Driving off the edge of the roadway can be very dangerous and could lead to a rollover crash, in which the chance of injury is very high.

HOW *to* **DRIVE**

SCHOOL

Keep a firm grip. If you run your right or left wheels off the roadway, maintain a firm grip on the steering wheel and keep the vehicle traveling straight ahead. Straddle the edge of the pavement. You will need to resist the tendency of the vehicle to pull toward the shoulder if it is soft. You also must resist the urge to immediately whip the vehicle back onto the pavement.

If your path of travel is clear. If there are no obstacles directly in front of you, do not rush to return to the roadway. Remain calm and do the following:

1. Ease off the accelerator and allow the vehicle to slow gradually. If possible, avoid braking. If you must brake, use a gentle squeeze-braking technique to maintain steering control. Unless some object beside the road is directly in your path, do not try to return to the roadway until you have reduced your speed. Search ahead, to the sides and to the rear.

2. Steer the off-road tires to about 1½ to 2 feet from the edge of the pavement.

3. When your speed is under control and it is safe to do so, quickly turn the steering wheel about an eighth of a turn back toward the roadway. This permits the front tire to climb the pavement edge and move back onto the roadway, rather than scrubbing along the roadway edge. As soon as the front tire is back on the roadway, counter-steer quickly left or right as necessary to stay in the correct lane. Continue to look and steer where you want to go.

1. Firm grip on steering wheel
2. Ease off accelerator and coast down your speed
3. Gentle pressure on brake
4. Quick steer when safe

If you must return to the road quickly. In some cases an object beside the road such as a tree, bridge abutment or pedestrian may force you to return to the road quickly. Because you have little or no opportunity to slow down, do the following:

1. Steer left or right so the off-road wheels are about 12 inches away from the edge of the pavement.

2. Remove your foot from the accelerator and stay off the brakes. Turn the steering wheel quickly about one-eighth turn toward the roadway. This allows the tire to roll up over the edge of the pavement back onto the road surface.

3. Immediately, as the outer wheel makes contact with the edge of the pavement, counter-steer about a quarter turn. Then make steering corrections to center or straighten steering. Continue to look and steer where you want to go.

Evasive Actions

Avoiding a collision. To avoid a collision, you may have to make a sudden and extreme change in your vehicle's speed and direction. These might include abrupt vehicle moves to the left or right, sudden application of brakes, abrupt acceleration or a combination of these actions.

Which is the best plan? It is generally better to use evasive steering rather than braking. That is because at speeds greater than 25 mph, less distance is required to steer around an object than to brake to a stop. The key to successful evasive steering is to have already identified an alternate path of travel to move into.

It is sometimes difficult to determine whether or not you have sufficient time/distance to stop to avoid a crash. Remember, at speeds greater than 25 miles per hour it takes less distance to steer than it does to brake to a stop. However, to use evasive steering, you must have identified an alternate path of travel.

SCHOOL

Evasive steering. As described in Chapter 4, hand-to-hand steering maximizes steering control and reduces the risk of injury should the airbag deploy. Since the arms never cross, you are able to provide continuous input to the steering wheel in either direction as necessary.

However, in an emergency situation, there may not be time for you to turn the steering wheel using this technique. In this case, fixed-hand steering using the 9 o'clock and 3 o'clock or 8 o'clock and 4 o'clock hand positioning can also be effective. This method provides:

- 180 degree steering input without removing your hands from the steering wheel

- A high level of vehicle control

- An awareness of where the wheels are pointing and how to straighten them

- With your hands at 9 and 3, or 8 and 4, your reaction time is quicker, making you better able to take evasive action

- NOTE: As the steering wheel is turned, the driver's torso remains in place (due to the opposing nature of the steering movement)

Evasive braking. In some emergency situations, you may be forced to brake because there is no space to the side into which you can steer or because you have failed to identify such a space. In many cases, such as when a crash at an intersection is about to occur, the best action is a combination of controlled braking and evasive steering. The purpose of controlled braking is to achieve the shortest possible stopping distance while maintaining directional control. In vehicles not equipped with ABS, slamming on the brakes and locking the wheels can result in a complete loss of directional control.

The heel-pivot method. If you do not have anti-lock brakes, the best way to make a controlled stop is the heel-pivot method. Keep the heel of your foot on the floor and use your toes to apply firm, steady pressure on the brake pedal just short of lockup — the point at which the wheels stop turning. The instant you lift your heel from the floor to place the ball of your foot on the brake pedal, the wheels will tend to lock because you will then be controlling the brake with your larger thigh muscles, which are incapable of fine muscle control. Under the stress of trying to stop quickly, drivers almost always apply the brakes too hard and lock the wheels. If this happens, use the heel-pivot method to release the brake just a bit, then immediately reapply it with slightly less pressure.

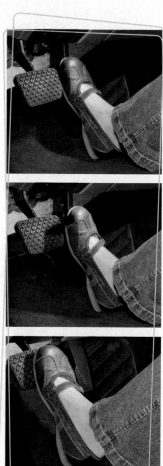

Keep your foot on the brake if you have ABS. If you have an anti-lock braking system, use the heel-pivot method but do not remove your foot from the brake. When you put on the brakes hard enough to engage the ABS, you will typically feel the brake pedal pulse back against your foot. This sensation is normal, and indicates that the system is working properly. Do not pump the pedal or remove your foot from the brake.

Evasive acceleration. The emergency technique used least frequently is acceleration, mainly because the dangerous event that drivers have to respond to is in front of them. However, the accelerator can be used effectively to avoid crashes at intersections and in merging situations.

For example, as you enter an intersection or approach a blind alley, you see a vehicle about to cross your path. Hard braking could bring you to a stop directly in the path of the approaching vehicle. Accelerating may be your only means of escape. In such a case, hard acceleration may remove you from the path of the crossing vehicle. Even if you cannot get completely out of the way, acceleration may move the point of impact to the rear of your vehicle, away from the passenger compartment.

Skidding

Skidding. Skidding is a situation in which your tires lose all or part of their grip on the road. As your tires lose traction, they will begin to slide, and can cause your vehicle to deviate from your intended path of travel. Skids can result from accelerating or braking too hard, steering too much or too quickly, or entering a curve with too much speed. Regardless of the cause, a skid means your actions demanded more traction than your vehicle could provide.

Front-tire Skid (Understeer)

Rear-tire Skid (Oversteer)

Cause	Description
Over-braking	Occurs when you apply the brakes so hard that one or more wheels lock in a vehicle not equipped with ABS. The vehicle generally skids in a straight line and steering control is lost.
Over-accelerating	Occurs if you abruptly depress the accelerator too much and spin the drive wheels. If such a skid is not corrected immediately, the vehicle can abruptly veer to one side, or spin around completely.
Cornering too fast	Occurs if you drive into or through a corner at a speed that exceeds the traction capability of your vehicle. If such a skid is not corrected immediately, the vehicle can abruptly veer to one side, or spin around completely.

Preventing skids. The key to maintaining traction at all times is to recognize when a skid is possible and take action to prevent one from occurring. Skids can be prevented by:

◆ Applying the brakes in a smooth and progressive manner.

◆ Making smooth, precise steering wheel movements.

◆ Slowing down well in advance of curves.

◆ Maintaining speeds appropriate for conditions.

Avoid shifting to lower gears in slick conditions. The sudden increase in either power or braking can cause a sudden weight shift in your vehicle, especially in conditions of reduced traction. You do not have to be going fast for a skid to happen when roads are slick. That is why you should always drive slower on wet, slippery or debris-covered roads.

Responding to skids. The first step in regaining traction is to recognize that you are experiencing a skid. Regardless of the cause of the skid, if you are maintaining your visual focus ahead of your vehicle, you should be able to detect when the front of your vehicle deviates from your intended path of travel. As soon as you detect this, you need to take corrective action. Once you begin to respond to a skid, do not stop trying to regain traction.

Types of Skids and Recovery Techniques

Regardless of the cause, there are two types of skids; front-tire and rear-tire.

Front-tire skid. In a front-tire ("understeer") skid, your front tires lose traction and the vehicle pushes wide through the turn and tends to run off the outside of the turn. To regain traction:

1. **Continue to look and steer toward your intended path of travel.** Keep your eyes focused on where you want the vehicle to go.

HOW *to* **DRIVE**

2. **Smoothly ease up on the accelerator.** This will transfer more weight to the front wheels, increasing the front tires' traction. If you lift off the accelerator too quickly in a skid, the weight may shift rapidly such that the rear of the vehicle may slide sideways. You may need to smoothly apply the brakes a bit to regain enough traction to turn the vehicle toward your intended path of travel.

Rear-tire skid. In a rear-tire ("oversteer") skid, your rear tires lose traction and the rear of the vehicle begins to slide sideways. As this happens, the front of the vehicle will deviate from your intended path of travel. If you do not take corrective action, the vehicle may spin around completely. To regain traction:

1. Continue to look and steer toward your intended path of travel. Keep your eyes focused on where you want the vehicle to go.

2. Avoid using the brakes.

3. As the rear tires regain traction, continue steering toward your intended path of travel. You may need to make a number of counter-steering corrections before traction is fully regained.

If your vehicle goes into a skid, continue to look and steer where you want to go.

Counter-steering. Counter-steering means steering in the direction you want the front of the vehicle to go, toward your intended path of travel. Most drivers tend to steer this way instinctively in their attempt to correct a rear-tire skid. When you counter-steer, straighten the wheels as soon as you feel the rear of the vehicle begin to realign with your intended path of travel.

Caution. Be careful when you counter-steer — it is not enough to correct for only the first oversteer skid. The rear of the vehicle may swing back in the opposite direction of the first skid ("fishtailing"). Be ready to counter-steer quickly if more skidding continues. You need quick and correct reactions for successful skid recovery.

Getting Unstuck

Getting unstuck. Despite your best efforts, you may find yourself stuck in mud, deep snow or sand. When wheels are stuck, apply power slowly and steadily.

1. Keep the front wheels pointed straight ahead so the vehicle can move in a straight line. If you cannot go forward, try to back out and steer in the tracks the vehicle has just made.

2. Try moving the vehicle using second gear, which helps to prevent wheel spin. Accelerate gently — give just enough pedal pressure to move the vehicle. Ease along gradually until traction is improved. When you must drive in mud, sand or snow, keep your vehicle moving slowly. Shift to a lower gear in advance and accelerate just enough to keep the vehicle moving.

HOW *to* **DRIVE**

Rocking your vehicle back and forth may help if you are stuck.

3. If your vehicle remains stuck, you may have to rock it out. You can rock a vehicle with either a manual or automatic transmission. (Check the owner's manual for the recommended procedure.) To rock a vehicle, start slowly in second gear (manual transmission) or low gear (automatic transmission). When the vehicle will go no farther forward, release the accelerator to permit the vehicle to roll back. When the vehicle stops its backward motion, apply minimum pressure on the accelerator again. Repeat these actions in rapid succession. Each rock should move the vehicle a little farther forward or out of the hole you are in. When you rock, you must use minimum power to help prevent the wheels from spinning and digging deeper.

4. If the wheels simply spin, stop rocking and find a way to create traction under the drive wheels. Usually, if one drive wheel spins, the vehicle is just as stuck as if both were spinning. Obviously, you need traction at both drive wheels. Any rough material such as gravel, cat litter, cinders, burlap or branches may help. You could even use a floor mat. You may have to shovel out in front of the stuck wheels before you use such materials. Then apply power slowly and steadily, using second gear or an even higher gear. In winter, you may find it useful to carry a bag of sand or cat litter, a shovel and traction mats in your trunk.

Vehicle Failures

On Undivided Highways

On Divided Highways

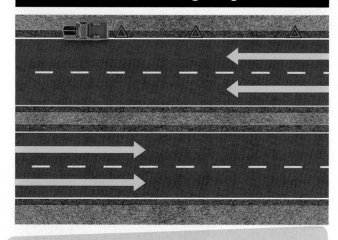

Recommended placement of emergency-warning devices.

Mechanical problems when you are driving. Regardless of how well you maintain your car, there always is a possibility that it may break down with little or no warning. The most serious failures are those that affect steering, braking or engine power. If your vehicle develops mechanical problems when you are driving, your main objective should be to steer safely off the roadway onto the shoulder, then call for help.

Be visible when stopped. After you have brought your vehicle to a stop off the roadway, set out flares or other high-visibility warning devices such as reflective triangles. Position them at 100- and 200-foot increments behind your car. If you do not have flares or triangles but have a passenger with you, direct the person to walk back 200 to 300 feet, stand well off the roadway and signal drivers. If you decide you cannot correct the problem, signal for help. Raise the hood and tie a white handkerchief on your antenna, door handle or side-view mirror, or place it in the window. Remain in your vehicle, and call for help.

HOW *to* **DRIVE**

SCHOO

Emergency road service.

Emergency road-service vehicle operators usually can change a flat tire or perform minor repairs on the spot. In addition, many carry gasoline and jumper cables to take care of the most common breakdowns. If you must be towed to a service garage, you should first find out whether towing is covered under your automobile insurance, roadside assistance program or auto club membership. You also should find out where the tow truck will take your vehicle, how many miles away the garage is and exactly what the towing will cost. Also, you may have to arrange transportation, since passengers are not usually allowed to ride in the towed vehicle. Joining an auto club can give you peace of mind regarding potential emergencies along the roadway.

A raised hood, flashing hazard lights and a white handkerchief help signal police and emergency road-service vehicles.

Most common engine failures.

The most common engine failures are stalling, overheating or failure to start. Many failures result from a malfunctioning fuel-injection system, a discharged battery, trouble in the ignition system, low coolant level, a defective thermostat or broken belts. Most such failures are preventable through proper maintenance.

Engine Failure

Getting off the road.

Engine failure in traffic requires that you check for other cars, signal and steer to the shoulder of the road to a position as safe as possible. This may be more difficult if your vehicle is equipped with power steering or power brakes, because a stalled engine or broken drive belt in effect eliminates power-booster systems. Such failures do not result in a complete loss of braking or steering. However, you must steer harder and apply much greater pressure on the brake pedal. If your engine should begin to miss or stall, shift to Neutral and safely steer off the road as soon as possible.

Unintended acceleration. A less frequent type of engine failure is caused by unintended acceleration. Such failures may occur at highway speeds but usually involve unintended acceleration when the vehicle is shifted into gear from a stopped position. There are two actions you should take — one preventive and the other responsive:

1. Before you shift a vehicle with an automatic transmission into gear, place your foot firmly on the brake pedal. Many newer vehicles do not allow the shifter to be moved from Park until the brake pedal is depressed.

2. If you experience sudden acceleration or the accelerator pedal sticks, shift to Neutral and apply the brakes. If you are driving a vehicle with a manual shift, depress the clutch pedal. Once you come to a stop safely off the roadway, shut off the engine.

In a vehicle with an automatic transmission, be careful when you shift to Neutral from Drive because it may be possible to move the shift lever through Neutral directly into Reverse.

Floor-mounted shift lever. To prevent the floor-mounted shift lever from moving accidentally, manufacturers have added a locking device to the shifting stem or the thumb side of the T-bar that must be depressed before the shift lever can be moved. However, in a few vehicles, the locking device must be depressed below the top of the knob. In others, you might have to squeeze the handle. Check the owner's manual for the proper operation.

Practice. Having information is not the same as using it. If you are to respond in an emergency, you must be able to act without conscious thought. Know the type of shifting mechanism in your vehicle, and practice until you can shift to Neutral without taking your eyes off the road.

A common problem is headlight, brake-light or turn-signal light failure. Analysis of data collected on vehicles passing though AAA automotive diagnostic centers revealed that more than 24 percent of vehicles tested have one or more lights burned out due to electrical malfunctions. Most failures should be detected during routine vehicle checks. Regardless of whether you perform all routine maintenance, sudden light failure can occur.

Sudden headlight failure. While failure of either brake or turn-signal lights increases your risk of being involved in a crash, sudden headlight failure on a dark, winding road can be disastrous. Apply the brakes and at the same time hit the dimmer switch. High and low beams are on different circuits, so one or the other may still work. If this does not help, turn on the parking lights, emergency flashers or turn signals. It is critical to concentrate on getting the vehicle safely off the road and parked. Warn other drivers of your presence and once you are parked, do not drive again until you take care of the problem.

Most light failures should be detected during the driver's routine vehicle checks.

Tire Failure

If a tire suddenly goes flat while you are driving, continue to look down your intended path of travel, keep a firm, steady grip on the steering wheel and maintain a straight course. You must concentrate on keeping or regaining control. Stay off the brakes.

Use the accelerator to help you control the vehicle with one of these methods:

1. Ease up on the accelerator, allowing the engine to slow the vehicle.

2. Accelerating slightly may help improve the vehicle's directional stability. Once you have the vehicle under control, lightly apply the brakes with an easy, steady pressure. If a front tire has failed, you will feel a strong pull toward the side where that tire is located. A rear tire failure can cause a rear-tire ("oversteer") skid.

If a tire suddenly goes flat while you are driving, keep a firm, steady grip on the steering wheel and maintain a straight course.

Pull off the road. When the vehicle is under control, look for a place to pull off the road. Do not worry about ruining your tire if you must drive on it for a short distance. Chances are it is not safe for future use anyway. Park well off the highway. If possible, have at least five feet of clearance between you and the traveled portion of the highway. Set the parking brake and move the selector to the Park position. If you have a manual transmission, place the gearshift lever in first or "Reverse." If you plan to change the tire, make sure you are not close to moving traffic and that other drivers can see you.

Fire

If fire breaks out under the hood or in the passenger compartment, steer the vehicle off the road. Turn off the ignition, then get passengers out and well away from the vehicle. Call 911 and notify the fire department. If the fire is under the hood and flames are shooting out, do not raise the hood. Usually, automotive fires are caused by electrical short circuits. If the fire is out of control, move at least 100 feet away, since a fuel fire may cause the fuel tank to explode.

HOW to DRIVE

Brake Failure

Most brake failures are the result of poor maintenance or inferior replacement materials.

If your brakes fail but the engine still appears to be functioning normally, pump the brake pedal rapidly. You may be able to build enough brake pressure to steer off the roadway and stop safely. If this does not work, apply steady pressure to the parking brake, which generally controls just the rear wheels. Be careful and prepare to release the brake if the wheels lock. You can reapply the parking brake if needed. There are several different types of parking brake systems. Take the time to review the vehicle owner's manual to determine how yours works.

Slowing your vehicle. Downshifting your vehicle can also help slow it down. Find an escape route — a safe exit from the roadway. Sound your horn and flash your lights to signal an emergency to other drivers. In extreme cases, you may have to use more severe methods to slow your car. You may have to run along an embankment, scrape against a curb or drive into bushes or other obstructions.

Child Restraint Laws

Safety restraints for children. All states have child-restraint laws that require children, at least up to age 4, to be properly secured in child safety seats. Rear-facing infant seats are designed for infants, usually from birth to 20 or more pounds. After a baby has outgrown the infant seat, parents should use a convertible child safety seat to secure the baby. Babies should ride rear-facing until age two or they reach the upper weight and height limit of their rear-facing convertible seat. A rear-facing child-safety seat should never be placed in front of an active frontal airbag, which could cause serious injury or even death if deployed.

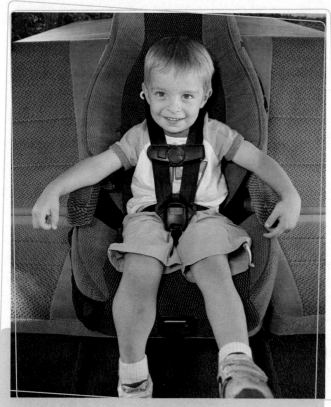
Infants and toddlers must be secured in child-safety seats.

Weight limit. A child can then safely ride in a forward-facing child safety seat. They should continue to use their forward facing seat until they reach the upper weight limit of the harnesses at 40 or more pounds.

Protecting children who have outgrown the safety seat.

Once a child has outgrown the child safety seat, he or she should be secured with the vehicle's lap/shoulder seat belts in a belt-positioning booster seat. Booster seats are important because they help position the seat belt correctly on the child, with the lap portion of the seat belt low on the child's hips and the shoulder belt across the collarbone and sternum. Children are ready for the vehicle seat belt when they are 4'9" usually between 8 to 12 years of age. Remember, all children under age 13 should ride in the back seat.

Buckle up — everyone. It is crucial that all occupants be buckled up properly during every ride in the vehicle. Crash forces are estimated by multiplying speed and weight. For example, in a 30 mph crash, a 15-pound baby would absorb 450 pounds of crash forces. Chances of injury and death are reduced by 71 percent for infants and by 54 percent for toddlers properly restrained in child-safety seats. When seat belts are used by front-seat occupants, chances of fatal injury are reduced by 45 percent.

HOW to DRIVE

How to Minimize the Consequences of a Collision

Minimizing consequences. A goal of any driver is to avoid crashes or injuries. Unfortunately, this goal is not always possible. If a collision appears inevitable, you should attempt to minimize the consequences. You must plan strategies before such a situation arises.

Protect yourself. When you use the safety equipment on your vehicle properly, you can reduce the possibility of death or injury. The more secure you are in the car, the lower your chance of being injured. Think of yourself as a fragile object that you want to package and ship. You would not throw an egg into a box, hoping it would arrive undamaged. Nor would you want the contents to spill out during shipment. This analogy applies just as easily to you and your vehicle.

Buckle up for safety. Your passengers are at much greater risk if they are not properly using their safety belts. You also are at much greater risk when your passengers are not belted. During a collision, your passengers could be thrown about inside your car and collide with you, injuring you or causing you to lose control of your vehicle.

Keep everyone safe by ensuring that:

◆ All passengers are belted.
◆ No passengers are seated where belts are unavailable.
◆ No passengers are in a pickup truck's bed.
◆ No passengers are in the in cargo area of an SUV.
◆ Pets are secured.

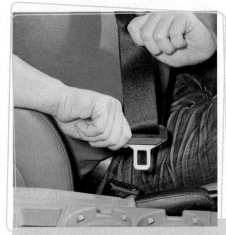

To help avoid injury in a crash, secure yourself and your passengers with the proper restraints.

Air bag/safety belt combination. Energy-absorbing materials protect fragile objects shipped in containers. Padded instrument panels, collapsible steering wheels, head restraints and air bags illustrate this principle in automobiles. The benefits of an air bag/seat belt combination become readily apparent when you realize that at least 70 percent of all vehicle-occupant fatalities are drivers. Of these deaths, approximately 70 percent are caused by injuries to the upper chest, neck and lower face. An air bag/safety belt combination helps keep the driver from coming in contact with the steering wheel and column.

Set a good example. One final point about safety belts applies to you if you have passengers in the car. You set a good example if you wear your safety belt whenever children ride with you. By insisting that they also wear safety belts, you can help them develop a habit that may save their lives.

Lock the doors. Locked doors may be less likely to open in a rollover or side collision, and can decrease the possibility of the driver or passengers being ejected. Wear your lap/shoulder belt drawn up snugly, even in an air bag-equipped vehicle, to reduce the chance of being thrown from the vehicle or tossed around inside in the event of a collision. Studies show you are likely to suffer less severe injuries if you are restrained inside the vehicle in a crash rather than ejected. Safety belts also keep you in place so you can control the vehicle and perhaps avoid a collision altogether.

The collision. In any motor vehicle crash, there is usually more than one collision. Although a vehicle decelerates rapidly in a collision, unsecured occupants continue to move. The first collision occurs between the vehicle and another vehicle, an abutment, a tree or some other object. The second collision occurs a fraction of a second later between the occupants and some part of the vehicle's interior. A third collision generally occurs a fraction of a second after the second collision. This is when the body's internal organs strike other body parts such as the ribs or the skull. The first collision causes vehicular and possible property damage. The second and third collisions may result in occupant injury or death.

The three-collision concept.

Minimizing the first collision. If you are packaged safely inside the vehicle, what can you do to minimize the first collision? Be constantly alert to the environment and stay focused on driving. If you use the vehicle's maneuverability to maintain control, in many cases you can change the nature and consequences of the collision.

HOW *to* **DRIVE**

Choose how to collide. If a collision appears unavoidable, perhaps you can choose an off-road path. A head-on collision with another vehicle or an immovable object such as a tree, pole or bridge abutment is the worst type of collision. If possible, steer to the right side of the road when you take evasive action. Steering left to avoid a collision is more likely to bring you into the path of oncoming traffic.

Hit with a glancing blow. Another general rule is to hit an object with a glancing blow (at an angle) rather than head-on. For example, many collisions have been minor because the vehicle has sideswiped a guardrail, bounced off, and the driver maintained steering control.

Choose what to hit. If you have the opportunity to decide what to hit, choose something that gives, such as a bush or other object capable of absorbing some of the energy.

Take the hit at or behind your rear wheels. If you see you are about to be involved in a crash, adjust your speed and steer so you can hit, or be hit, at or behind the rear wheels. Such actions substantially reduce impact forces and allow the vehicle to spin instead of absorbing the force of the vehicle that strikes it.

Recognize that it can happen. No one can predict in advance exactly what to do to minimize the effects of a collision. Each situation presents different possibilities. Time is limited in emergencies, so it becomes impossible to judge what each person can or cannot do when a collision appears inevitable. By accepting the fact that a collision can happen to you, you will be taking a step in the right direction. Data indicate that about one in ten drivers, and one in two new drivers, will be involved in a crash of some type each year.

REMEMBER: Only one-tenth of a second is enough to turn a fender bender into a potentially fatal collision.

If You Are Involved in a Collision

Know what to do. Even competent drivers sometimes become involved in a crash. It does not matter who is at fault. A collision can cause human suffering, loss of time, legal problems and great expense. Doing the right thing at the right time might save a life or minimize injuries. Therefore, all drivers should know what to do if they become involved in a traffic collision.

Responsibility. Drivers and owners of motor vehicles must be prepared to assume legal and financial responsibilities if they are involved in a collision. People are liable for actions that cause injury or damage to others or their property. Being prepared can lessen, and often prevent, legal problems.

Duties at the Scene of a Collision

Stop immediately. If you are driving a vehicle involved in a collision, you must stop your vehicle at the scene, or as near as possible, and try to avoid obstructing traffic. In some jurisdictions, vehicles must remain unmoved until a police officer arrives. In others, unless someone has been injured, the vehicles are to be moved from the roadway if they can be driven. All states apply severe penalties to drivers who flee the scene of a collision (hit-and-run drivers).

Assist the injured. Your first duty in the event of a collision is to quickly check for injured people and call 911. Make the injured comfortable but do not move them unless there is a risk of another collision or fire. You do not want your good intentions to result in further injury to anyone. If you are certified to render first aid, administer basic first aid to address blocked breathing, shock and severe bleeding.

HOW to DRIVE

Control the scene. After checking for injuries, take steps to prevent further damage or injury:

- If possible, post someone near the scene to warn approaching traffic.
- Place warning flares or reflective triangles several hundred feet in back of, and in front of, the crash site to warn approaching drivers. Be extra careful of approaching vehicles when you set out warning devices or examine your vehicle.
- Turn on hazard flashers. At night, leave on the low-beam headlights.
- If a disabled vehicle must remain on the road, stay as far away from the vehicle as possible.

Even when damage is slight, notify police so they can investigate and file a report.

Notify the police. The law requires you to notify the police immediately when your vehicle is involved in a collision that results in personal injury, death or property damage over a specific dollar amount. Call the law enforcement agency that has jurisdiction in the area where the collision occurs. Even when there seem to be no injuries or property damage, you should notify the proper authority immediately so an officer can investigate the collision. The officer's report may help later if a liability claim is filed.

A report must be submitted to the state. If a police officer is not present at the scene, a report still must be submitted within a specified number of days following a collision. Regardless of which driver is at fault, the state can suspend the driver's license of any person who fails to make such a report. Report forms are available from local police departments and auto insurance companies. As a general rule, these reports are confidential and cannot be used as evidence in any civil or criminal trial that results from the collision.

Remain at the scene. Unless your injuries force you to do otherwise, do not leave the crash scene until you have helped the injured, protected the crash scene and talked with a police officer. Make notes and diagrams, including weather and road conditions, to help you complete the necessary state and insurance collision reports. If you have a camera, taking photographs of the scene can also provide important documentation of the event.

If you are involved in a crash, exchange information such as names, addresses, vehicle registration numbers, driver's license numbers and names of insurance companies.

Exchange required information. If you are driving a vehicle involved in a collision, you should exchange information with the other driver and any passengers. Give each other your names, addresses, vehicle identification numbers and registration numbers. Both drivers must show their driver's licenses when requested. Passengers must provide the required information when the driver is physically unable to do so. Any crash witnesses also should be identified.

Notify your insurance carrier. Be sure to contact your insurance representative promptly to ensure proper claims filing.

Unattended vehicle or property. Should you hit an unattended vehicle or property, try to inform the owner. If you cannot locate the owner, attach a written notice with the required information to the vehicle or property. Write down the license number of the other vehicle, if what you hit was another vehicle.

Stopping when not personally involved. You have a moral responsibility to stop if you come upon a collision and assistance is needed. Be sure to find a safe place to pull off the roadway. Drive on if there is adequate assistance available, because stopping may create additional problems.

Know what to say. What you say or do may be very important in the follow-up of a collision. Do not argue, accuse anyone, admit fault or sign any statement except as required by police. No one can force you — at the crash scene, police headquarters or elsewhere — to give an opinion about the crash's cause. You might have the right to consult an attorney before you make any statement.

Financial responsibility. Motor vehicle owners must assume financial responsibility for their driving actions and those of others permitted to use their vehicles. In many cases, both the driver and the owner may be liable for injuries to passengers or others.

HOW to DRIVE

Adverse Driving Conditions and Emergencies

Study and respond to each of the following questions. Then review the chapter to see if your responses are correct.

Multiple Choice:

1. _____ occurs when water between the tires and the road builds until the tires begin to ride on a film of water, resulting in loss of traction.

   a. Hydroplaning
   b. Hydrolocking
   c. Aqualocking
   d. Tire skipping

2. To avoid a collision, you can use:

   a. Evasive steering
   b. Evasive braking
   c. Evasive acceleration
   d. All of the above

3. A(n) _____ skid occurs when your front tires begin to lose contact with the road surface.

   a. Power
   b. Understeer
   c. Oversteer
   d. Fishtail

4. If you begin to experience a skid, the best response is to _____.

   a. Downshift to a lower gear
   b. Turn on the emergency flashers
   c. Continue to look and steer where you want the vehicle to go
   d. Smoothly apply the brakes

5. If you believe that your brakes may have failed, your first action should be to _____.

   a. Position warning devices at 100- and 200-foot increments behind your car
   b. Scrape against a solid surface to reduce speed
   c. Downshift to a lower gear
   d. Pump the brakes

Short Answer:

1. Name five rules that will help reduce the challenges of night driving.

2. Explain the process of executing an off-road recovery.

3. List five types of vehicle failures and how you would avoid or compensate for them.

4. Explain the "three-collision concept."

5. Explain your duties if you are driving a vehicle involved in a collision.

HOW to DRIVE

CHAPTER 15

Purchasing and Insuring a Vehicle

Chapter Objectives:

◆ Explain the factors to consider when purchasing a vehicle.
◆ Define financial responsibility.
◆ Identify and explain the types of automobile insurance.
◆ List guidelines for selecting and buying insurance.
◆ Explain the need to evaluate insurance rates when you buy a new vehicle.

Purchasing a Vehicle

Significant commitment. Buying a vehicle represents a significant commitment in terms of expense and responsibility. Operating a vehicle over time is a process, not a one-time event. A vehicle is one of the largest purchases a person makes, and it is critical to find the right vehicle for you. When preparing to purchase a vehicle, consider three main factors: safety, reliability, and affordability.

Safety

A midsize sedan is a better choice than a van, SUV or sports car.

It is critical to choose a vehicle with features that can help prevent crashes and minimize injuries. You may be thinking "sporty," but you should think twice about buying a car that could tempt you to speed or drive recklessly. Also, a midsize sedan is a better choice than a van or sport utility vehicle (SUV) because such "top-heavy" vehicles are more susceptible to rolling over in a crash.

Consider a late-model vehicle equipped with safety features such as:

◆ Anti-lock braking system (ABS).

◆ Daytime running lights (DRLs).

◆ Electronic stability control (ESC).

◆ Multiple airbags.

◆ Adjustable/lockable head restraints.

Ask your AAA office for a copy of *Buying a Safer Car,* which provides crash-test ratings for a wide range of vehicles. For more information, visit AAA.com or safercar.gov.

Reliability

Vehicle reliability. Peace of mind is an important factor for new drivers. Selecting and maintaining a reliable vehicle can prevent most breakdowns. When vehicle shopping, consider these tips:

◆ **Look for a warranty.** Select a vehicle with a remaining warranty or purchase an extended warranty. AAA can help you find sources for extended warranties.

◆ **Avoid excessive mileage.** A car driven beyond standard mileage for its age may mean heavy or abusive driving that could lead to abnormal wear on components.

◆ **Check the history.** Review all maintenance and crash-repair histories. AAA members can obtain a CARFAX vehicle history report at a discount through AAA.com. It can help you learn about possible past crashes and damage due to floods or other causes.

◆ **Conduct a pre-purchase inspection.** Have the vehicle inspected at a repair facility to ensure that it is roadworthy, mechanically sound, and equipped with operational safety components. AAA Approved Auto Repair facilities offer this service for a nominal fee.

Think twice about older vehicles. Though relatively inexpensive to purchase, they can cost more to maintain in the long run and often get poor gas mileage. They also might not feature important safety systems.

HOW *to* **DRIVE**

Affordability

Total costs involved. Owning and operating a vehicle can be costly. But there are ways to minimize both the initial costs of buying a vehicle and the ongoing operating costs. Smart buying decisions up front can make the difference.

The cost of the vehicle. You may have your heart set on a new car, but it could be out of your price range. Your best solution might be to buy a previously-owned model. Research all the options to determine the best investment. In order to avoid paying too much for a vehicle, do your homework and investigate the market. AAA clubs also can provide pre-owned vehicle pricing information by year, make and model.

Consider a certified used car. Many auto manufacturers have certification programs that offer low-mileage vehicles that were leased or have had only one owner. Certified vehicles typically feature an extension of the factory warranty, offering increased peace of mind. This option typically is more expensive but could pay off in the long run with increased safety, reliability and resale value.

Operating costs. Beyond the initial purchase price, you should expect ongoing expenses to operate your vehicle, such as insurance, maintenance, repairs and fuel. Insurance costs can be especially high for teenagers. Research your insurance options and explore opportunities to obtain discounts by completing a driver training program and/or providing proof of good grades.

Fuel costs. Every motor vehicle consumes some form of fuel. Vehicles that get good mileage are easier on the wallet — and the environment. Ask your AAA club for a copy of *Gas Watcher's Guide*, a AAA brochure that provides tips and other information for maximizing miles per gallon.

Alternatively-powered vehicles. While most vehicles are powered purely by gasoline, other options are available. Alternatively-powered vehicles have the potential to use less fuel per mile traveled, have less impact on the environment, or both.

Diesel. Vehicles powered by diesel, including biodiesel, tend to get more miles per gallon than gasoline-powered vehicles. However, diesel fuel may not be as readily available as gasoline. More popular in Europe, diesel vehicles are expected to become more prevalent in the U.S. over the next few years.

Ethanol. Ethanol, a form of alcohol, is sometimes mixed with gasoline to reduce the amount of petroleum used while driving. Although ethanol produces fewer harmful emissions, it contains less energy per unit than gasoline, and thus does not provide as many miles per gallon.

Electric. Some vehicles are powered entirely by electricity. These vehicles do not have an internal combustion motor, and thus emit no harmful emissions. Range is more limited than that of gasoline- or diesel-powered vehicles, but battery technology is expected to improve to allow greater range.

Hybrids. Hybrid vehicles feature two forms of propulsion; a gasoline motor and an electric motor. The electric motor is powered by a battery pack that is charged by the vehicle's brakes and the gasoline engine. Because the two motors operate together, hybrid vehicles' gasoline motors can be smaller, using less fuel and emitting fewer harmful gases. In some hybrids, the gasoline motor remains inactive as long as the electric motor can generate enough power to meet the driver's immediate needs. Some hybrid vehicles allow the vehicle to be plugged into an electrical socket while parked to increase the amount of electric energy stored in the battery. Other models convert the friction caused by braking into additional energy (regenerative braking), tending to result in higher mileage in the city.

Other power sources. Other fuels used to power vehicles include compressed natural gas and liquid hydrogen. Vehicles that run on solar power are also being explored. In the future, drivers may have many more vehicle fuel options than currently exist.

HOW to DRIVE

Insuring a Vehicle

The most common types of automobile insurance. Auto insurance is complicated and may be confusing. Different policies, terms and conditions influence the cost. Below are listed the most common types of insurance. Note that insurance laws vary from state to state. For additional information, contact an insurance agent who can explain the coverage available in your area.

Liability. The purpose of liability insurance is to protect you from claims made by others who suffer injury or loss in a crash in which you may be declared at fault. Liability insurance is the most important motor vehicle insurance protection you can have. If you cannot pay for damages you have caused, the court could mandate the sale of your real estate and personal property. Also, your license could be suspended until a judgment is satisfied. Your liability insurance policy protects you and anyone else who has permission to drive your vehicle.

Bodily injury liability coverage insures you for injury or death to others.

There are two types of liability insurance:

1. **Bodily injury:** For injury or death to others, up to the amount of the coverage provided by the policy.

2. **Property damage:** For property that belongs to others, up to the amount of coverage provided by the policy.

Property damage liability coverage insures you for damages you cause to the property of others.

Medical payment. Medical payment coverage includes medical, hospital or funeral expenses. It covers you and any passengers injured or killed in your vehicle. In some circumstances, it pays expenses for you or others injured or killed while riding in, or struck by, someone else's vehicle. Medical payment coverage pays regardless of who causes the crash. The amount of payment is determined by the policy.

Collision. Collision insurance covers damage to your vehicle caused by a collision. This part of your policy covers repairs to your vehicle regardless of who is at fault. For example, collision insurance covers damage to your vehicle if you run off the road. Your collision coverage also pays for repairs if your unattended vehicle is damaged by another's vehicle and the owner of the other vehicle does not assume responsibility for the damage.

Comprehensive coverage insures you against damage caused by hail, theft, falling objects, floods and vandalism.

Comprehensive. Comprehensive insurance covers damage to your vehicle caused by something other than a collision, such as fire, theft, falling objects, explosions, earthquakes, windstorms, hail, floods or vandalism.

Uninsured motorist. Uninsured motorist coverage protects you and your passengers from bodily injury losses caused by an uninsured or hit-and-run driver legally liable for the damage. If you do not have this coverage and are involved in a crash with a person who has no liability insurance and is unable to pay, you may have to assume your costs, even though you are not at fault. Many states now require inclusion of uninsured motorist coverage in all automobile liability policies.

No-fault insurance. With conventional insurance, the driver found not-at-fault must collect either from the at-fault driver or that driver's insurance company. The process can involve months or even years of legal action. With no-fault insurance, the injured party can collect from his or her own insurance company without litigation. For more serious incidents, the injured party still can use the courts to collect from the other party's insurance company. The advantage of no-fault insurance is that the injured party gets immediate financial relief without costly legal action.

HOW *to* **DRIVE**

Deductible. Because full collision coverage is costly, most motorists carry a deductible policy — usually between $100 and $500. In this instance, if you are involved in a crash, you would pay the first $100 (or $500) of collision costs, and your insurance company would pay the balance. Accepting a higher deductible can help reduce insurance costs.

Selecting Insurance

Amount and cost of coverage. Many factors influence the amount and cost of motor vehicle insurance.

Know what to buy. The most important protection against financial loss from a collision is liability insurance, which covers damages to other people. A second type of loss is injury to you or your passengers, and you need medical payment insurance to cover that.

Deductibles, collision and comprehensive coverage. Decisions concerning deductibles, as well as collision and comprehensive coverage, are personal ones. Your need for collision and comprehensive insurance coverage depends on the age and value of your vehicle. In some cases, the savings on annual premiums over a period of years may cover any damages that might occur. Another factor to consider is the risk of theft or vandalism in your neighborhood.

Proper insurance coverage is like an invisible shield.

Know how much coverage you need. State laws set a minimum amount of money or security that drivers are required to show as proof of financial responsibility in the event of a collision. This amount is usually expressed in figures such as 25/50/10. These figures, for instance, mean you must be able to pay up to $25,000 for bodily injury or death to any one person, $50,000 for bodily injury or death to one or more people in any one occurrence and $10,000 for damage to the property of others.

Cheaper than a legal judgment. Although these amounts may sound high, judgments against you awarded by a court of law may be much higher. Considering the rate of inflation and recent court awards to victims of auto collisions, the limits stated may be inadequate. Increasing the amount of insurance coverage does not necessarily mean a sharp increase in premiums. Contact your insurance agent to determine what limits are best for you.

Compare policy conditions and exclusions. A policy is a contract that provides protection against specified types of financial loss. It spells out your rights and responsibilities as well as those of the insurance company. The policy also describes the kinds, amounts and conditions of coverage. These conditions establish the circumstances that must exist or be met by you and the insurance company in various situations. For example, policies spell out grounds for canceling the contract and reporting a claim.

Consider the costs associated with settling claims before you decide how much insurance coverage you need.

Compare costs. Variations in policy provisions may cause differences in the costs of automotive insurance. When you compare companies, be sure the policy provisions and coverage are similar. Get a full explanation from an agent before you decide.

Special rates. Many factors determine the total cost of auto insurance. Your coverage, the number of miles you drive, your age, where you live, your vehicle, who drives it, driving records, car or van pooling, and many other factors all affect insurance costs. You should find out about the various discounts available. Here are some factors to consider:

1. **Safe driving record.** Some companies offer discounts to those who drive a set number of years without a collision or traffic ticket. However, if you have one collision or traffic ticket, these companies may charge much higher renewal premiums than other companies.

2. **Two or more cars with the same company.** Most companies offer a discount for a second or third car.

HOW to DRIVE

3. **Student.** Some companies give a discount for young drivers who maintain high grade-point averages.

4. **Driver education credit.** Some companies give an additional discount to young drivers who successfully complete a standard course in driver education. A similar discount might be available to adults who voluntarily complete a classroom or an Internet-based driver improvement program.

5. **Occupation and habits.** Some companies offer more favorable rates to teachers, former military officers, government employees, farm bureau members, nondrinkers and other special groups.

6. **Safety features.** Vehicles equipped with safety features such as airbags, anti-lock brakes, alarm systems and tracking systems also may earn you a discount.

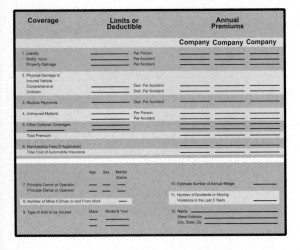

Consider insurance rates when you shop for a vehicle.

The make and model of the vehicle you drive can make quite a difference in your insurance rates. Before you decide to buy that high performance sports car, check the cost and availability of insurance. On the other hand, a low-horsepower, compact vehicle may earn you a discount. In addition, a three- to five-year-old used vehicle with low mileage may cost less to insure because its market value has decreased.

Check with your insurance company first.

Under any circumstances, always check with your insurance company before you buy or lease a vehicle. When you finance a new or used vehicle, the dealer or finance company may include the cost of insurance as part of the monthly payment. Be careful: such insurance coverage may consist of only collision and comprehensive to protect the dealer or finance company against damage to the vehicle. Because the insurance may not include liability and medical payments coverage to protect you, you should discuss your coverage with an independent insurance agent.

Shop around. Once you decide on the amount and kind of coverage you need, shop around for the best deal. You may be surprised to find a wide difference in insurance costs. This is partly because some companies have more claims and higher operating costs. Others may write insurance only in a limited geographical area or to a special class of people. Look for an insurer with adequate claims service in your community and a reputation for timely claims handling.

Changing insurance companies. If you wish to change companies before your current policy expires, be sure to get a firm commitment from the new company. When you cancel your insurance with one company, you are entitled to a refund for the unused portion of the premium paid. Companies may lower or raise premiums subject to changing conditions.

Rental Vehicles and Insurance

When you rent a vehicle. It is important to check all of your insurance options when renting a vehicle. Car rental companies must offer you the option of purchasing collision and liability insurance, usually at a set rate per day. However, before you select this option, check your own automobile insurance policy to see if you are covered. Many credit card companies also offer rental vehicle protection.

Loss-damage waiver. For an additional fee, rental companies also offer a loss-damage waiver, which relieves you of any liability for loss or damage to the vehicle. Such waivers cover only the vehicle.

Check for restrictions. Always check for restrictions in the vehicle-rental contract. For example, there may be geographic restrictions that prevent you from driving out of the state or country, or the insurance may cover only the driver, not passengers. In addition, the insurance may be void if the car is kept beyond the return date unless you request a rental extension.

TEST **15**

Purchasing and Insuring a Vehicle

Study and respond to each of the following questions. Then review the chapter to see if your responses are correct.

Multiple Choice:

1. Generally, the safest type of vehicle for a new driver is a:
   a. Sport-utility vehicle (SUV)
   b. Sports car
   c. Full-size van
   d. Mid-size sedan

2. When shopping for a vehicle, you should:
   a. Investigate the market
   b. Consider a previously-owned model
   c. Consider a certified used car
   d. All of the above

3. The most important protection against financial loss from a collision is _____ insurance, which covers damages to other people.
   a. Comprehensive
   b. Collision
   c. Liability
   d. Uninsured motorist

4. _____ protects you and your passengers from bodily injury losses caused by an uninsured or hit-and-run driver legally liable for the damage.
   a. Comprehensive
   b. Collision
   c. Liability
   d. Uninsured motorist

5. _____ insurance covers damage to your vehicle caused by something other than a collision.
   a. Comprehensive
   b. Collision
   c. Liability
   d. Uninsured motorist

Short Answer:

1. Describe three tips to maximize reliability when shopping for a vehicle.

2. Describe three vehicle operating costs.

3. List and describe three alternatively-powered vehicles.

4. Explain the two types of liability insurance.

5. Identify three factors that may qualify you for an insurance premium discount.

CHAPTER 16

Consumer's Guide to Economical and Trouble-Free Driving

Chapter Objectives:

- Explain why it is important to read the owner's manual for the vehicle you drive.
- Describe techniques to minimize fuel consumption.
- Describe vehicle problems that could develop to which you should be alert.
- Explain how to minimize air pollution resulting from vehicle exhaust.
- Describe your vehicle's various systems and how their proper operation affects your safety when driving.
- Describe how to maintain a vehicle.

HOW *to* **DRIVE**

Economical, Trouble-Free Driving

Efficient, safe, economical operation. It is important to know how to operate your vehicle efficiently, safely and economically. Fuel and maintenance are a driver's biggest ongoing costs. Keeping them under control can result in substantial savings, both for you and the environment. Tailpipe emissions are harmful to the environment, so it is critical to drive with economy in mind and maintain your vehicle for optimal efficiency.

Driving for Maximum Fuel Economy and Minimal Impact on the Environment

How you drive can significantly affect the amount of fuel you use. By developing fuel-saving driving habits, you can increase your fuel economy and decrease the impact on the environment throughout your driving career.

Starting. Avoid excessive idling upon startup. It only takes a few seconds for modern vehicles' fluids and engines to warm up enough to drive without risk of damage.

Idling. When stopped on the roadway, do not turn your vehicle off unless you will be idling for an extended period of time, such as waiting at a construction area or road blockage due to emergency vehicles.

Accelerating. Vehicles use the greatest amount of fuel when accelerating. As the rate of acceleration increases, more and more fuel is used. Accelerate slowly and smoothly to increase fuel economy and decrease tailpipe emissions.

Braking. When you need to decelerate, either to reduce speed or to come to a stop, lift off the accelerator as early as reasonably possible. To slow to a lower speed, you may not need to apply the brakes. If you must come to a stop, avoid continuing at a higher speed and having to use the brakes harder than necessary as you near the stop point.

Cruising speed. Vehicles run most efficiently at a constant speed. That is one reason most vehicles achieve maximum fuel economy on the highway where there are fewer reasons to change speed than in the city. Always maintain adequate space between your vehicle and the vehicle ahead, and use your vehicle's cruise control when possible. Avoid using cruise control in slick conditions, however, as slippery pavement warrants having as much immediate manual control of the accelerator as possible. Unless you are towing or driving up a steep grade, use overdrive gear, which minimizes engine revolutions and increases fuel economy.

Other fuel-saving techniques include:

- **Parking.** When possible, pull through parking spots so you can drive forward when leaving. This minimizes the number of times you move your vehicle from a dead stop.

- **Route planning.** Before driving, carefully plan your route to include all of your destinations. This can help reduce the total number of trips you need to make during the week.

- **Look ahead.** Looking far enough ahead can help you minimize speed changes, and identify potential risks well in advance. You may find it useful to look through the vehicle ahead, if possible. Never fixate on the vehicle directly ahead of you — you could miss important cues to possible risks.

- **Turns.** If you regularly drive a route with a left turn where you end up idling for an extended time while waiting to complete your turn, consider making three right turns instead — it may save both time and fuel.

- **Carpooling.** Consider carpooling, where you share driving responsibilities with others. This helps reduce the number of vehicles on the road, tailpipe emissions and your personal fuel costs.

- **Vehicle preparation.** Roof racks and other vehicle attachments can increase your vehicle's wind resistance significantly. This requires more energy to move your vehicle through the air, which increases fuel use. When such attachments are not being used, remove them to obtain maximum mileage.

It makes sense. Efforts to save fuel can pay off — literally. You will minimize your fuel costs, as well as your impact on the environment. Always remember to be smooth with your steering and pedal inputs, and never sacrifice safety for any reason.

HOW to **DRIVE**

Tires and brakes probably are the most important safety features on your vehicle.

Tire pressure not only affects fuel mileage, it also greatly affects tire life and the traction that a vehicle's tires provide. That is one reason that tires are often considered the most important part on a vehicle.

Never skimp on tires. People who skimp on tires are cheating themselves. When you drive, four small patches of rubber are all that is in contact with the road. Never shortchange yourself — always have proper tires with adequate tread and a reliable spare. Replace tires when the tread wear indicator bars show across the tread. When purchasing new tires, do not let cost be the only factor. Quality, tread life, temperature rating and traction rating should all be considered.

Traction. On smooth, clean, dry surfaces, the amount of tread on your tires has little effect on braking distance and traction. However, on wet surfaces and in snow and mud, the amount of tread is a critical traction factor. Adequate tread depth helps evacuate water from under the tires. Tires with low tread depth double the risk of hydroplaning on wet surfaces and are more likely to blow out if they hit an obstacle. Plus, bald tires are twice as likely as new tires to go flat.

Checking tread depth. Place a quarter into several tread grooves across the width of the tire. If part of Washington's head is always covered by the tread, your tires have more than 4/32 of a inch of tread depth remaining and are safe for use. If the top of Washington's head is exposed at any point, you should replace the tires.

Tire types. Composed of two or more layers of cords covered by rubber tread, tires come in a variety of designs and construction. Each type of tire has certain advantages and disadvantages. For the greatest safety, do not mix different types of tires. To help consumers make informed choices when purchasing passenger car tires, the Uniform Tire Quality Grading Standards give information about tread wear, traction and temperature resistance.

Rotating tires. Usually tires do not wear at the same rate. To equalize wear, rotate the position of the tires according to the manufacturer's recommended interval and pattern. Most new cars come with an emergency-only space-saver spare tire that cannot be rotated among the others for regular tire use. After rotating the tires, be sure each tire is inflated to the proper pressure according to the vehicle manufacturer's recommendation.

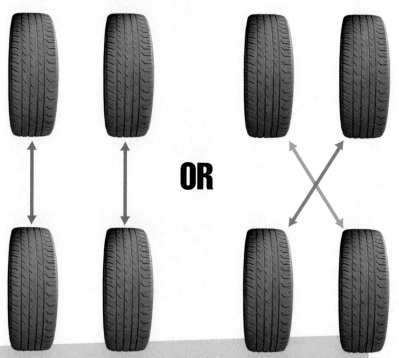

Rotate tires according to the manufacturer's recommended interval. Check your owner's manual for the appropriate rotation pattern.

HOW *to* **DRIVE**

Alignment and balancing. Uneven tire wear means that the wheels need to be aligned or balanced. If your steering wheel vibrates, you may need to have your wheels balanced. Excessive wear of tread edges may mean the tires are under-inflated. Some cars also may require rear-wheel alignment.

Under-inflated tires may look fine—always check the pressure to make sure.

Proper inflation. A summary report by AAA on more than 134,000 cars tested at automotive diagnostic centers over a 10-year period revealed that more than 42 percent had one or more tires under-inflated by at least four pounds. An under-inflated tire may look perfectly normal, so air pressure in the tires, including the spare, should be checked with an accurate tire gauge at least once a month. Tire pressure should be tested when the tire is cold, before the vehicle has been driven. Carry an accurate gauge unless you are sure of the accuracy of a service-station gauge.

Under-inflation by 20 percent decreases fuel economy and has the same effect on a tire as a 30 percent increase in speed. While it may result in a somewhat firmer ride, inflating tires to the pressures recommended for long-distance, high-speed travel will provide greater tread life.

How much air pressure? You can find the vehicle's recommended air pressure in your owner's manual or on a placard typically located on the driver's doorjamb. The placard may also be located in the glove box or inside the trunk lid or fuel filler door.

Maintaining Your Vehicle for Maximum Economy and Minimum Expense

Prevention is key. You need not be a mechanic to ensure economical and trouble-free driving. Simply maintain your vehicle according to the manufacturer's specifications. Stay alert for signs that something is not working properly and either fix it or have it repaired before there is a malfunction. It is important to prevent problems before they occur.

Technology has lengthened the maintenance intervals for most newer models. Read your owner's manual carefully and follow the maintenance schedules designed especially for your vehicle and driving habits to help reduce costly repairs and increase fuel economy.

Know what to do. You should be familiar with different vehicle systems so you can detect when something is not operating properly. It is important to know the condition of your vehicle's battery, coolant, belts, hoses, tires, oil, windshield wipers and brakes. In general, know what to do to keep your vehicle in peak working condition.

Fuel System

Use the correct fuel. Some drivers mistakenly believe using a higher octane fuel will increase the performance of all vehicles. It will not. Using a higher octane fuel than your vehicle requires is a waste of money and may cause your vehicle to run less efficiently. Check your owner's manual for the correct octane requirements.

Gasoline typically is offered in several octane ratings. Check your owner's manual for the recommended octane rating for your vehicle.

Most modern computer-controlled vehicles are equipped with a system that prevents engine knock. If your engine still knocks when using the recommended grade of fuel, go up one grade at a time until you find the lowest-octane fuel that eliminates engine knocking when you accelerate or drive up a steep hill.

Exhaust System

Prevent carbon monoxide problems. The exhaust pipe, catalytic converter, muffler and tail pipe should be checked annually for pinholes, rust and looseness. Any part of the exhaust system that does not function properly can limit vehicle performance.

A leaking muffler can also allow escaping carbon monoxide — a deadly gas — to enter the interior of the vehicle. To prevent carbon monoxide from building up, never run the engine of your vehicle in an enclosed area such as a garage, other than to start the vehicle to move it.

Change the engine oil and filter on the schedule shown in your vehicle's owner's manual.

Lubricating System

Maintain oil levels. Consult your owner's manual for information on how to check your engine's oil level, what type of oil to use and how often it should be changed. Intervals between oil changes, which once were typically 3,000 miles, now vary from vehicle to vehicle upward to 7,500 miles. An increasing number of vehicles have electronic systems that monitor operating conditions and let the driver know when an oil change is required.

Never let the oil get too low. Engine oil serves two purposes: it lubricates and it cools. Low oil levels can make an engine run hot, which increases wear. Insufficient oil can cause a loss of oil pressure that will destroy an engine. Any unusual oil pressure gauge reading means you should check the oil level. If the vehicle is equipped with a warning light instead of a gauge and the light comes on, immediately and safely pull off the roadway, shut off the engine and do not restart it until the cause of the problem has been determined.

Check the oil level regularly. It is best to follow the suggestions in the owner's manual regarding regular lubrication, filter changes and the grade and weight of oil to use.

Cooling System

Check it out. When a vehicle's cooling system works properly, the engine temperature is controlled within a narrow range for maximum efficiency. Every time your vehicle is at a service facility for an oil change, ask the technician to check the coolant level, drive belts, radiator, radiator hoses and heater hoses. Remember that too much heat can destroy an engine, and too little robs it of power and fuel economy. Taking a little time to ensure the cooling system is working properly is worth the effort.

Use antifreeze year-round to prevent freezing and overheating.

Seasonal Checks. In cold climates, check your vehicle's cooling system each fall and spring. Normally, antifreeze should be checked and added, if necessary, before the first freeze. Be certain your vehicle is protected for the lowest temperatures expected. Because it also helps prevent overheating, antifreeze must be used throughout the year.

Changing coolant. The previous standard of changing engine coolant every two years may not apply if your vehicle is only a few years old. Many newer vehicles have been designed with coolant that lasts up to five years or more than 100,000 miles. Consult the owner's manual for information on the coolant used in your vehicle. Always use the coolant type and change interval recommended by the manufacturer. A 50/50 solution of coolant and water is the usual mixture. Changing coolant when recommended will prevent rust buildup and corrosion.

Temperature gauge. When you drive, check the temperature gauge or indicator light frequently. Unusual readings may indicate strain on the engine from coolant loss, a clogged radiator, broken drive belt, sticky thermostat or low-oil level. If the warning light comes on, or if the gauge reads high during normal operation, stop the engine immediately and do not start it again until you find the cause of overheating.

Electrical System

Electrical system problems. Each year, electrical system failures (battery, starter, alternator and ignition) disable more vehicles than the next two vehicle breakdown causes combined. In most instances, proper maintenance can prevent such problems.

The battery. Most newer batteries are sealed and do not require periodic fluid level checks. Other than a visual inspection for corrosion on the terminals and cable ends, the only way to determine the condition of a battery is to test it with equipment designed for that purpose. Some batteries have an indicator "eye" on top that allows a quick check of condition. Generally, if the indicator is colored, the battery has some level of charge. If the indicator is dark, the battery is discharged. And, if the indicator is light colored, the battery is low on fluid and should not be charged or used unless a proper fluid level can be restored.

Corroded battery connections are a common cause of no-start problems.

Check more frequently in winter and summer. Extreme temperatures can reduce the battery's efficiency. To enhance the charge, ensure that cable connections are tight and free of corrosion.

Other electrical components. Other parts of the electrical system also must be maintained, including ignition and charging system components, wiring and connections. Except for spark plugs and plug wires, ignition components should be serviced only by a properly trained technician. Refer to the owner's manual for service intervals.

Warning gauges and lights. Remember, without a properly functioning electrical system, starting the vehicle may be difficult or impossible, gas mileage may be reduced and the overall performance of your vehicle will be poor. During normal operation of vehicles equipped with gauges monitoring electrical functions, a voltmeter will register about 13 to 14 volts, and an ampmeter will register slightly above the midpoint of the range. If an indicator continually registers discharge, you should have the charging system checked immediately. Unlike gauges, warning lights give no advance notification. If an alternator warning light comes on, have the vehicle checked immediately.

Brake System

Brakes. Brakes, along with tires, are probably your vehicle's most important safety feature. How well the brakes work and how much they wear depend on the type of driving you do. If you brake frequently in stop-and-go traffic, have your brakes checked every 10,000 miles. You should also have your brakes checked any time they make unusual noises, or if the brake pedal pulsates when it is pressed. If your driving is a combination of city and highway miles, have the brakes checked at least every year and any time you experience difficulty.

Maintaining ABS. If your vehicle is equipped with anti-lock brakes, the maintenance schedule may require that the brake fluid be drained and replaced at regular intervals. Check your owner's manual for more information about maintaining this critical system.

Other Systems

Do not overlook wipers and bulbs. All the systems described can affect your safety, directly or indirectly. Safety checks reveal that the most obvious safety-related parts and accessories such as windshield wiper blades and turn signal bulbs are the most overlooked. Emergency equipment also should be part of your safety system check.

Windshield wipers. If wipers begin to streak or smear, it is time to replace the blades. Keep plenty of washer fluid in the reservoir, and during cold weather use a solution that helps prevent the liquid from freezing.

Lights. Burned-out light bulbs are hard to detect from the driver's seat, and create a serious safety issue. At least once a month, check turn signals, emergency flashers, brake lights, headlights and taillights. A burned-out turn signal lamp may cause a change in the speed at which the turn signal indicator flashes on the instrument panel, warning you of a problem.

How is your aim? In addition to checking headlight operation, you should also pay attention to how your headlights are aimed. If people flash their headlights while you are using your low beams, or if the road directly ahead of you is not evenly illuminated, your headlights are probably misaimed. They should be checked by a service center and aimed properly.

Emergency Equipment

Emergency equipment checklist. Properly maintained vehicles seldom become disabled. But if they do, certain equipment will be extremely helpful:

- Flashlight with fresh batteries
- Jack and a flat board for soft surfaces
- Screwdriver
- Pliers
- Lug wrench
- Wiping cloth
- Flares or reflective triangles
- Tire gauge
- Extra drive belts
- Ice scraper
- Pencil and notebook
- Gloves
- Blanket
- Jumper (booster) cables

Doing your part. While it is good to be concerned about the performance of your vehicle, you also should be concerned

about the air pollution it creates. Tailpipe emissions are harmful to the environment, and should be minimized. A properly operating engine not only emits fewer pollutants, it provides better fuel mileage.

Check your PCV system regularly. Vehicles built after 1966 have a positive crankcase ventilation system (PCV) that plays an important role in controlling engine emissions. Have the PCV system checked each time you have the engine tuned. The PCV valve should be replaced at least every 30,000 miles.

Know Your Service Center

Selecting a service center. Check your local AAA office or visit AAA.com for a list of AAA Approved Auto Repair facilities near your home or work. Never accept inferior repair work. Make sure you are not charged for work covered under warranty. Study the owner's manual and have the service manager explain any charges you do not understand. Before you buy a new vehicle, investigate the dealer's service reputation.

Routine checks. Although self-serve gasoline stations save you money, they do not provide the services of a full-service station, such as cleaning your windshield and headlights, and checking the oil and battery. Since this is not being done by someone else, it becomes your responsibility to do these things on a regular basis, or have someone else do them for you.

Taking your car in for repairs. When you take your vehicle to a service center, describe the nature of the trouble as accurately as possible. Do not try to tell the technician what you think is wrong. Describe only the symptoms. Ask that the service adviser or manager call you after an inspection to describe what needs to be done. Ask for a written estimate of all repair costs. This helps discourage unnecessary work. If you feel that you may be charged for parts that were not actually replaced, ask the shop to save and return your old parts.

Your Maintenance Checklist

Maintenance schedule. Ideally, every driver should follow the vehicle manufacturer's recommended maintenance schedule for proper upkeep of their car or truck. As a general rule, people who drive an average of 12,000 miles a year should take 15 minutes a month to check the items listed below that affect their vehicle's safety and efficiency.

Spring and fall. Depending on manufacturer recommendations, the following should be performed each spring and fall:

- Rotate tires
- Change engine oil
- Check coolant (antifreeze)
- Check brakes

Driver Inspections

When to Check	Item	What to Check
Daily	Windows	Cracks, scratches, dirt, pits
	Brakes	Pedal pressure/travel, smooth/straight stops
	Exhaust	Noise, fumes, leaks
	Steering	Steering wheel play, stiffness in steering
Weekly	Lights	Dirty lens, burned out bulbs, alignment
	Tires	Air pressure, cuts, tread wear, alignment. Remember to include spare tire.
	Under the hood	Fluids, hoses, belts, filters, connections
Monthly	Wipers	Wiper blade condition, washer fluid
Annually	Suspension	Excessive bouncing, leaning, swaying

Scheduled Inspections

Item	When to Check	What to Check
Engine oil	Check owner's manual for recommended intervals	Leaks, correct level, cleanliness
Cooling system	Every two to three years; change coolant at manufacturer's recommended intervals	Hoses, belts, radiator, water pump, heater operation
Engine tune-up	Check owner's manual for recommended intervals	Spark plugs, filters, fuel system, hoses, exhaust
Brakes	Check owner's manual for recommended intervals	Rotors, pads, drums, brake lines, fluids

Maintenance intervals may vary with different makes and models. For information on your vehicle, consult your owner's manual.

HOW to DRIVE

Consumer's Guide to Economical and Trouble-Free Driving

Study and respond to each of the following questions. Then review the chapter to see if your responses are correct.

Multiple Choice:

1. Vehicles use the greatest amount of fuel when _____.
    a. Accelerating
    b. Braking
    c. Idling
    d. Turning

2. _____ should be considered when purchasing tires.
    a. Tire quality
    b. Tread life
    c. Traction rating
    d. All of the above

3. The recommended tire air pressure can typically be found:
    a. In the owner's manual
    b. On a placard located on the driver's doorjamb
    c. On the side of the tire
    d. Both A and B

4. To be safe for use, your tires should have a minimum tread depth of _____.
    a. 2/32 of an inch
    b. 4/32 of an inch
    c. 1/4 of an inch
    d. The thickness of a quarter

5. Engine oil should be changed _____.
    a. Every 3,000 miles
    b. Every 5,000 miles
    c. Every 7,500 miles
    d. According to the maintenance schedule in your owner's manual

Short Answer:

1. Explain three driving techniques for minimizing fuel consumption.

2. Explain how to use a quarter to check tire tread depth.

3. Explain the effects of low tire pressure on fuel economy and exhaust emissions.

4. Explain how to determine the proper fuel octane level for your vehicle.

5. Identify 10 items a driver should have available in case of an emergency.

HOW *to* **DRIVE**

CHAPTER **17**

Travel Planning, Loading, Towing and Driving Special Vehicles

Chapter Objectives:

- Describe how to effectively plan for travel.
- Explain how to prepare your vehicle for travel.
- Describe the skills required for safely towing a boat or camper trailer.
- Explain the techniques required to back a trailer successfully.
- List the basic equipment needed to tow a trailer safely.
- Explain the procedure for distributing weight when loading a trailer.
- Identify your state's requirements for insurance coverage when towing a trailer, or operating a motor home or recreational vehicle.

Effective Travel Planning and Preparation

Preparing for a road trip. If you are planning an extended drive, advance preparation can pay off in terms of fewer troubles, fuel savings and enhanced safety. A little bit of time and effort before you leave will be worth it.

Planning your route. Identifying your route before you leave can help you save fuel, minimize driving time, and maximize your enjoyment of the drive. For actual route directions, consult a map or visit websites that provide travel directions. Alternatively, you can visit your local AAA branch office or visit AAA.com to obtain a TripTik™, a customized travel itinerary complete with information on attractions, restaurants, fuel stations and lodging.

Some drivers choose to use an electronic system to assist with navigation. Generally GPS-based, such devices can come integrated into the vehicle or added by the driver. With proper precautions to prevent driver distraction, these units can be very effective in helping drivers reach their destination and support a comfortable trip.

Checking your route. Be sure to check the weather and traffic reports along your route before you leave. Based on this information, you may choose to adjust your start time, or reschedule the entire trip during better driving conditions.

Preparing your vehicle. A well-prepared and maintained vehicle can be the key to a trouble-free driving trip. Be sure to fully inspect your vehicle before you leave. At a minimum, you should check your vehicle's tires (including tread depth and air pressure), belts, hoses and fluids. Alternatively, have a technician check your vehicle. AAA's Approved Auto Repair facilities offer this service at no charge or for a nominal fee.

Loading your vehicle. Be sure to take what you need, but resist overloading the vehicle. Extra weight in the vehicle results in more fuel consumed, increasing the cost of the trip. When loading a vehicle with a trunk, load the trunk area first. With all types of vehicles, be sure to secure loose items. Items not secured can become projectiles in a collision, injuring the occupants. A hairbrush or CD holder can become deadly if left loose in the vehicle.

Preparing the driver. Although a well-prepared vehicle is important, the driver is the most important factor in having a safe road trip. If you are not ready to drive, do not begin the trip.

Start fresh. Get plenty of rest before you start your trip. Rather than starting a drive late at night, it is better to get a good night's rest and leave in the morning.

Drive during waking hours. Always drive during the time you are normally awake. This will help minimize the chance of your falling asleep while driving, and maximize your alertness during the daytime. Also, avoid driving more than 500 miles per day. This will allow you to get adequate rest between days spent driving. If you feel yourself getting sleepy, stop in a safe place and get some rest. Attempting to "push through" to your destination while tired can be dangerous.

Stop periodically. Be sure to stop regularly for breaks. One rule of thumb is to stop every two hours. Alternatively, you could stop every 100 miles. Get some exercise and fresh air during your breaks. Stretching can help ease stiff limbs resulting from sitting in the vehicle for extended periods of time. These efforts can help maintain your alertness while driving.

HOW *to* **DRIVE**

Handling Large Vehicles

Large vehicles. There are many types of large vehicles, including motor homes and recreational vehicles, moving trucks, wide-axle pickup trucks and delivery trucks. To operate these vehicles safely, it is important to understand their dimensions and limitations, as well as the special care needed to prevent collisions and other problems.

Weight Factor. Keep in mind that most large vehicles weigh much more than the average passenger sedan. This extra weight can affect your ability to accelerate, turn and slow down.

Accelerating. Heavier vehicles accelerate more slowly, so it is important to allow enough room to get up to speed. Pay careful attention when moving into gaps in traffic, and plan ahead for longer distances needed to reach cruising speed.

Turning. Heavier vehicles also tend to have a higher center of gravity, which can make turning maneuvers more challenging. Because a higher center of gravity can cause a vehicle to be more likely to roll over in abrupt turning maneuvers, it is critical to slow down well in advance of turns. It is also important to use smooth, gradual steering movements. Basically, you want to slow the rate at which the vehicle's weight shifts during turns, which will help keep the vehicle stable and less prone to rolling over.

Decelerating. Since large vehicles tend to be heavy, slowing down requires more distance than other vehicles. To allow for this, it is important to allow enough space ahead of you to bring your vehicle to a stop. This means you should allow more room between you and the vehicle ahead. Maintaining more following distance will also give you more time to safely steer around any obstacles in your path.

Handling Special Vehicles: Towing and RVs

Before you tow. Many drivers tow boats, campers and other kinds of trailers behind their vehicles. Others may drive motor homes or recreational vehicles (RVs). Before you tow a vehicle or drive an RV, you need to learn some special skills.

Trailers. Trailers come in all shapes and sizes, including utility trailers, tandem axles, horse and boat trailers, and travel trailers. Boat trailers are the most commonly used trailers today.

Load Limits. All vehicles have gross vehicle weight or weight-to-trailer towing-capacity limits, so it is critical not to exceed a vehicle's recommended load or trailer load limits. Refer to your owner's manual for information regarding these limits. This information also may be on your vehicle's doorjamb.

Practice where there is no traffic.

Regardless of how skillful you are with an automobile, you must acquire new skills when you pull a trailer or drive a motor home. Before you venture onto a busy highway, practice driving in your driveway or a vacant parking lot.

Adjusting to Special Vehicles

Starting. Bear in mind that you will experience restricted maneuverability and acceleration when pulling a trailer or driving an RV. Check traffic carefully and signal before moving. Allow a larger gap in traffic before you pull out. Start slowly and frequently check other traffic, using side mirrors. Check both side mirrors to be sure the trailer does not intrude into an adjoining lane of traffic.

Beginning to turn. How far beyond the curb line you begin to turn depends on several things: the length of your vehicle or trailer, the turning radius of the vehicle, the intersection's angle and the presence of parked vehicles. You will need practice and experience to determine the best way to make a turn. It is critical that you use the right outside mirror to check your vehicle's or trailer's clearance from the curb.

Right turns. As you prepare to turn right, watch traffic. Signal early and move farther from the curb or edge of the pavement than you would with your car. Keep the vehicle straight until the front wheels are well beyond the curb line. Then turn the steering wheel sharply right.

Right Turns

Signal early and delay turning until well beyond the curb line, using all available space in the right lane.

Left turns. When you turn left, proceed farther into the intersection than normal to allow adequate space for the trailer or motor home. Swing out wide enough so that the trailer will not cut across the center of the intersection. Carefully observe other traffic. Signal far enough in advance that other drivers can adjust to your action. Be sure to check the left outside mirror to see that you clear any vehicles waiting at the intersection. Also be sure the vehicle and trailer clear any median islands or other obstacles. You can learn a lot from watching professional truck drivers' turning techniques with semi-trailers.

Overtaking and passing. You need much more time and space to overtake and pass another vehicle. A trailer or RV's extra weight and length reduce acceleration ability and increase the distance needed to return to the right lane. Be sure there is plenty of open, straight road ahead. Check blind spots to the left and right before you pass. After you have overtaken the vehicle you are passing, be sure to check your blind areas to ensure you are far enough ahead to signal and move back into the travel lane. Guard against sudden swerves that might cause a trailer to tilt or sway, which can cause you to lose control.

Left Turns

Turning later in the intersection will keep the trailer from jumping the median island or sideswiping cars waiting at the intersection.

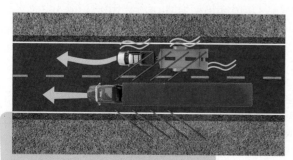

Turbulent, displaced air can make your vehicle and trailer sway. Be prepared to counter-steer.

HOW *to* **DRIVE**

Being passed and overtaken. Other drivers probably will pass you if you drive slower than they do. When a larger vehicle overtakes you, the air it displaces tends to push you to the side. Be prepared to adjust your steering to keep your vehicle and trailer under control. As the large vehicle passes, the pressure of displaced air will be rapidly reduced, causing your vehicle to move abruptly toward the passing vehicle. Be prepared to counter-steer again.

Let others pass. If you notice a lot of vehicles behind you, it is courteous to stay in the right lane or pull off the road and stop so others may pass. Use the stop as an opportunity to recheck wiring connections and the hitch if you are pulling a trailer.

Curves. It is easier to control your vehicle if you reduce speed before you enter curves. On roads that curve right, allow more distance from the edge of the pavement. Otherwise, your trailer wheels could drop to the shoulder, causing a dangerous weight shift and accelerated tire wear. Keep toward the center line. On left curves, stay to the right so you do not cross the center line.

Staying toward the center line on right curves keeps trailer wheels on the pavement and off the shoulder.

Slowing and stopping. Few recreational or utility trailers are equipped with their own braking system. Thus the towing vehicle's brakes must control the combined weight of both vehicle and trailer. Be sure to give yourself plenty of room to complete all slowing and stopping maneuvers.

Avoid sudden stops. Search for enough ahead that you avoid having to stop suddenly. Avoid high-speed lanes on highways and allow additional time and space for unfavorable road and weather conditions.

Adjusting Following Distance

Increase your following distance. Remember that the stopping distance for a large vehicle or a vehicle pulling a trailer is much greater than for a passenger sedan. That means you should increase your following distance one second for each additional 10 feet beyond 15 feet of overall vehicle and trailer length. The table on the next page summarizes the adjustments to following distances.

Vehicle	Normal Following Distance	Additional Following Distance	Total Following Distance
Automobile with no trailer	3 to 4 seconds	None needed	3 to 4 seconds
Automobile with 20-foot trailer	3 to 4 seconds	2 seconds	5 to 6 seconds
35-foot motor home	3 to 4 seconds	2 seconds	5 to 6 seconds

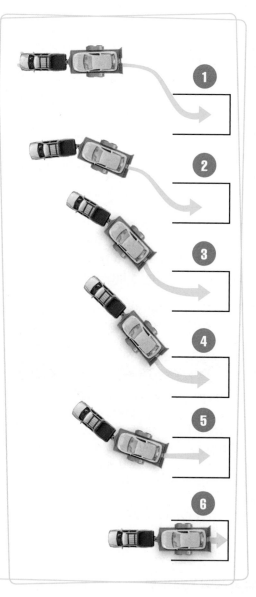

Backing a Trailer

Backing a trailer. Backing a trailer is difficult for many new trailer operators. It is best to avoid backing if possible. However, sometimes backing is necessary, so it is something you should learn to do. First, walk behind the trailer to make sure the area is clear. Then return to your vehicle and back slowly, turning the steering wheel opposite the direction you want the trailer to go. Turn the wheel right to go left. Turn the wheel left to go right.

1. To back to the left, turn the steering wheel to the right.
2. Straighten the wheel.
3. Turn the wheel in the opposite direction.
4. Straighten the wheel as the trailer responds to the towing vehicle's action.
5. Turn the steering wheel to the right.
6. Straighten the wheel and back the towing vehicle and trailer.

HOW to DRIVE

Alternative technique. Another technique is to hold the bottom of the steering wheel when backing a trailer. Move your hand in the direction you wish the trailer to turn. This technique may make it easier to remember which way to steer when backing a trailer.

Backing to the left is easier. When you back into a position that requires turning, it is easier to back the trailer to the left, where you can see over your left shoulder into the open space. (This also applies when you back an RV.)

Ask someone to help. Some people can back a trailer using only the outside mirrors. However, you might need to stop and get out of the vehicle to check for clearance before you continue to back. The best approach is to get help from a second person outside the vehicle on the driver's side. Even experts appreciate help in this difficult task.

Two common errors to avoid:

1. Turning the steering wheel too far
2. Holding the steering wheel in a turned position too long

These actions can cause the trailer and towing vehicle to jackknife.

Practice is essential. Regardless of whether you are backing a large vehicle or a trailer, practice is essential, especially when you must maneuver into a tight spot such as a parking space or driveway. Many problems associated with backing a trailer — particularly those due to limited line of sight — also apply to backing a large vehicle.

Laws and Regulations for Trailers

The driver's responsibility. Using a trailer involves driver and owner responsibility. This includes proper registration and insurance, brake requirements, lights, reflectors, towing hitches, safety chains, speed, weight and size limits. Many states require auxiliary brakes and other safety devices for all loaded trailers heavier than 40 percent of the towing vehicle's weight. Some states prohibit trailers on specially designated highways, and nearly all states prohibit passengers from riding in a trailer. Know the regulations that apply in each state where you travel.

Additional Equipment for Towing

Extra equipment. The ordinary passenger car or light truck is not designed to tow trailers. Additional equipment is necessary if you intend to use a vehicle to tow a trailer. You will need a heavy-duty suspension, an increased-capacity cooling system and a high-ratio (numerical) axle. Also, for pulling most trailers, you will need additional, oversize mirrors.

Emergency equipment. Regular emergency equipment usually is adequate for towing light trailers. However, towing a heavier boat or travel trailer requires special equipment. A hydraulic jack, red flags and flares, wheel chocks, flashlights and trouble lights, and tow chains/ropes are essential. Minor repairs may be able to be performed with pliers, a screwdriver, electrician's tape, light wire and cotter pins. You will also need an adequate jack and lug wrench to change flat tires.

Trailer hitch. For ordinary loads on utility or boat trailers, a well-engineered hitch welded or bolted to the vehicle frame should be adequate. You can buy these from auto parts stores or car dealerships. Specially developed load-equalizing hitches are available for heavier loads on all trailers. When trailer hitches are installed, include safety chains and an electrical connection for trailer brake lights and taillights.

Use the correct hitch ball. For different use classifications, automotive engineers recommend a minimum-size hitch ball for passenger car-trailer couplings. This information can be found in the trailer manual. Usually the hitch and draw-bar attachment allows a distance of 28 inches between the two vehicles. Attachments that meet Society of Automotive Engineers (SAE) standards are plainly marked.

Loading Trailers Properly

Stay under the limits. When properly loaded and hitched, the rear of your towing vehicle should support 10 to 15 percent of the trailer load. Never load your vehicle to the owner's manual limits when you tow a trailer. Assign the heaviest passenger to the front seat and load only light items in the rear seat and trunk of your vehicle.

Total weight. The total weight of the load should not exceed the weight capacity of the trailer. Arrange 60 percent of the weight in the front half of the trailer and distribute the weight equally from side to side. Place the heaviest items over the trailer wheels and toward the bottom of the load. Tightly pack and secure all items to prevent shifting.

Be sure the hitch is loaded properly, it should support 10 to 15% of the trailer's load.

Arrange 60% of the weight in the front half of the trailer.

Be sure it is level. After the tow vehicle and trailer are loaded, walk around to see if they are level. Properly loaded and hitched, the tow vehicle and trailer should be about parallel to the ground. Too much weight in the rear of the trailer will lift the rear of the towing vehicle. Too much weight in the front of the trailer will raise the towing vehicle's front end. Either of these conditions can cause steering and braking problems, and aim the headlights too low or too high. When the tow vehicle's front end is raised, it can hydroplane on wet pavement at speeds as slow as 35 mph, even if the front tires are new and properly inflated. Improper positioning of the trailer load also may cause fishtailing and increase risk of loss of control. Check the load and hitch regularly during rest stops.

Insurance Requirements

Are you covered? Before you drive an RV or tow a trailer, check with your insurance agent to determine whether your policy covers such vehicles. Additional coverage may be needed.

Care and Maintenance

Take extra care of the tow vehicle. Because the car, truck or van used for towing is often not intended for such use, you should take extra care in its maintenance. Your radiator must work at maximum efficiency in order to keep engine temperatures stable. Ensure that coolant is fresh and topped off. Change the oil and lubricate the chassis and running gear more frequently. Due to the greater load, towing speeds up tire wear. Not even heavier tires and higher air pressure will eliminate the problem entirely.

Check your trailer regularly. Trailer springs, shackles, brakes and wheel bearings need frequent inspection and lubrication. Also, inspect the trailer frame, hitch and tires at regular intervals.

Electrical system. The tow vehicle's electrical system operates additional trailer lights — stop, clearance, turn signals and brake. In some cases, the tow vehicle's electrical system also operates trailer brakes. Install a heavy duty flasher and ensure the alternator and its drive belt are in proper condition before towing.

TEST 17

Travel Planning, Loading, Towing and Driving Special Vehicles

Study and respond to each of the following questions. Then review the chapter to see if your responses are correct.

Multiple Choice:

1. If you are planning an extended drive, preparation can pay off in terms of:
   a. Fewer troubles
   b. Fuel savings
   c. Enhanced safety
   d. All of the above

2. When on an extended drive, avoid driving more than _____ miles per day.
   a. 300
   b. 400
   c. 500
   d. 800

3. You should maintain a _____following distance when driving a heavy vehicle or towing a trailer.
   a. 2–3 second
   b. 3–4 second
   c. 5–6 second
   d. 7–8 second

4. Two common errors to avoid when backing are (1) turning the steering wheel too far, and (2) _____.
   a. Holding the steering wheel in a turned position too long
   b. Turning the steering wheel too quickly
   c. Turning the steering wheel too slowly
   d. Backing too quickly

5. When you load a trailer, arrange ___ percent of the weight in the front half of the trailer.
   a. 30
   b. 40
   c. 50
   d. 60

Short Answer:

1. Explain three benefits of identifying your route before you leave on an extended drive.

2. Describe two rules of thumb regarding when to stop regularly for breaks on an extended drive.

3. Explain how the additional weight of heavy vehicles affects the ability to accelerate, turn and slow down.

4. Explain how to steer when backing with a trailer.

5. List three pieces of vehicle equipment needed to tow a trailer safely.

HOW *to* **DRIVE**

GLOSSARY

A

accelerate To increase in speed or velocity.

acceleration lane An auxiliary lane primarily for vehicles changing speeds as they enter or leave through-traffic lanes.

accelerator The gas pedal, which is linked to the throttle valve in the engine; controls speed by adjusting the flow of fuel to the engine.

adaptive cruise control A special form of speed control that aids the driver in maintaining a safe distance from the vehicle ahead, often by automatically adjusting speed to maintain the desired headway.

adhesion Traction or friction, in automotive terms.

adjacent Next to.

adverse driving conditions Weather conditions such as rain, sleet, ice, snow or fog.

administrative laws Laws that regulate driver licensing, motor vehicle registration and operation, financial responsibility, and vehicle-equipment standards.

aggressive driving Occurs when a driver operates a vehicle in a pushy, bold or otherwise unsafe manner.

airbag A safety device that automatically inflates upon impact in a frontal and/or side collision to prevent occupants from striking the vehicle's interior.

alcohol An intoxicating, depressant drug that slows down the central nervous system and impairs driving ability.

alcohol dehydrogenase An enzyme that breaks down alcohol in the stomach. Women have smaller quantities than men.

all-wheel drive A vehicle in which the engine drives all four wheels.

alternate path of travel An emergency route to be taken if the intended (immediate) travel path is suddenly blocked.

alternator A device that produces electricity in a vehicle, driven by the engine.

alignment Generally refers to wheel alignment, which is the adjustment of a vehicle's front or rear suspension for proper steering, comfortable ride, maximum traction, and minimization of tire wear.

amphetamines Drugs that speed up the central nervous system; may give the driver a false feeling of alertness such that risk is increased.

angle parking Parking so that vehicles are arranged diagonally/at an angle with a curb or other boundary.

antifreeze A substance with a low freezing point, usually added to the liquid in a vehicle's radiator to prevent freezing.

anti-lock braking system (ABS) Brake system designed to keep a car's wheels from locking when the driver brakes hard or abruptly, or applies the brakes on a slick surface.

automatic transmission A system that changes the vehicle's gears automatically.

B

banked curve A curve that is sloped up from the inside edge.

basic speed law A law that specifies that drivers must always drive at a speed that is reasonable and proper for existing road, traffic, weather, and light conditions.

barbiturates Depressant drugs that slow down the central nervous system and affect emotions, alertness, attention, judgment, and reaction time.

blind spot An area outside the vehicle that is not visible to the driver in the rear- or side-view mirrors.

blood alcohol concentration (BAC) The concentration of alcohol in a person's bloodstream, represented as a percentage; the ratio between the amounts of alcohol and blood in the body.

blood alcohol level (BAL) Same as blood alcohol concentration.

brake friction Increased friction between the tires and road surface caused by brake application, which slows the turning of the wheels.

brake pedal Pedal that enables a driver to slow or stop a vehicle; positioned to the left of the accelerator pedal.

brake system The system that enables a vehicle to slow down and stop by means of hydraulic pressure.

braking distance The distance a vehicle covers from the time the driver applies the brakes until the vehicle comes to a stop.

HOW *to* **DRIVE**

C

centrifugal force Natural force that tends to push a vehicle outward (in a straight line) when rounding a curve.

certificate of title Proof of ownership issued by the state when a motor vehicle is purchased.

circadian rhythm The body's natural cycle of energy and general functioning over a 24-hour period.

closing probability The chances that your vehicle and some other object will move closer together as you move along your projected travel path.

clutch The pedal-operated device in a manual-shift (standard) transmission vehicle that disengages the engine power from the drive wheels so that gears can be shifted.

cocaine A highly addictive stimulant drug.

collapsible steering wheel Steering wheel designed to collapse in a frontal crash to prevent injury to the driver.

collision insurance Insurance that covers the cost of repairs for collision damage to your vehicle, even if no other vehicle is involved.

collision A crash when one object hits another with sudden force.

comprehensive insurance Insurance that covers damage to your vehicle caused by something other than a collision.

compromise In risk-management terms, if faced with two or more dangerous situations, give the most room to the one with the greatest chance of happening and that has the most severe consequences.

communicate To exchange information by sending and receiving. In a vehicle, use your signals, horn, headlamps, gestures, and vehicle position.

construction warning signs Orange diamond-shaped warning signs used to advise drivers that road crews are working on or near the road.

coolant Liquid added to a vehicle's radiator to reduce heat.

countersteer To turn the steering wheel back in the opposite direction in order to maintain or regain directional control of the vehicle.

courtesy lane change A safe lane change by a driver on a highway to allow additional room for a vehicle to enter the highway

cover-brake position Placing the toes of the foot over, but not pressing on, the brake pedal in order to facilitate quicker stops because the driver has already begun to respond.

crash To collide with force.

crossing An intersection of user paths.

crosswalk A marked pathway for use by pedestrians when they cross a street.

crowned roadway A road that is higher in the center than at the edges. A curved section of road that is crowned can make left turns more challenging and risky.

cruise control Device that allows the driver to choose and maintain a speed without continuous accelerator pressure.

D

daytime running lights (DRLs) A system that automatically turns on a vehicle's low beam headlights when the vehicle is turned on.

decelerate To slow down.

deceleration lane A lane used for vehicles to slow down as they leave through-traffic lanes.

deductible The amount an insured person must pay for damages before the insurance company pays the remainder.

defroster A heating unit that clears moisture from the inside the front and/or rear windows and ice from the outside surfaces.

directional control The ability of a driver to direct and maintain a motor vehicle along a desired travel path.

directional signal (turn signal) A signal that tells other drivers that a driver plans to turn or move a motor vehicle to the right or left. It may be given by blinking a light on the right or left side on the front and rear of the vehicle, or as a hand signal given by putting the left arm out the window.

divided highway A highway with a center median strip that separates vehicles traveling in opposite directions.

double parking To park a vehicle directly parallel to another parked along a curb.

downshift To shift to a lower gear from a higher one.

drive shaft A shaft that transmits motion or power from the engine via the transmission to the drive axle(s) of a motor vehicle.

drivetrain The main propulsive components of a vehicle, including the engine, transmission, and clutch.

drive wheels The wheels to which power is sent by the engine to push and/or pull the vehicle.

driver condition laws Laws requiring drivers to be in suitable physical and mental condition to drive legally.

driver licensing The issuing by the state of permits legally granting persons the privilege of operating a motor vehicle in the highway transportation system.

driver record Record of a driver's traffic violation history.

driving under the influence (DUI), driving while impaired, or driving while intoxicated (DWI) An offense a driver may be charged with, depending on the state, if the BAC at the time of arrest is above a certain point or if the driver is perceived to have lost normal use of mental or physical faculties because of alcohol or other drugs.

drowsiness Tiredness; the tendency to fall asleep

drugs Chemical substances that have physical and/or psychological effects on those who use them. Taken by people to achieve a real or imagined improved physical or mental state.

dual-service brake system An arrangement of separate braking systems for front and rear wheels.

E

edge line Solid white line to mark the outside edge of the outermost lane of traffic.

electronic fuel injection (EFI) system A system that times and meters fuel flow (injection) into the engine.

electronic stability control A system that helps prevent loss of traction and aids a driver in maintaining directional control.

embankment A mound of earth, rubble, etc., used to support a roadway.

emergency flasher A device that flashes the front and rear directional signals on and off.

emergency vehicle A police, fire or emergency medical vehicle that is given the right-of-way when its lights are flashing and siren is activated.

emission-control device A device that prevents or controls pollution by regulating exhaust gases.

engine Part of a vehicle that produces power by igniting an air-fuel mixture within its cylinders.

engine braking Increase in engine back pressure (drag) when the accelerator is released and the transmission is in gear.

evasive acceleration Using hard acceleration to avoid or lessen the consequences of a crash.

evasive action A quick change in speed or direction to avoid a collision.

expressway A divided highway for high-speed through-traffic, with full or partial control of access and overpasses or underpasses at major intersections.

F

fatigue Physical or mental exhaustion, which may involve a tendency to fall asleep.

felony offense A major crime usually punishable by jail sentence.

field of vision The area to the left and right that you can see when you look straight ahead.

financial responsibility laws A legal requirement that all drivers must be able to prove ability to pay damages resulting from collisions for which they are responsible.

fishtail When the rear end of a vehicle swings back-and-forth during a rear-wheel (oversteer) skid.

fixed (absolute) speed limit A posted speed limit that may not be exceeded for any reason.

flashing red traffic signal Light to indicate that a driver must come to a full stop before proceeding.

flashing yellow traffic signal Light to indicate a possible hazard. It means slow down, check traffic, proceed with caution, and be prepared to stop.

flashing yellow X A special lane-control light to indicate that a particular lane is for left-turning vehicles only.

following distance The time and space gap between vehicles traveling in the same direction and lane of traffic.

freeway A divided highway for high-speed through-traffic, with fully controlled access, overpasses or underpasses at intersections or railroads and interchanges at selected public crossroads.

friction Resistance to motion between two objects when they are in contact.

friction point The point at which the clutch and other power train parts begin to connect to transfer the engine power to the drive wheels.

front-wheel drive A vehicle in which the engine drives the front wheels.

fuel economy A vehicle's fuel-use ratio over a specified distance; usually expressed in miles per gallon (mpg).

fuel system Consists of the fuel tank, fuel pump, carburetor, and intake manifold.

HOW *to* **DRIVE**

G

gear A wheel with teeth that interlocks with another tooth part, and in doing so, transmits motion. The choice of gears determines a car's direction (forward or reverse), power, and speed.

gear-selector lever The lever that allows the driver to select a gear.

graduated drivers licensing (GDL) An approach to ease new drivers into driving by providing practice and skill development under low-risk conditions. As drivers become more experienced, they are gradually allowed to drive under increasingly complex conditions.

green arrow Used on a traffic signal to permit drivers to move only in the direction shown by the arrow. Used also as a special lane-control light if the lane is open to traffic facing the signal.

green downward-pointing arrow A signal light over a lane of traffic that indicates the lane is open to traffic facing the signal.

ground viewing A low-level search by a driver for objects in or near the vehicle's path that may be hidden by shrubs, parked cars or other large objects.

guide signs Guide vehicle operators along streets and highways; inform of interesting routes; direct drivers to cities or other important destinations; identify nearby parks, forests and historical sites.

H

hallucinogen Substance that produces hallucinations—sights, sounds, etc., that are not actually present.

hand-over-hand steering A steering method in which the driver's hands cross when turning the steering wheel.

head restraint A padded device, sometimes adjustable, extending above the front seat back designed to reduce whiplash or neck injuries in the event of a collision.

high beam Bright headlight setting that projects light further than low beams.

high-occupancy vehicle (HOV) lane A lane reserved for use by vehicles carrying two or more passengers; sometimes called a carpool lane.

highway A public roadway, especially one that runs between cities. It includes roads, bridges, and tunnels.

highway transportation system (HTS) The network of roadway environments, people who use the roadways, and the vehicles they use.

hybrid vehicle A vehicle that uses two different power sources for propulsion, generally resulting in decreased fuel use. A common combination uses a gas engine and an electric motor.

hydraulic brake system A system of brakes that works on the principle that fluid cannot be compressed. The fluid in the master brake cylinder is pushed under pressure through brake-fluid lines. The resistance to this force activates brake cylinders in each wheel.

hydroplane When a vehicle's tires lose contact with the road and ride on top of a film of water.

I

idle When the engine is running but the vehicle is not moving.

ignition A switch-controlled system that provides the spark that causes the fuel and air mixture in the engine to ignite and start the engine.

immediate path of travel The route to the point where the driver wants to be, in normal traffic, at least four seconds ahead.

Implied consent law A law that requires a driver charged with being under the influence to take a chemical test that measures the amount of alcohol in the blood. Drivers who refuse to take the test may have their license suspended or may be charged with impaired driving based on erratic driving or behavior.

inertia The tendency of an object in motion to resist any change in direction and of an object at rest to resist motion.

information sign Sign which has easily recognized symbols, used to guide and direct drivers.

internal combustion engine An engine in which a fuel mixture is burned within the engine. The energy that produces the car's motion comes from burning within the engine cylinders, not from burning outside, as in a steam engine.

interchange Any of the places on a limited-access roadway that traffic can enter or exit, usually by means of ramps.

international symbols Traffic sign symbols that use graphics for quick recognition.

intersection A place where two or more user paths cross.

interstate Over 46,000 miles of roadways throughout the United States which is part of a national system of Interstate and Defense Highways.

J

jackknife When a towed trailer swivels while backing so far that a V-shape is formed between the trailer and the towing vehicle.

L

lane signals Signals that show which lanes are open to traffic.

lane-use lights Electronic traffic signal lights mounted above reversible lanes that indicate which lanes can or cannot be used.

lap belt A restraining belt (seat belt, safety belt) designed to protect the driver and riders in a motor vehicle which fastens low across hips.

lateral evasive maneuver A quick, accurate turning of the steering wheel and swerving to avoid a collision.

lateral maneuvers A sideways motion, either to the front or to the rear.

liability insurance Insurance to protect you against claims in the event you are in a collision and are found to be at fault.

line of sight Area you can see when you look straight ahead.

loading zone Area reserved for authorized vehicles to deliver goods to a business or warehouse.

low beam Headlight setting used often during city driving; projects light over less distance than high beams.

LSD Hallucinogenic drug that affects the central nervous system, changes mood, and alters behavior.

lubricating system A system that reduces heat and engine wear by coating the engine parts with oil; also includes the oil pump, oil pan, and oil filter.

M

manual transmission A vehicle transmission that must be shifted using a hand-operated shifter and a foot-operated clutch.

managing risk Using the available traction to continuously adjust vehicle speed and position to maximize visibility, time, and space in various traffic situations.

mandatory Required.

marijuana A mild hallucinogenic drug that has varied effects on users.

median A grassed, landscaped or paved area on a highway that separates opposing directions of travel.

merging The gradual blending of vehicles in traffic moving in the same direction.

mirror checks Quick glances in the mirrors to look for the presence of objects.

misdemeanor offense Any minor legal offense. The penalty is usually a fine and/or imprisonment for under a year.

momentum Energy of motion, also called kinetic energy.

motor vehicle A self-propelled vehicle on wheels, not running on rails or tracks; for example a car, truck, bus, or motorcycle; may include bicycles.

motor vehicle inspection State inspections to ensure that motor vehicles meet minimum operation or safety standards.

N

narcotics Highly addictive depressant drugs that affect the central nervous system and produce side effects such as incoherence, dizziness, nausea, and vomiting.

national driver register A record of chronic problem drivers across the country that state licensing officials can check any time a driver applies for a new license.

neutral The position in which the vehicle gears are not engaged and cannot transmit power.

no-fault insurance System in which your insurance company pays your expenses up to a certain amount arising from injuries sustained in a motor vehicle crash. Payment is made without regard of fault or who caused collision.

no-passing zone Area indicated by a solid yellow center line where drivers are not allowed to pass, usually on an approach to a hill or curve.

O

obstacle Anything that gets in the way or hinders an obstruction.

off-road recovery Returning to the road from the shoulder.

oncoming traffic Vehicles traveling toward you.

ongoing traffic Vehicles traveling in the same direction as you.

overdriving headlights Driving so fast at night that you are unable to stop within the range of the headlights.

overpass A bridge that carries a roadway or railroad tracks over a street or highway.

P

parallel parking Parking so that a vehicle is in line with a group of vehicles arranged one behind the other, parallel to and close to a road edge or curb.

parent-teen driving agreement A written agreement between parents and their new driver to outline responsibilities and rules related to the teen's safe driving.

park The gear-selector reading that shows the transmission is locked; to bring a vehicle to rest in a parking space.

parking brake A mechanical brake that holds the rear wheels, used to keep a parked car from moving.

parking downgrade Parking facing down a hill.

parking upgrade Parking facing up a hill.

passive safety devices Devices, such as air bags or head restraints, that function without the user having to operate them.

pavement markings Markings painted onto the road surface to indicate lanes, crosswalks, no-passing zones, school zones, and the edge of the travel path.

pedestrian A person traveling on foot.

perception The process of obtaining information about the traffic scene, about which drivers will make decisions and take action.

peripheral vision The area of vision above, below, or to the right and left of central vision.

perpendicular At right angles.

point system Method of treating drivers in a uniform manner for traffic violations. Points are assigned each traffic violation, and the number of points determines the type of license action taken.

power brakes Type of braking system that requires less effort or pressure on the brake pedal to slow or stop the vehicle.

power skid A skid caused when the gas pedal suddenly is pressed too hard.

powertrain The main propulsive components of a vehicle, including the engine, transmission, and clutch.

preventive maintenance Inspection and servicing of vehicle systems to prevent costly repairs or breakdowns.

push-pull-feed steering A steering method in which the hands do not cross, even when turning.

R

reaction distance Distance a vehicle travels during reaction time.

reaction time Time it takes a driver to identify and react to a potential danger.

rear-wheel drive A vehicle in which the engine drives the rear wheels.

reckless driving Driving a vehicle with willful or wanton disregard for the safety of other persons or property.

reckless homicide Reckless driving that results in the death of another person.

recreational vehicle (RV) A large vehicle, such as a motorhome, primarily used for pleasure.

registration Record of legal vehicle documentation which includes title license plates or tags, and registration card. Generally, registration must be renewed yearly.

regulate Control, direct or govern according to a rule, principle, or system.

regulatory signs Roadway signs that control right-of-way, speed, turning, alignment, passing, one-way driving, pedestrian crossing, parking, and weight limits. Miscellaneous signs may include NO DUMPING, NO LITTERING.

reverse The gear used to back a vehicle.

reversible lanes Lanes on which the direction of traffic changes at certain times of day, typically rush hours.

revocation State cancellation of a legal permit to drive a vehicle.

right-of-way The right of a vehicle or pedestrian to go first before other traffic moves when there is a conflict; it is granted by law or custom.

risk The chance of injury, damage, or loss.

risk management The efficient use of available traction to continuously adjust vehicle speed and position in various traffic situations to maximize visibility, time, and space.

road rage Occurs when a driver uses the vehicle or some other weapon to threaten or cause harm to another roadway user in response to a traffic incident.

roadway markings Markings painted onto the road surface to indicate lanes, crosswalks, no-passing zones, school zones, and the edge of the travel path.

route Planned travel path.

S

safety belt A restraining belt designed to protect the driver and riders in a motor vehicle. Lap belts fasten across hips; shoulder belts fasten across the shoulder and chest.

shared left-turn lane A lane that drivers moving in either direction use to make a left turn.

selective search pattern A pattern of observation that avoids or passes over distractions and focuses on things important to the current driving task.

selector lever The lever in an automatic transmission vehicle that allows you to select the gear you want.

separating Adjusting speed to deal with multiple risks one at a time.

serial number Number on a motor vehicle used as identification. No two vehicles have the same serial number.

shift To change gears.

shoulder The off-road strip of land along the edge of a roadway.

shoulder belt A passenger restraint system that fastens across the chest and shoulder.

sideswipe To strike another vehicle along its side when you try to pass it.

skid Loss of traction by the front, rear or all tires, generally resulting in a deviation from the desired path of travel.

slow-moving vehicle sign A sign used on the back of tractors and other slow-moving vehicles that warns they travel at speed of 25 miles per hour or slower.

space Distance.

space margin The amount of space around a vehicle that separates it from possible sources of danger in traffic.

speed control System that allows the driver to choose and maintain a speed without continuous accelerator pressure.

speed limits Fixed minimum and maximum speeds set to reflect the level of congestion, roadway conditions, and types of vehicles. Drivers must not travel faster than the maximum or slower than the minimum unless conditions warrant it.

squeeze braking A gradual increase of brake pressure.

stimulant Substance that temporarily excites or accelerates the function of a vital process or organ, in particular the central nervous system.

suspension (of license) To take away a driver's license for a time.

suspension system The assembly of springs, shock absorbers, and related parts that insulate (protect) the chassis of a vehicle against road shocks coming through the wheels.

synergism A total effect that is greater than the sum of the two effects separately; often used in reference to combining alcohol and other drugs.

T

tailgate To drive behind another vehicle too closely.

three-point turn A turnabout made by turning left, backing to the right, then moving forward.

threshold braking A quick, hard brake application to a point just short of lockup.

traction The contact between the tire and road surface; the adhesive or holding quality of friction.

traffic control devices The signs, signals and markings used in the highway transportation system.

tranquilizers Depressant drugs that slow down the central nervous system and may cause drowsiness; if combined with alcohol, they can stop the heart, reduce blood pressure and halt the oxygen supply to the brain.

tunnel vision A very narrow field of vision with little or no peripheral vision.

turnabout A turning maneuver in which a driver uses a series of moves to reverse a vehicle's direction.

two-point turn A turnabout made by first backing into a driveway or alley. Although more dangerous, a turnabout can also be made by heading into an alley or driveway and then backing into the street.

U

U-turn A turnabout that is a full, U-shaped left turn back in the opposite direction.

under the influence Impaired ability to operate a motor vehicle, usually caused by alcohol or other drugs.

underpass A passage or road running under another one.

uniform vehicle code Vehicle laws recommended by a national committee and used in part by all states.

uninsured motorist protection Protection from certain financial losses resulting from a collision involving a driver who does not have insurance protection.

V

variable speed limits Speed limits that change based on road, traffic, and weather conditions, generally communicated to drivers by changeable electronic road signs.

vehicle identification number (VIN) Number on a motor vehicle used as identification. No two vehicles have the same serial number.

visibility The maximum distance at which an object can be seen under the prevailing conditions; range of vision.

visual acuity Ability to see clearly.

visual field Area a driver can see ahead and to the sides. The entire area of the highway and its surroundings that can be seen at any given moment.

visual habits How the eyes are used to collect information (scan the roadway).

visual lead The time and space a driver has available for identifying and reacting to a traffic situation.

W

wanton Senseless, unjustifiable or deliberately malicious.

warning signs Traffic signs that alert drivers to potential dangers ahead; usually yellow and diamond shaped.

weave lane Lane near the entrance or exit of an expressway to be used by vehicles preparing to enter (speed up) or exit (slow down).

whiplash A sudden, severe bending and jolting of the neck backward and then forward as caused by the impact of a rear-end motor vehicle collision; sometimes results in injury to the soft tissues and vertebrae of the neck.

willful Deliberate.

Y

yield To let another motorist have the right-of-way.

INDEX

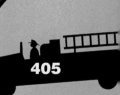

HOW to DRIVE

HOW *to* **DRIVE**

HOW *to* DRIVE

HOW to DRIVE